Machine Learning with Li and Python

A practitioner's guide to developing production-ready machine learning systems

Andrich van Wyk

<packt>

BIRMINGHAM—MUMBAI

Machine Learning with LightGBM and Python

Group Product Manager: Niranjan Naikwadi
Publishing Product Manager: Tejashwini R
Senior Editor: Gowri Rekha
Content Development Editor: Manikandan Kurup
Technical Editor: Kavyashree K S
Copy Editor: Safis Editing
Project Coordinator: Farheen Fathima
Proofreader: Safis Editing
Indexer: Subalakshmi Govindhan
Production Designer: Shyam Sundar Korumilli
Marketing Coordinator: Vinishka Kalra

First published: September 2023

Production reference: 1220923

Published by Packt Publishing Ltd.
Grosvenor House
11 St Paul's Square
Birmingham
B3 1RB, UK.

ISBN: 978-1-80056-474-9

www.packtpub.com

Countless nights and weekends have been dedicated to completing this book, and I would like to thank my wife, Irene, for her eternal support, without which, nobody would be reading any of this. Further, I'm grateful to my daughter, Emily, for inspiring me to reach a little further.

– Andrich van Wyk

Contributors

About the author

Andrich van Wyk has 15 years of experience in machine learning R&D, building AI-driven solutions, and consulting in the AI domain. He also has broad experience as a software engineer and architect with over a decade of industry experience working on enterprise systems.

He graduated cum laude with an M.Sc. in Computer Science from the University of Pretoria, focusing on neural networks and evolutionary algorithms.

Andrich enjoys writing about machine learning engineering and the software industry at large. He currently resides in South Africa with his wife and daughter.

About the reviewers

Valentine Shkulov is a renowned visiting lecturer at a top tech university, where he seamlessly melds academia with real-world expertise as a distinguished Data Scientist in Fintech and E-commerce. His ingenuity in crafting ML-driven solutions has transformed businesses, from tech giants to budding startups. Valentine excels at introducing AI innovations and refining current systems, ensuring they profoundly influence vital business metrics. His passion for navigating product challenges has established him as a pioneer in leveraging ML to elevate businesses.

Above all, a heartfelt thanks to my spouse, the unwavering pillar of support in my remarkable journey.

Kayewan M Karanjia has over 7 years of experience in machine learning, artificial intelligence (AI), and data technologies, and brings a wealth of expertise to his current role at DrDoctor. Here, as a machine learning engineer, he is dedicated to implementing advanced machine learning models that have a direct impact on enhancing healthcare services and process optimization for the NHS. In the past, he has also worked with multiple MNCs such as Reliance Industries Limited, and implemented solutions for the government of India.

Table of Contents

6

Solving Real-World Data Science Problems with LightGBM   103

7

AutoML with LightGBM and FLAML   135

Part 3: Production-ready Machine Learning with LightGBM

8

Machine Learning Pipelines and MLOps with LightGBM   149

9

LightGBM MLOps with AWS SageMaker   165

10

LightGBM Models with PostgresML   195

11

Distributed and GPU-Based Learning with LightGBM   209

Preface

Welcome to *Machine Learning with LightGBM and Python: A Practitioner's Guide to Developing Production-Ready Machine Learning Systems*. In this book, you'll embark on a rich journey, taking you from the foundational principles of machine learning to the advanced realms of MLOps. The cornerstone of our exploration is LightGBM, a powerful and flexible gradient-boosting framework that can be harnessed for a wide range of machine-learning challenges.

This book is tailor-made for anyone passionate about transforming raw data into actionable insights using the power of **Machine Learning** (**ML**). Whether you're an ML novice eager to get your hands dirty or an experienced data scientist seeking to master the intricacies of LightGBM, there's something in here for you.

The digital era has equipped us with a treasure trove of data. However, the challenges often lie in extracting meaningful insights from this data and deploying scalable, efficient, and reliable models in production environments. This book will guide you in overcoming these challenges. By diving into gradient boosting, the data science life cycle, and the nuances of production deployment, you will gain a comprehensive skill set to navigate the ever-evolving landscape of ML.

Each chapter is designed with practicality in mind. Real-world case studies interspersed with theoretical insights ensure your learning is grounded in tangible applications. Our focus on LightGBM, which sometimes gets overshadowed by more mainstream algorithms, provides a unique lens to appreciate and apply gradient boosting in various scenarios.

For those curious about what sets this book apart, it's our pragmatic approach. We take pride in transcending beyond merely explaining algorithms or tools. Instead, we will prioritize hands-on applications, case studies, and real-world challenges, ensuring you're not just reading but also "doing" ML.

As we traverse through the chapters, remember that the world of ML is vast and constantly evolving. This book, while comprehensive, is a stepping stone in your lifelong journey of learning and exploration in the domain. As you navigate the world of LightGBM, data science, MLOps, and more, keep your mind open, your curiosity alive, and your hands ready to code.

Who this book is for

Machine Learning with LightGBM and Python: A Practitioner's Guide to Developing Production-Ready Machine Learning Systems is tailored for a broad spectrum of readers passionate about harnessing data's power through ML. The target audience for this book includes the following:

- **Beginners in ML**: Individuals just stepping into the world of ML will find this book immensely beneficial. It starts with foundational ML principles and introduces them to gradient boosting using LightGBM, making it an excellent entry point for newcomers.

- **Experienced data scientists and ML practitioners**: For those who are already familiar with the landscape of ML but want to deepen their knowledge of LightGBM and/or MLOps, this book offers advanced insights, techniques, and practical applications.

- **Software engineers and architects looking to learn more about data science**: Software professionals keen on transitioning to data science or integrating ML into their applications will find this book valuable. The book approaches ML theoretically and practically, emphasizing hands-on coding and real-world applications.

- **MLOps engineers and DevOps professionals**: Individuals working in the field of MLOps or those who wish to understand the deployment, scaling, and monitoring of ML models in production environments will benefit from the chapters dedicated to MLOps, pipelines, and deployment strategies.

- **Academicians and students**: Faculty members teaching ML, data science, or related courses, as well as students pursuing these fields, will find this book to be both an informative textbook and a practical guide.

Knowledge of how to program Python is necessary. Familiarity with Jupyter notebooks and Python environments is a bonus. No prior knowledge of ML is required.

In essence, anyone with a penchant for data, a background in Python programming, and an eagerness to explore the multifaceted world of ML using LightGBM will find this book a valuable addition to their repertoire.

What this book covers

Chapter 1, Introducing Machine Learning, starts our journey into ML, viewing it through the lens of software engineering. We will elucidate vital concepts central to the field, such as models, datasets, and the various learning paradigms, ensuring clarity with a hands-on example using decision trees.

Chapter 2, Ensemble Learning – Bagging and Boosting, delves into ensemble learning, focusing on bagging and boosting techniques applied to decision trees. We will explore algorithms such as random forests, gradient-boosted decision trees, and more advanced concepts such as **Dropout meets Additive Regression Trees (DART)**.

Chapter 3, An Overview of LightGBM in Python, examines LightGBM, an advanced gradient-boosting framework with tree-based learners. Highlighting its unique innovations and enhancements to ensemble learning, we will guide you through its Python APIs. A comprehensive modeling example using LightGBM, enriched with advanced validation and optimization techniques, sets the stage for a deeper dive into data science and production systems ML.

Chapter 4, Comparing LightGBM, XGBoost, and Deep Learning, pits LightGBM against two prominent tabular data modeling methods – XGBoost and **deep neural networks (DNNs)**, specifically TabTransformer. We will assess each method's complexity, performance, and computational cost through evaluations of two datasets. The essence of this chapter is ascertaining LightGBM's competitiveness in the broader ML landscape, rather than an in-depth study of XGBoost or DNNs.

Chapter 5, LightGBM Parameter Optimization with Optuna, focuses on the pivotal task of hyperparameter optimization, introducing the Optuna framework as a potent solution. Covering various optimization algorithms and strategies to prune the hyperparameter space, this chapter guides you through a hands-on example of refining LightGBM parameters using Optuna.

Chapter 6, Solving Real-World Data Science Problems with LightGBM, methodically breaks down the data science process, applying it to two distinct case studies – a regression and a classification problem. The chapter illuminates each step of the data science life cycle. You will experience hands-on modeling with LightGBM, paired with comprehensive theory. This chapter also serves as a blueprint for data science projects using LightGBM.

Chapter 7, AutoML with LightGBM and FLAML, delves into **automated machine learning** (**AutoML**), emphasizing its significance in simplifying and expediting data engineering and model development. We will introduce FLAML, a notable library that automates model selection and fine-tuning with efficient hyperparameter algorithms. Through a practical case study, you will witness FLAML's synergy with LightGBM and the transformative Zero-Shot AutoML functionality, which renders the tuning process obsolete.

Chapter 8, Machine Learning Pipelines and MLOps with LightGBM, moves on from modeling intricacies to the world of production ML. It introduces you to ML pipelines, ensuring consistent data processing and model building, and ventures into MLOps, a fusion of DevOps and ML, which is vital to deploying resilient ML systems.

Chapter 9, LightGBM MLOps with AWS SageMaker, steers our journey toward Amazon SageMaker, Amazon Web Services' comprehensive suite to craft and maintain ML solutions. We will deepen our understanding of ML pipelines by delving into advanced areas such as bias detection, explainability in models, and the nuances of automated, scalable deployments.

Chapter 10, LightGBM Models with PostgresML, introduces PostgresML, a distinct MLOps platform and a PostgreSQL database extension that facilitates ML model development and deployment directly via SQL. This approach, while contrasting the scikit-learn programming style that we've embraced, showcases the benefits of database-level ML, particularly regarding data movement efficiencies and faster inferencing.

Chapter 11, Distributed and GPU-Based Learning with LightGBM, delves into the expansive realm of training LightGBM models, leveraging distributed computing clusters and GPUs. By harnessing distributed computing, you will understand how to substantially accelerate training workloads and manage datasets that exceed a single machine's memory capacity.

To get the most out of this book

This book is written assuming that you have some knowledge of Python programming. None of the Python code is very complex, so even understanding the basics of Python should be enough to get you through most of the code examples.

Jupyter notebooks are used for the practical examples in all the chapters. Jupyter Notebooks is an open source tool that allows you to create code notebooks that contain live code, visualizations, and markdown text. Tutorials to get started with Jupyter Notebooks are available at https://realpython.com/jupyter-notebook-introduction/ and at https://plotly.com/python/ipython-notebook-tutorial/.

Software/hardware covered in the book	Operating system requirements
Python 3.10	Windows, macOS, or Linux
Anaconda 3	Windows, macOS, or Linux
scikit-learn 1.2.1	Windows, macOS, or Linux
LightGBM 3.3.5	Windows, macOS, or Linux
XGBoost 1.7.4	Windows, macOS, or Linux
Optuna 3.1.1	Windows, macOS, or Linux
FLAML 1.2.3	Windows, macOS, or Linux
FastAPI 0.103.1	Windows, macOS, or Linux
Amazon SageMaker	
Docker 23.0.1	Windows, macOS, or Linux
PostgresML 2.7.0	Windows, macOS, or Linux
Dask 2023.7.1	Windows, macOS, or Linux

We recommend using Anaconda for Python environment management when setting up your own environment. Anaconda also bundles many data science packages, so you don't have to install them individually. Anaconda can be downloaded from https://www.anaconda.com/download. Notably, the book is accompanied by a GitHub repository, which includes an Anaconda environment file, to create the environment required to run the code examples in this book.

If you are using the digital version of this book, we advise you to type the code yourself or access the code from the book's GitHub repository (a link is available in the next section). Doing so will help you avoid any potential errors related to the copying and pasting of code.

Download the example code files

You can download the example code files for this book from GitHub at https://github.com/PacktPublishing/Practical-Machine-Learning-with-LightGBM-and-Python. If there's an update to the code, it will be updated in the GitHub repository.

We also have other code bundles from our rich catalog of books and videos available at `https://github.com/PacktPublishing/`. Check them out!

Conventions used

There are several text conventions used throughout this book.

`Code in text`: Indicates code words in text, database table names, folder names, filenames, file extensions, pathnames, dummy URLs, user input, and Twitter handles. Here is an example: "The code is almost identical to our classification example – instead of a classifier, we use `DecisionTreeRegressor` as our model and calculate `mean_absolute_error` instead of the F1 score."

A block of code is set as follows:

```
import numpy as np

import pandas as pd


from matplotlib import pyplot as plt

import seaborn as sns


from sklearn.linear_model import LinearRegression

from sklearn.metrics import mean_absolute_error
```

When we wish to draw your attention to a particular part of a code block, the relevant lines or items are set in bold:

```
model = DecisionTreeRegressor(random_state=157, max_depth=3, min_
samples_split=2)
model = model.fit(X_train, y_train)

mean_absolute_error(y_test, model.predict(X_test))
```

Any command-line input or output is written as follows:

```
conda create -n your_env_name python=3.9
```

Bold: Indicates a new term, an important word, or words you see on screen. For instance, words in menus or dialog boxes appear in **bold**. Here is an example: "Therefore, **data preparation and cleaning** are essential parts of the machine-learning process."

> **Tips or important notes**
> Appear in blocks such as these.

Get in touch

Feedback from our readers is always welcome.

General feedback: If you have questions about any aspect of this book, email us at customercare@packtpub.com and mention the book title in the subject of your message.

Errata: Although we have taken every care to ensure the accuracy of our content, mistakes do happen. If you have found a mistake in this book, we would be grateful if you would report this to us. Please visit www.packtpub.com/support/errata and fill in the form.

Piracy: If you come across any illegal copies of our works in any form on the internet, we would be grateful if you would provide us with the location address or website name. Please get in touch with us at copyright@packt.com with a link to the material.

If you are interested in becoming an author: If there is a topic that you have expertise in and you are interested in either writing or contributing to a book, please visit authors.packtpub.com.

Share Your Thoughts

Once you've read *Machine Learning with LightGBM and Python*, we'd love to hear your thoughts! Scan the QR code below to go straight to the Amazon review page for this book and share your feedback.

https://packt.link/r/1-800-56474-0

Your review is important to us and the tech community and will help us make sure we're delivering excellent quality content.

Download a free PDF copy of this book

Thanks for purchasing this book!

Do you like to read on the go but are unable to carry your print books everywhere? Is your eBook purchase not compatible with the device of your choice?

Don't worry, now with every Packt book you get a DRM-free PDF version of that book at no cost.

Read anywhere, any place, on any device. Search, copy, and paste code from your favorite technical books directly into your application.

The perks don't stop there, you can get exclusive access to discounts, newsletters, and great free content in your inbox daily.

Follow these simple steps to get the benefits:

1. Scan the QR code or visit the link below

https://packt.link/free-ebook/9781800564749

2. Submit your proof of purchase
3. That's it! We'll send your free PDF and other benefits to your email directly

Part 1: Gradient Boosting and LightGBM Fundamentals

In this part, we will initiate our exploration of machine learning by grounding you in its fundamental concepts, ranging from basic terminologies to intricate algorithms like random forests. We will delve deep into ensemble learning, highlighting the power of decision trees when combined, and then shift our focus to the gradient-boosting framework, LightGBM. Through hands-on examples in Python and comparative analyses against techniques like XGBoost and deep neural networks, you'll gain both a foundational understanding and practical competence in the realm of machine learning, especially with LightGBM.

This part will include the following chapters:

- *Chapter 1, Introducing Machine Learning*
- *Chapter 2, Ensemble Learning – Bagging and Boosting*
- *Chapter 3, An Overview of LightGBM in Python*
- *Chapter 4, Comparing LightGBM, XGBoost, and Deep Learning*

Introducing Machine Learning

Our journey starts with an introduction to machine learning and the fundamental concepts we'll use throughout this book.

We'll start by providing an overview of machine learning from a software engineering perspective. Then, we'll introduce the core concepts that are used in the field of machine learning and data science: models, datasets, learning paradigms, and other details. This introduction will include a practical example that clearly illustrates the machine learning terms discussed.

We will also introduce decision trees, a crucially important machine learning algorithm that is our first step to understanding LightGBM.

After completing this chapter, you will have established a solid foundation in machine learning and the practical application of machine learning techniques.

The following main topics will be covered in this chapter:

- What is machine learning?
- Introducing models, datasets, and supervised learning
- Decision tree learning

Technical requirements

This chapter includes examples of simple machine learning algorithms and introduces working with scikit-learn. You must install a Python environment with scikit-learn, NumPy, pandas, and Jupyter Notebook. The code for this chapter is available at `https://github.com/PacktPublishing/Practical-Machine-Learning-with-LightGBM-and-Python/tree/main/chapter-1`.

What is machine learning?

Machine learning is a part of the broader artificial intelligence field that involves methods and techniques that allow computers to "learn" specific tasks without explicit programming.

Machine learning is just another way to write programs, albeit automatically, from data. Abstractly, a program is a set of *instructions* that transforms *inputs* into specific *outputs*. A programmer's job is to understand all the relevant inputs to a computer program and develop a set of instructions to produce the correct outputs.

However, what if the inputs are beyond the programmer's understanding?

For example, let's consider creating a program to forecast the total sales of a large retail store. The inputs to the program would be various factors that could affect sales. We could imagine factors such as historical sales figures, upcoming public holidays, stock availability, any special deals the store might be running, and even factors such as the weather forecast or proximity to other stores.

In our store example, the traditional approach would be to break down the inputs into manageable, understandable (by a programmer) pieces, perhaps consult an expert in store sales forecasting, and then devise handcrafted rules and instructions to attempt to forecast future sales.

While this approach is certainly possible, it is also brittle (in the sense that the program might have to undergo extensive changes regarding the input factors) and wholly based on the programmer's (or domain expert's) understanding of the problem. With potentially thousands of factors and billions of examples, this problem becomes untenable.

Machine learning offers us an alternative to this approach. Instead of creating rules and instructions, we repeatedly show the computer examples of the tasks we need to accomplish and then get it to figure out how to solve them automatically.

However, where we previously had a set of instructions, we now have a **trained model** instead of a programmed one.

The key realization here, especially if you are coming from a software background, is that our machine learning program still functions like a regular program: it accepts input, has a way to process it, and produces output. Like all other software programs, machine learning software must be tested for correctness, integrated into other systems, deployed, monitored, and optimized. Collectively, this forms the field of *machine learning engineering*. We'll cover all these aspects and more in later chapters.

Machine learning paradigms

Broadly speaking, machine learning has three main paradigms: supervised, unsupervised, and reinforcement learning.

With **supervised learning**, the model is trained on labeled data: each instance in the dataset has its associated correct output, or label, for the input example. The model is expected to learn to predict the label for unseen input examples.

With **unsupervised learning**, the examples in the dataset are unlabeled; in this case, the model is expected to discover patterns and relationships in the data. Examples of unsupervised approaches are clustering algorithms, anomaly detection, and dimensionality reduction algorithms.

Finally, **reinforcement learning** entails a model, usually called an agent, interacting with a particular environment and learning by receiving penalties or rewards for specific actions. The goal is for the agent to perform actions that maximize its reward. Reinforcement learning is widely used in robotics, control systems, or training computers to play games.

LightGBM and most other algorithms discussed later in this book are examples of supervised learning techniques and are the focus of this book.

The following section dives deeper into the machine learning terminology we'll use throughout this book and the details of the machine learning process.

Introducing models, datasets, and supervised learning

In the previous section, we introduced a model as a construct to replace a set of instructions that typically comprise a program to perform a specific task. This section covers models and other core machine learning concepts in more detail.

Models

More formally, a model is a mathematical or algorithmic representation of a specific process that performs a particular task. A machine learning model learns a particular task by being trained on a **dataset** using a **training algorithm**.

> **Note**
>
> An alternative term for training is **fit**. Historically, fit stems from the statistical field. A model is said to "fit the data" when trained. We'll use both terms interchangeably throughout this book.

Many distinct types of models exist, all of which use different mathematical, statistical, or algorithmic techniques to model the training data. Examples of machine learning algorithms include linear regression, logistic regression, decision trees, support vector machines, and neural networks.

A distinction is made between the model type and a trained instance of that model: the majority of machine learning models can be trained to perform various tasks. For example, decision trees (a model type) can be trained to forecast sales, recognize heart disease, and predict football match results.

However, each of these tasks requires a different *instance* of a decision tree that has been trained on a distinct dataset.

What a specific model does depends on the model's **parameters**. Parameters are also sometimes called **weights**, which are technically particular types of model parameters.

A **training algorithm** is an algorithm for finding the most appropriate model parameters for a specific task.

We determine the quality of fit, or how well the model performs, using an **objective function**. This is a mathematical function that measures the difference between the predicted output and the actual output for a given input. The objective function quantifies the performance of a model. We may seek to minimize or maximize the objective function depending on the problem we are solving. The objective is often measured as an error we aim to minimize during training.

We can summarize the model training process as follows: a training algorithm uses data from a dataset to optimize a model's parameters for a particular task, as measured through an objective function.

Hyperparameters

While a model is composed of parameters, the training algorithm has parameters of its own called **hyperparameters**. A hyperparameter is a controllable value that influences the training process or algorithm. For example, consider finding the minimum of a parabola function: we could start by guessing a value and then take small steps in the direction that minimizes the function output. The step size would have to be chosen well: if our steps are too small, it will take a prohibitively long time to find the minimum. If the step size is too large, we may overshoot and miss the minimum and then continue oscillating (jumping back and forth) around the minimum:

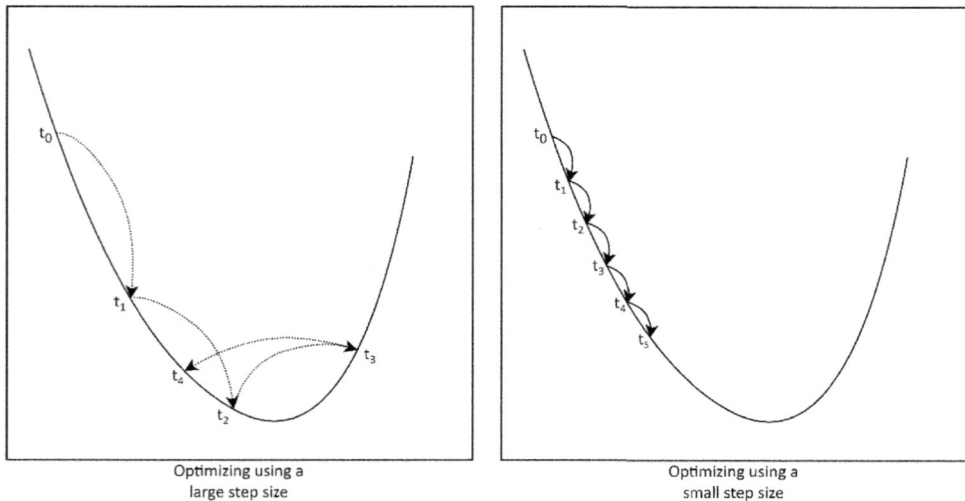

Optimizing using a
large step size

Optimizing using a
small step size

Figure 1.1 – Effect of using a step size that is too large (left) and too small (right)

In this example, the step size would be a hyperparameter of our minimization algorithm. The effect of the step size is illustrated in *Figure 1.1*.

Datasets

As explained previously, the machine learning model is trained using a dataset. Data is at the heart of the machine learning process, and data preparation is often the part of the process that takes up the most time.

Throughout this book, we'll work with *tabular* datasets. Tabular datasets are very common in the real world and consist of rows and columns. Rows are often called samples, examples, or observations, and columns are usually called features, variables, or attributes.

Importantly, there is no restriction on the data type in a column. Features may be strings, numbers, Booleans, geospatial coordinates, or encoded formats such as audio, images, or video.

Datasets are also rarely perfectly defined. Data may be incomplete, noisy, incorrect, inconsistent, and contain various formats.

Therefore, *data preparation and cleaning* are essential parts of the machine learning process.

Data preparation concerns processing the data to make it suitable for machine learning and typically consists of the following steps:

1. **Gathering and validation**: Some datasets are initially too small or represent the problem poorly (the data is not representative of the actual data population it's been sampled from). In these cases, the practitioner must collect more data, and validation must be done to ensure the data represents the problem.

2. **Checking for systemic errors and bias**: It is vital to check for and correct any systemic errors in the collection and validation process that may lead to bias in the dataset. In our sales example, a systemic collection error may be that data was only gathered from urban stores and excluded rural ones. A model trained on only urban store data will be biased in forecasting store sales, and we may expect poor performance when the model is used to predict sales for rural stores.

3. **Cleaning the data**: Any format or value range inconsistencies must be addressed. Any missing values also need to be handled in a way that does not introduce bias.

4. **Feature engineering**: Certain features may need to be transformed to ensure the machine learning model can learn from them, such as numerically encoding a sentence of words. Additionally, new features may need to be prepared from existing features to help the model detect patterns.

5. **Normalizing and standardizing**: The relative ranges of features must be normalized and standardized. Normalizing and standardizing ensure that no one feature has an outsized effect on the overall prediction.

6. **Balancing the dataset**: In cases where the dataset is imbalanced – that is, it contains many more examples of one class or prediction than another – the dataset needs to be balanced. Balancing is typically done by oversampling the minority examples to balance the dataset.

In *Chapter 6, Solving Real-World Data Science Problems with LightGBM*, we'll go through the entire data preparation process to show how the preceding steps are applied practically.

> **Note**
>
> A good adage to remember is "garbage in, garbage out". A model learns from any data given to it, including any flaws or biases contained in the data. When we train the model on garbage data, it results in a garbage model.

One final concept to understand regarding datasets is the training, validation, and test datasets. We split our datasets into these three subsets after the data preparation step is done:

- The **training set** is the most significant subset and typically consists of 60% to 80% of the data. This data is used to train the model.

- The **validation set** is separate from the training data and is used throughout the training process to evaluate the model. Having independent validation data ensures that the model is evaluated on data it has not seen before, also known as its generalization ability. Hyperparameter tuning, a process covered in detail in *Chapter 5, LightGBM Parameter Optimization with Optuna*, also uses the validation set.

- Finally, the **test set** is an optional hold-out set, similar to the validation set. It is used at the end of the process to evaluate the model's performance on data that was not part of the training or tuning process.

Another use of the validation set is to monitor whether the model is overfitting the data. Let's discuss overfitting in more detail.

Overfitting and generalization

To understand overfitting, we must first define what we mean by model **generalization**. As stated previously, generalization is the model's ability to accurately predict data it has not seen before. Compared to training accuracy, generalization accuracy is more significant as an estimate of model performance as this indicates how our model will perform in production. Generalization comes in two forms, **interpolation and extrapolation**:

- Interpolation refers to the model's ability to predict a value between two known data points – stated another way, to generalize within the training data range. For example, let's say we train our model with monthly data from January to July. When interpolating, we would ask the model to make a prediction on a particular day in April, a date within our training range.

- Extrapolation, as you might infer, is the model's ability to predict values outside of the range defined by our training data. A typical example of extrapolation is forecasting – that is, predicting the future. In our previous example, if we ask the model to make a prediction in December, we expect it to extrapolate from the training data.

Of the two types of generalization, extrapolation is much more challenging and may require a specific type of model to achieve. However, in both cases, a model can overfit the data, losing its ability to interpolate or extrapolate accurately.

Overfitting is a phenomenon where the model fits the training data too closely and loses its ability to generalize to unseen data. Instead of learning the underlying pattern in the data, the model has memorized the training data. More technically, the model fits the *noise* contained in the training data. The term noise stems from the concept of data containing *signal* and *noise*. Signal refers to the underlying pattern or information captured in the data we are trying to predict. In contrast, noise refers to random or irrelevant variations of data points that mask the signal.

For example, consider a dataset where we try to predict the rainfall for specific locations. The signal in the data would be the general trend of rainfall: rainfall increases in the winter or summer, or vice versa for other locations. The noise would be the slight variations in rainfall measurement for each month and location in our dataset.

The following graph illustrates the phenomenon of overfitting:

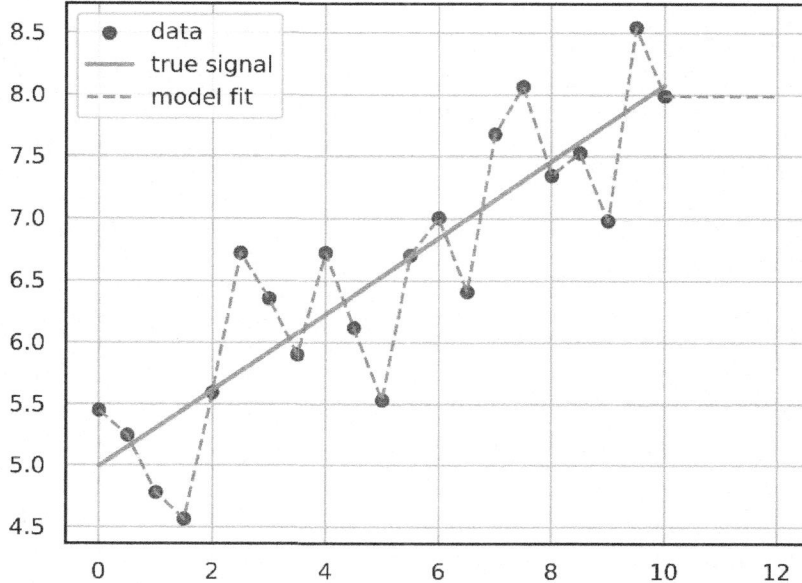

Figure 1.2 – Graph showing overfitting. The model has overfitted and predicted the
training data perfectly but has lost the ability to generalize to the actual signal

The preceding figure shows the difference between signal and noise: each data point was sampled from the actual signal. The data follows the general pattern of the signal, with slight, random variations. We can see how the model has overfitted the data: the model has fit the training data perfectly but at the cost of generalization. We can also see that if we use the model to *interpolate* by predicting a value for 4, we get a result much higher than the actual signal (6.72 versus 6.2). Also shown is the model's failure to *extrapolate*: the prediction for 12 is much lower than a forecast of the signal (7.98 versus 8.6).

In reality, all real-world datasets contain noise. As data scientists, we aim to prepare the data to remove as much noise as possible, making the signal easier to detect. Data cleaning, normalization, feature selection, feature engineering, and regularization are techniques for removing noise from the data.

Since all real-world data contains noise, overfitting is impossible to eliminate. The following conditions may lead to overfitting:

- **An overly complex model**: A model that is too complex for the amount of data we have utilizes additional complexity to memorize the noise in the data, leading to overfitting
- **Insufficient data**: If we don't have enough training data for the model we use, it's similar to an overly complex model, which overfits the data
- **Too many features**: A dataset with too many features likely contains irrelevant (noisy) features that reduce the model's generalization
- **Overtraining**: Training the model for too long allows it to memorize the noise in the dataset

As the validation set is a part of the training data that remains unseen by the model, we use the validation set to monitor for overfitting. We can recognize the point of overfitting by looking at the training and generalization errors over time. At the point of overfitting, the validation error increases. In contrast, the training error continues to improve: the model is fitting noise in the training data and losing its ability to generalize.

Techniques that prevent overfitting usually aim to address the conditions that lead to overfitting we discussed previously. Here are some strategies to avoid overfitting:

- **Early stopping**: We can stop training when we see the validation error beginning to increase.
- **Simplifying the model**: A less complex model with fewer parameters would be incapable of learning the noise in the training data, thereby generalizing better.
- **Get more data**: Either collecting more data or augmenting data is an effective method for preventing overfitting by giving the model a better chance to learn the signal in the data instead of the noise in a smaller dataset.
- **Feature selection and dimensionality reduction**: As some features might be irrelevant to the problem being solved, we can discard features we think are redundant or use techniques such as Principal Component Analysis to reduce the dimensionality (features).

- **Adding regularization**: Smaller parameter values typically lead to better generalization, depending on the model (a neural network is an example of such a model). Regularization adds a penalty term to the objective function to discourage large parameter values. By driving the parameters to smaller (or zero) values, they contribute less to the prediction, effectively simplifying the model.

- **Ensemble methods**: Combining the prediction from multiple, *weaker* models can lead to better generalization while also improving performance.

It's important to note that *overfitting and the techniques to prevent overfitting are specific to our model*. Our goal should always be to minimize overfitting to ensure generalization to unseen data. Some strategies, such as regularization, might not work for specific models, while others might be more effective. There are also more bespoke strategies for models, an example of which we'll see when we discuss overfitting in decision trees.

Supervised learning

The store sales example is an instance of **supervised learning** – we have a dataset consisting of features and are training the model to predict a target.

Supervised learning problems can be divided into two main types of problem categories: **classification problems** and **regression problems**.

Classification and regression

With a *classification problem*, the label that needs to be predicted by the model is categorical or defines a class. Some examples of classes are `spam` or `not spam`, `cat` or `dog`, and `diabetic` or `not diabetic`. These are examples of binary classifications: there are only two classes.

Multi-class classification is also possible; for example, email may be classified as `Important`, `Promotional`, `Clutter`, or `Spam`; images of clouds could be classified as `Cirro`, `Cumulo`, `Strato`, or `Nimbo`.

With *regression problems*, the goal is to predict a continuous, numerical value. Examples include predicting revenue, sales, temperature, house prices, and crowd size.

A big part of the *art* of machine learning is correctly defining or transcribing a problem as a classification or regression problem (or perhaps unsupervised or reinforcement). Later chapters will cover multiple end-to-end case studies of both types of problems.

Model performance metrics

Let's briefly discuss how we measure our model's performance. Model performance refers to the ability of a machine learning model to make accurate predictions or generate meaningful outputs based on the given inputs. An evaluation metric quantifies how well a model generalizes to new, unseen data.

High model performance indicates that the model has learned the underlying patterns in the data effectively and can make accurate predictions on data it has not seen before. We can measure the model's performance relative to the known targets when working with supervised learning problems (either classification or regression problems).

Importantly, how we measure the model's performance on classification tasks and regression tasks differs. scikit-learn has many built-in metrics functions ready for use with either a classification or regression problem (`https://scikit-learn.org/stable/modules/model_evaluation.html`). Let's review the most common of these.

Classification metrics can be defined in terms of positive and negative predictions made by the model. The following definitions can be used to calculate classification metrics:

- **True positive (TP)**: A positive instance is correctly classified as positive

- **True negative (TN)**: A negative instance is correctly classified as negative

- **False positive (FP)**: A negative instance is incorrectly classified as positive

- **False negative (FN)**: A positive instance is incorrectly classified as negative

Given these definitions, the most common *classification* metrics are as follows:

- **Accuracy**: Accuracy is the most straightforward classification metric. Accuracy is the number of correct predictions divided by the total number of predictions. However, accuracy is susceptible to an imbalance in the data. For example, suppose we have an email dataset with 8 examples of spam and 2 examples of non-spam, and our model predicts only spam. In that case, the model has an accuracy of 80%, even though it never correctly classified non-spam emails. Mathematically, we can define accuracy as follows:

$$Accuracy = \frac{TP + TN}{TP + FP + TN + FN}$$

- **Precision**: The precision score is one way of getting a more nuanced understanding of the classification performance. Precision is the ratio between the true positive prediction (correctly predicted) and all positive predictions (true positive and false positive). In other words, the precision score indicates how precise the model is in predicting positives. In our spam emails example, a model predicting only spam is not very precise (as it classifies all non-spam emails as spam) and has a lower precision score. The following formula can be used to calculate precision:

$$Precision = \frac{TP}{TP + FP}$$

- **Recall**: The recall score is the counterpoint to the precision score. The recall score measures how effectively the model finds (or recalls) all true positive cases. The recall is calculated as the ratio between true positive predictions and all positive instances (true positive and false negative). In our spam example, a model predicting only spam has perfect recall (it can find all the spam). We can calculate recall like so:

$$Recall = \frac{TP}{TP + FN}$$

- **F1 score**: Finally, we have the F1 score. The F1 score is calculated as the harmonic mean between precision and recall. The F1 score balances precision and recall, giving us a singular value that summarizes the classifier's performance. The following formula can be used to calculate the F1 score:

$$F_1 = \frac{2 \times Precision \times Recall}{Precision + Recall} = \frac{2 \times TP}{2 \times TP + FP + FN}$$

The preceding classification metrics are the most common, but there are many more. Even though the F1 score is commonly used in classification problems (as it summarizes precision and recall), choosing the best metric is specific to the problem you are solving. Often, it might be the case that a specific metric is required, but other times, you must choose based on experience and your understanding of the data. We will look at examples of different metrics later in this book.

The following are common *regression* metrics:

- **Mean squared error (MSE)**: The MSE is calculated as the average of the squared differences between predicted and actual values. The MSE is commonly used because of one crucial mathematical property: the MSE is *differentiable* and is therefore appropriate for use with gradient-based learning methods. However, since the difference is squared, the MSE penalizes large errors more heavily than small errors, which may or may not be appropriate to the problem being solved.

- **Mean absolute error (MAE)**: Instead of squaring the differences, the MAE is calculated as the average of the absolute differences between predicted and actual values. By avoiding the square of errors, the MAE is more robust against the magnitude of errors and less sensitive to outliers than the MSE. However, the MAE is not differentiable and, therefore, can't be used with gradient-based learning methods.

As with the classification metrics, choosing the most appropriate regression metric is specific to the problem you are trying to solve.

> **Metrics versus objectives**
>
> We defined training a model as finding the most appropriate parameters to minimize an *objective function*. It's important to note that the objective function and metrics used for a specific problem may differ. A good example is decision trees, where a measure of impurity (entropy) is used as the objective function when building a tree. However, we still calculate the metrics explained previously to determine the tree's performance on the data.

With our understanding of basic metrics in place, we can conclude our introduction to machine learning concepts. Now, let's review the terms and concepts we've discussed using an example.

A modeling example

Consider the following data of sales by month, in thousands:

Jan	Feb	Mar	Apr	May	Jun
4,140	4,850	7,340	6,890	8,270	10,060
Jul	Aug	Sept	Oct	Nov	Dec
8,110	11,670	10,450	11,540	13,400	14,420

Table 1.1 – Sample sales data, by month, in thousands

This problem is straightforward: there is only one feature, the month, and the target is the number of sales. Therefore, this is an example of a supervised regression problem.

> **Note**
>
> You might have noticed that this is an example of a time series problem: time is the primary variable. Time series can also be predicted using more advanced time series-specific algorithms such as ANOVA, but we'll use a simple algorithm for illustration purposes in this section.

We can plot our data as a graph of sales per month to understand it better:

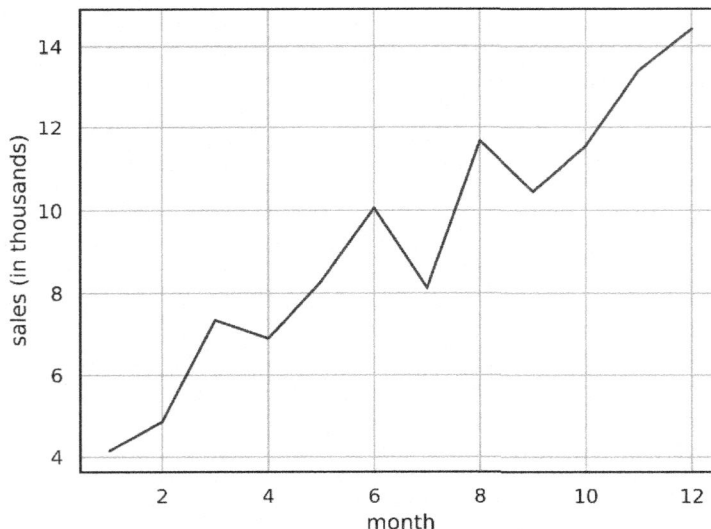

Figure 1.3 – Graph showing store sales by month

Here, we're using a straight-line model, also known as simple linear regression, to model our sales data. The definition of a straight line is given by the following formula:

$$y = mx + c$$

Here, m is the line's slope and c is the Y-intercept. In machine learning, the straight line is the model, and m and c are the model parameters.

To find the best parameters, we must measure how well our model fits the data for a particular set of parameters – that is, the error in our outputs. We will use the MAE as our metric:

$$MAE = \frac{\sum_{i=1}^{n}|\hat{y} - y|}{n}$$

Here, $\hat{y}$ is the predicted output, y is the actual output, and n is the number of predictions. We calculate the MAE by making a prediction for each of our inputs and then calculating the MAE based on the formula.

Fitting the model

Now, let's fit our linear model to our data. Our process for fitting the line is iterative, and we start this process by guessing values for m and c and then iterating from there. For example, let's consider $m = 0.1, c = 4$:

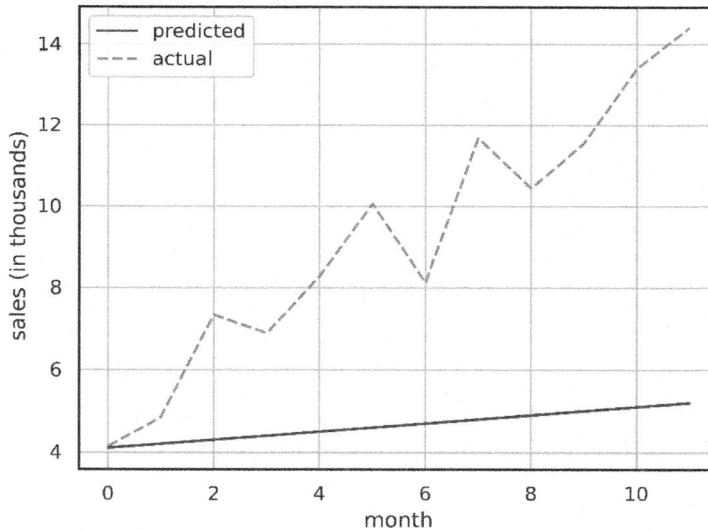

Figure 1.4 – Graph showing the prediction of a linear model with m = 0.1 and c = 4

With these parameters, we achieve an error of 4,610.

Our guess is far too low, but that's okay; we can now update the parameters to attempt to improve the error. In reality, updating the model parameters is done algorithmically using a training algorithm such as gradient descent. We'll discuss gradient descent in *Chapter 2, Ensemble Learning – Bagging and Boosting*.

In this example, we'll use our understanding of straight lines and intuition to update the parameters for each iteration manually. Our line is too shallow, and the intercept is too low; therefore, we must increase both values. We can control the updates we make each iteration by choosing a *step size*. We must update the *m* and *c* values with each iteration by adding the step size. The results, for a step size of 0.1, is shown in *Table 1.2*.

Guess#	*m*	*c*	*MAE*
1	0.1	4	4.61
2	0.2	4.1	3.89
3	0.3	4.2	3.17
4	0.3	4.3	2.5
5	0.4	4.4	1.83

Table 1.2 – Step wise guessing of the slope (***m***) and y-intercept (***c***) for a straight line to fit our data. The quality of fit is measured using the MAE

In our example, the *step size* is a *hyperparameter* of our training process.

We end up with an error of *1.83*, which means, on average, our predictions are wrong by less than *2,000*.

Now, let's see how we can solve this problem using scikit-learn.

Linear regression with scikit-learn

Instead of manually modeling, we can use scikit-learn to build a linear regression model. As this is our first example, we'll walk through the code line by line and explain what's happening.

To start with, we must import the Python tools we are going to use:

```
import numpy as np
import pandas as pd

from matplotlib import pyplot as plt
import seaborn as sns

from sklearn.linear_model import LinearRegression
from sklearn.metrics import mean_absolute_error
```

There are three sets of imports: we import numpy and pandas first. Importing NumPy and pandas is a widely used way to start all your data science notebooks. Also, note the short names np and pd, which are the standard conventions when working with numpy and pandas.

Next, we import a few standard plotting libraries we will use to plot some graphs: pyplot from matplotlib and seaborn. Matplotlib is a widely used plotting library that we access via the pyplot python interface. **Seaborn** is another visualization tool built on top of Matplotlib, which makes it easier to draw professional-looking graphs.

Finally, we get to our scikit-learn imports. In Python code, the scikit-learn library is called `sklearn`. From its `linear_model` package, we import `LinearRegression`. scikit-learn implements a wide variety of predefined metrics, and here, we will be using `mean_absolute_error`.

Now, we are ready to set up our data:

```
months = np.array([ 1,   2,   3,   4,   5,   6,   7,   8,   9, 10, 11, 12])
sales = np.array([4.14,   4.85,   7.34,   6.89,   8.27, 10.06,   8.11,
11.67, 10.45, 11.54, 13.4 , 14.42])

df = pd.DataFrame({"month": months, "sales": sales})
```

Here, we define a new numpy array for the months and the corresponding sales, and to make them easier to work with, we gather both arrays into a new pandas DataFrame.

With the data in place, we get to the interesting part of the code: modeling using scikit-learn. The code is straightforward:

```
model = LinearRegression()
model = model.fit(df[["month"]], df[["sales"]])
```

First, we create our model by constructing an instance of `LinearRegression`. We then fit our model using `model.fit` and passing in the month and sales data from our DataFrame. These two lines are all that's required to fit a model, and as we'll see in later chapters, even complicated models use the same recipe to instantiate and train a model.

We can now calculate our *MAE* by creating predictions for our data and passing the predictions and actual targets to the metric function:

```
predicted_sales = model.predict(df[["month"]])
mean_absolute_error(predicted_sales, df[["sales"]])
```

We get an error of *0.74*, which is slightly lower than our guesswork. We can also examine the model's coefficient and intercept (m and c from earlier):

```
print(f"Gradient: ${model.coef_}")
print(f"Intercept: ${model.intercept_}")
```

scikit-learn has fitted a model with a coefficient of *0.85* and an intercept of *3.68*. We were in the right neighborhood with our guesses, but it might have taken us some time to get to the optimal values.

That concludes our introduction to scikit-learn and the basics of modeling and machine learning. In our toy example, we did not split our data into separate datasets, optimize our model's hyperparameters, or apply any techniques to ensure our model does not overfit. In the next section, we'll look at classification and regression examples, where we'll apply these and other best practices.

Decision tree learning

This section introduces decision tree learning, a machine learning algorithm essential to understanding LightGBM. We'll work through an example of how to build decision trees using scikit-learn. This section will also provide some mathematical definitions for building decision trees; understanding these definitions is not critical, but it will help us understand our discussion of the decision tree hyperparameters.

Decision trees are tree-based learners that function by asking successive questions about the data to determine the result. A path is followed down the tree, making decisions about the input using one or more features. The path terminates at a leaf node, which represents the predicted class or value. Decision trees can be used for classification or regression.

The following is an illustration of a decision tree fit on the Iris dataset:

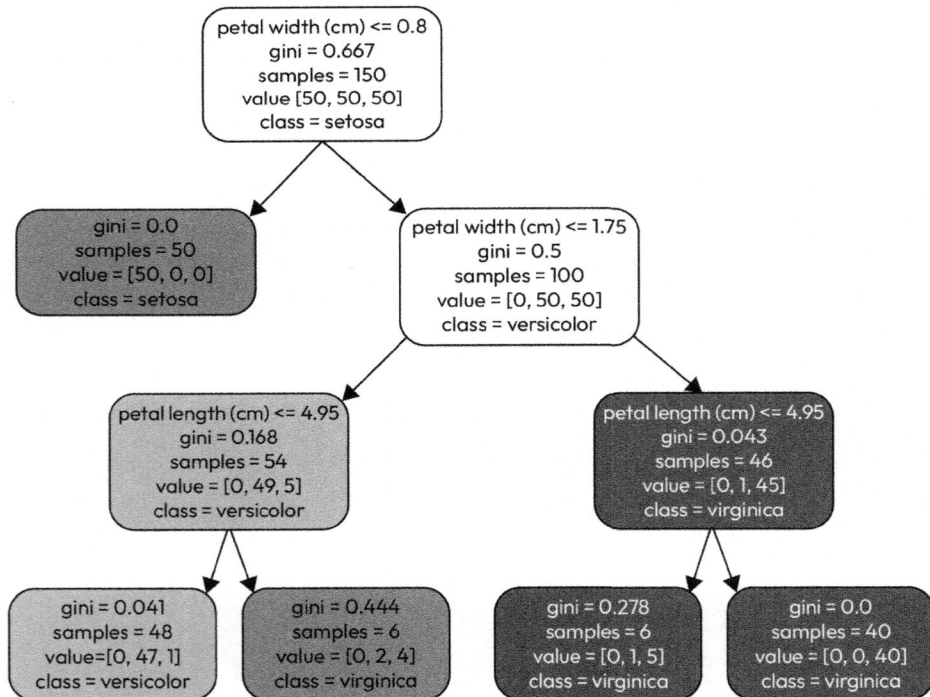

Figure 1.5 – A decision tree modeling the Iris dataset

The Iris dataset is a classification dataset where Iris flower sepal and petal dimensions are used to predict the type of Iris flower. Each non-leaf node uses one or more features to narrow down the samples in the dataset: the root node starts with all 150 samples and then splits them based on petal width, <= 0.8. We continue down the tree, with each node splitting the samples further until we reach a leaf node that contains the predicted class (versicolor, virginica, or setosa).

Compared to other models, decision trees have many advantages:

- **Features may be numeric or categorical**: Samples can be split using either numerical features (by splitting a range) or categorical ones without us having to encode either.

- **Reduced need for data preparation**: Decision splits are not sensitive to data ranges or size. Many other models (for example, neural networks) require data to be normalized to unit ranges.

- **Interpretability**: As shown previously, it's straightforward to interpret the predictions made by a tree. Interpretability is valuable in contexts where a prediction must be explained to decision-makers.

These are just some of the advantages of using tree-based models. However, we also need to be aware of some of the disadvantages associated with decision trees:

- **Overfitting**: Decision trees are very prone to overfitting. Setting the correct hyperparameters is essential when fitting decision trees. Overfitting in decision trees will be discussed in detail later.

- **Poor extrapolation**: Decision trees are poor at extrapolation since their predictions are not continuous and are effectively bounded by the training data.

- **Unbalanced data**: When fitting a tree on unbalanced data, the high-frequency classes dominate the predictions. Data needs to be prepared to remove imbalances.

A more detailed discussion of the advantages and disadvantages of decision trees is available at https://scikit-learn.org/stable/modules/tree.html.

Entropy and information gain

First, we need a rudimentary understanding of entropy and information gain before we look at an algorithm for building (or fitting) a decision tree.

Entropy can be considered a way to measure the disorder or randomness of a system. Entropy measures how surprising the result of a specific input or event might be. Consider a well-shuffled deck of cards: drawing from the top of the deck could give us any of the cards in the deck (a surprising result each time); therefore, we can say that a shuffled deck of cards has **high entropy**. Drawing cards from the top of an ordered deck is unsurprising; we know which cards come next. Therefore, an ordered deck of cards has **low entropy**. Another way to interpret entropy is the impurity of the dataset: a low-entropy dataset (neatly ordered) has less impurity than a high-entropy dataset.

Information gain, in turn, is the amount of information gained when modifying or observing the underlying data. Information gain involves reducing entropy from before the observation. In our deck of cards example, we might take a shuffled deck of cards and split it into four smaller decks by suit (spades, hearts, diamonds, and clubs). If we draw from the smaller decks, the outcome is less of a surprise: we know that the next card is from the same suit. By splitting the deck by suit, we have reduced the entropy of the smaller decks. Splitting the deck of cards on a feature (the suit) is very similar to how the splits in a decision tree work; each division seeks to maximize the information gain – that is, they minimize the entropy after the split.

In decision trees, there are two common ways of measuring information gain or the loss of impurity:

- The Gini index
- Log loss or entropy

A detailed explanation of each is available at `https://scikit-learn.org/stable/modules/tree.html#classification-criteria`.

Building a decision tree using C4.5

C4.5 is an algorithm for building a decision tree from a dataset [1]. The algorithm is recursive and starts with the following base cases:

1. If all the samples in a sub-dataset are of the same class, create a leaf node in the tree that chooses that class.
2. If no information can be gained by splitting using any of the features (the dataset can't be divided any further), create a leaf node that predicts the most frequent class contained in the sub-dataset.
3. If a minimum threshold of samples is reached in a sub-dataset, create a leaf node that predicts the most frequent class contained in the sub-dataset.

Then, we can apply the algorithm:

1. Check for any of the three base cases and stop splitting if any applies to the dataset.
2. For each feature or attribute of the dataset, calculate the information gained by splitting the dataset on that feature.
3. Create a decision node by splitting the dataset on the feature with the highest information gain.
4. Split the dataset into two sub-datasets based on the decision node and recursively reply to the algorithm on each sub-dataset.

Once the tree has been built, pruning is applied. During pruning, decision nodes with a relatively lower information gain than other tree nodes are removed. Removing nodes avoids overfitting the training data and improves the tree's generalization ability.

Classification and Regression Tree

You may have noticed that in the preceding explanations, we only used classes to split datasets using decision nodes; this is not by chance, as the canonical C4.5 algorithm only supports classification trees. **Classification and Regression Tree (CART)** extends C4.5 to support numerical target variables – that is, regression problems [2]. With CART, decision nodes can also split continuous numerical input variables to support regression, typically using a threshold (for example, x <= 0.3). When reaching a leaf node, the mean or median of the remaining numerical range is generally taken as the predicted value.

When building classification trees, only impurity is used to determine splits. However, with regression trees, impurity is combined with other criteria to calculate optimal splits:

- The MSE (or MAE)
- Half Poisson Deviance

A detailed mathematical explanation of each is available at `https://scikit-learn.org/stable/modules/tree.html#regression-criteria`.

scikit-learn uses an optimized version of CART to build decision trees.

Overfitting in decision trees

One of the most significant disadvantages of decision trees is that they are prone to overfitting. Without proper hyperparameter choices, C4.5 and other training algorithms create overly complex and deep trees that fit the training data almost exactly. Managing overfitting is a crucial part of building decision trees. Here are some strategies to avoid overfitting:

- **Pruning**: As mentioned previously, we can remove branches that do not contribute much information gain; this reduces the tree's complexity and improves generalization.
- **Maximum depth**: Limiting the depth of the tree also avoids overly complex trees and avoids overfitting.
- **Maximum number of leaf nodes**: Similar to restricting depth, limiting the number of leaf nodes avoids overly specific branches and improves generalization.
- **Minimum samples per leaf**: Setting a minimum limit on the number of samples a leaf may contain (stopping splitting when the sub-dataset is of the minimum size) also avoids overly specific leaf nodes.
- **Ensemble methods**: Ensemble learning is a technique that combines multiple models to improve the prediction over an individual model. Averaging the prediction of multiple models can also reduce overfitting.

These strategies can be applied by setting the appropriate hyperparameters. Now that we understand how to build decision trees and strategies for overfitting, let's look at building decision trees in scikit-learn.

Building decision trees with scikit-learn

It is time to examine how we may use decision trees by training classification and regression trees using scikit-learn.

For these examples, we'll use the toy datasets included in scikit-learn. These datasets are small compared to real-world data but are easy to work with, allowing us to focus on the decision trees.

Classifying breast cancer

We'll use the Breast Cancer dataset (`https://scikit-learn.org/stable/datasets/toy_dataset.html#breast-cancer-dataset`) for our classification example. This dataset consists of features that have been calculated from the images of fine needle aspirated breast masses, and the task is to predict whether the mass is malignant or benign.

Using scikit-learn, we can solve this classification problem with five lines of code:

```
dataset = datasets.load_breast_cancer()

X_train, X_test, y_train, y_test = train_test_split(dataset.data,
dataset.target, random_state=157)

model = DecisionTreeClassifier(random_state=157, max_depth=3, min_
samples_split=2)
model = model.fit(X_train, y_train)

f1_score(y_test, model.predict(X_test))
```

First, we load the dataset using `load_breast_cancer`. Then, we split our dataset into training and test sets using `train_test_split`; by default, 25% of the data is used for the test set. Like before, we instantiate our `DecisionTreeClassifier` model and train it on the training set using `model.fit`. The two hyperparameters we pass through when instantiating the model are notable: `max_depth` and `min_samples_split`. Both parameters control overfitting and will be discussed in more detail in the next section. We also specify `random_state` for both the train-test split and the model. By fixing the random state, we ensure the outcome is repeatable (otherwise, a new random state is created by scikit-learn for every execution).

Finally, we measure the performance using `f1_score`. Our model achieves an F1 score of 0.94 and an accuracy of 93.7%. F1 scores are out of 1.0, so we may conclude that the model does very well. If we break down our predictions, the model missed the prediction on only 9 of the 143 samples in the test set: 7 false positives and 2 false negatives.

Predicting diabetes progression

To illustrate solving a regression problem with decision trees, we'll use the Diabetes dataset (`https://scikit-learn.org/stable/datasets/toy_dataset.html#diabetes-dataset`). This dataset has 10 features (age, sex, body mass index, and others), and the model is tasked with predicting a quantitative measure of disease progression after 1 year.

We can use the following code to build and evaluate a regression model:

```
dataset = datasets.load_diabetes()

X_train, X_test, y_train, y_test = train_test_split(dataset.data,
dataset.target, random_state=157)

model = DecisionTreeRegressor(random_state=157, max_depth=3, min_
samples_split=2)
model = model.fit(X_train, y_train)

mean_absolute_error(y_test, model.predict(X_test))
```

Our model achieves an MAE of 45.28. The code is almost identical to our classification example: instead of a classifier, we use `DecisionTreeRegressor` as our model and calculate `mean_absolute_error` instead of the F1 score. The consistency in the API for solving various problems with different types of models in scikit-learn is by design and illustrates a fundamental truth in machine learning work: even though data, models, and metrics change, *the overall process for building machine learning models remains the same*. In the coming chapters, we'll expand on this general methodology and leverage the process' consistency when building machine learning pipelines.

Decision tree hyperparameters

We used some decision tree hyperparameters in the preceding classification and regression examples to control overfitting. This section will look at the most critical decision tree hyperparameters provided by scikit-learn:

- `max_depth`: The maximum depth the tree is allowed to reach. Deeper trees allow more splits, resulting in more complex trees and overfitting.

- `min_samples_split`: The minimum number of samples required to split a node. Nodes containing only a few samples overfit the data, whereas having a larger minimum improves generalization.

- `min_samples_leaf`: The minimum number of samples allowed in leaf nodes. Like the minimum samples in a split, increasing the value leads to less complex trees, reducing overfitting.

- `max_leaf_nodes`: The maximum number of lead nodes to allow. Fewer leaf nodes reduce the tree size and, therefore, the complexity, which may improve generalization.

- `max_features`: The maximum features to consider when determining a split. Discarding some features reduces noise in the data, which improves overfitting. Features are chosen at random.

- `criterion`: The impurity measure to use when determining a split, either `gini` or `entropy`/`log_loss`.

As you may have noticed, most decision tree hyperparameters involve controlling overfitting by controlling the complexity of the tree. These parameters provide multiple ways of doing so, and finding the best combination of parameters and their values is non-trivial. Finding the best hyperparameters is called **hyperparameter tuning** and will be covered extensively later in this book.

A complete list of the hyperparameters can be found at the following places:

- `https://scikit-learn.org/stable/modules/generated/sklearn.tree.DecisionTreeClassifier.html#sklearn-tree-decisiontreeclassifier`
- `https://scikit-learn.org/stable/modules/generated/sklearn.tree.DecisionTreeRegressor.html#sklearn.tree.DecisionTreeRegressor`

Now, let's summarize the key takeaways from this chapter.

Summary

In this chapter, we introduced machine learning as a method of creating software by learning to perform a task from a corpus of data instead of relying on programming the instructions by hand. We introduced the core concepts of machine learning with a focus on supervised learning and illustrated their applications through examples with scikit-learn.

We also introduced decision trees as a machine learning algorithm and discussed their strengths and weaknesses, as well as how to control overfitting using hyperparameters. We concluded this chapter with examples of how to solve classification and regression problems using decision trees in scikit-learn.

This chapter has given us a foundational understanding of machine learning, enabling us to dive deeper into the data science process and the LightGBM library.

The next chapter will focus on ensemble learning in decision trees, a technique where the predictions of multiple decision trees are combined to improve the overall performance. Boosting, particularly gradient boosting, will be covered in detail.

References

[1]   J. R. Quinlan, C4.5: Programs for machine learning, Elsevier, 2014.

[2]   R. J. Lewis, An introduction to classification and regression tree (CART) analysis, in Annual meeting of the Society For Academic Emergency Medicine in San Francisco, California, 2000.

2

Ensemble Learning – Bagging and Boosting

In the previous chapter, we covered the fundamentals of **machine learning** (**ML**), working with data and models, and concepts such as overfitting and **supervised learning** (**SL**). We also introduced decision trees and saw how to apply them practically in scikit-learn.

In this chapter, we will learn about ensemble learning and the two most significant types of ensemble learning: bagging and boosting. We will cover the theory and practice of applying ensemble learning to decision trees and conclude the chapter by focusing on more advanced boosting methods.

By the end of this chapter, you will have a good understanding of ensemble learning and how to practically build decision tree ensembles through bagging or boosting. We will also be ready to dive deep into LightGBM, including its more advanced theoretical aspects.

The main topics we will cover are set out here:

- Ensemble learning
- Bagging and random forests
- **Gradient-boosted decision trees** (**GBDTs**)
- Advanced boosting algorithm—**Dropouts meet Multiple Additive Regression Trees** (**DART**)

Technical requirements

The chapter includes examples of simple ML algorithms and introduces working with scikit-learn. You must install a Python environment with scikit-learn, NumPy, pandas, and Jupyter. The code for this chapter is available at `https://github.com/PacktPublishing/Practical-Machine-Learning-with-LightGBM-and-Python/tree/main/chapter-2`.

Ensemble learning

Ensemble learning is the practice of combining multiple predictors, or models, to create a more robust model. Models can either be of the same type (homogenous ensembles) or different types (heterogenous ensembles). Further, ensemble learning is not specific to decision trees and can be applied to any ML technique, including linear models, **neural networks** (**NNs**), and more.

The central idea behind ensemble learning is that by aggregating the results of many models, we compensate for the weaknesses of a single model.

Of course, training the same models on the same data is not helpful in an ensemble (as the models will have similar predictions). Therefore, we aim for **diversity** in the models. Diversity refers to the degree to which each model in the ensemble differs. A high-diversity ensemble has widely different models.

There are several ways we can ensure diversity in our ensemble. One method is to train models on different subsets of the training data. Each model is exposed to different patterns and noise in the training data, increasing the diversity of the trained models.

Similarly, we can train each model on a different subset of features in the training data. Some features are more valuable than others, and some might be irrelevant, leading to diversity in the model predictions.

We can also train each model with different hyperparameters, leading to different models of varying complexity and ability. The impact of hyperparameters is especially pronounced in the case of decision trees, where the hyperparameters significantly impact the structure of the trees, leading to very different models.

Finally, we could diversify the ensemble by using different types of models. Each model has unique strengths and weaknesses, leading to diversity in the ensemble.

The **ensemble learning method** refers to how we introduce diversity in ensemble models by specifying how we train the member models and how we combine the results of the models. The most common ensemble methods are set out here:

- **Bootstrap aggregation (bagging)**: These are methods where models are trained on subsets of the training data (either samples or features), and the predictions are aggregated.

- **Boosting**: This involves iteratively training models on the errors of previous models. The final prediction is made by combining the prediction of all models in the chain.

- **Stacking**: This involves methods where multiple base models are trained, then a higher-order model (known as a meta-model) is trained to learn from the base model predictions and make the final prediction.

- **Blending**: This is very similar to stacking. However, the meta-model is trained on predictions made by the base models on a *hold-out set* (a part of the training data the base learners were not trained on) instead of the whole training set.

The purpose of ensemble learning methods is to improve our prediction performance, and there are several ways ensembles improve the performance over individual models, as outlined here:

- **Improved accuracy**: By combining predictions, we increase the likelihood that the final prediction is accurate as, in aggregate, models make fewer mistakes.

- **Improved generalization and overfitting**: By aggregating predictions, we reduce the variance in the final prediction, improving generalization. Further, in some ensemble methods, the models cannot access all data (bagging ensembles), reducing noise and overfitting.

- **Improved prediction stability**: The aggregation of predictions reduces the random fluctuations of individual predictions. Ensembles are less sensitive to outliers, and outlying predictions of member models have a limited impact on the final prediction.

Decision trees are well suited for ensemble learning, and decision tree-specific algorithms exist for ensemble learning. The following section discusses bagging ensembles in decision trees focusing on **random forests**.

Bagging and random forests

Bagging is an ensemble method where multiple models are trained on subsets of the training data. The models' predictions are combined to make a final prediction, usually by taking the average for numerical prediction (for regression) or the majority vote for a class (for classification). When training each model, we select a subset of data from the original training dataset with replacement—that is, a specific training pattern can be a member of multiple subsets. Since each model is only presented with a sample of the training data, no single model can "memorize" the training data, which reduces overfitting. The following diagram illustrates the bagging process:

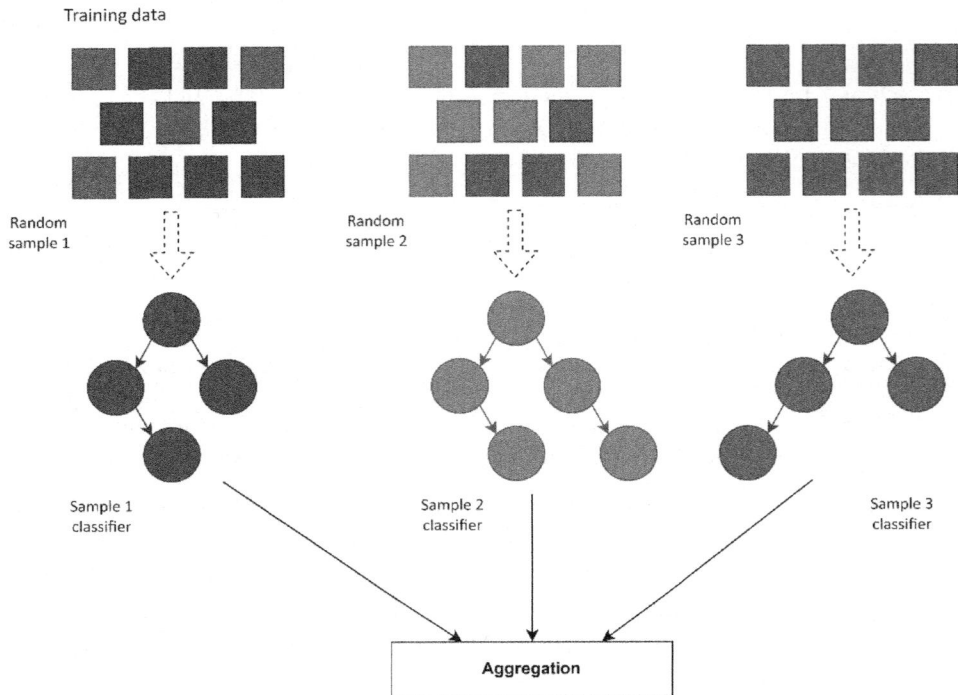

Figure 2.1 – Illustration of the bagging process; each independent classifier is
trained on a random subsample from the training data and a final prediction
is made by aggregating the predictions of all classifiers

Each model in a bagging ensemble is still a complete model, capable of standing on its own. As such, bagging works best with strong models—that is, in the case of decision trees, deep or wide decision trees.

While the previous example illustrates sampling patterns from the training set, it is also possible to subsample random features from the dataset for each model. Selecting features at random when creating a training set is known as a random subspace method or feature bagging. Feature bagging prevents occurrences where a specific attribute might dominate the prediction or mislead the model and further reduces overfitting.

In decision trees, a popular algorithm that applies both sample bagging and feature bagging is the random forest. Let's have a look at this algorithm now.

Random forest

Random forest is a decision tree-specific bagging ensemble learning method [1]. Instead of building a single decision tree, as the name implies, many decision trees are trained using bagging: each tree is trained on either random samples, random features from the training data, or both. Random forests support both classification and regression.

The training methodology for individual trees in random forests is the same as for a single decision tree, and as explained previously, each tree is a complete tree. The final prediction for the forest is made by taking the arithmetic mean of all trees in the case of prediction or the majority vote for a class (in the case of classification).

Regarding performance, random forest learning produces a more robust model with higher accuracy, which tends to avoid overfitting (since no single model can overfit on all training data).

Random forest hyperparameters

In scikit-learn, as may be expected, the hyperparameters available for random forests are the same as those available to train decision trees. We can specify `max_depth`, `min_samples_split`, `max_leaf_nodes`, and so on, which are then used to train the individual trees. However, there are three notable additional parameters, as follows:

- `n_estimators`: Controls the number of trees in the forest. Generally, more trees are better. However, a point of diminishing returns is often reached.

- `max_features`: Determines the maximum number of features to be used as a subset when splitting a node. Setting `max_features=1.0` allows all features to be used in the random selection.

- `bootstrap` determines whether bagging is used. All trees use the entire training set if `bootstrap` is set to `False`.

A list of all parameters available in scikit-learn is available here: `https://scikit-learn.org/stable/modules/generated/sklearn.ensemble.RandomForestClassifier.html`.

ExtraTrees

Extremely Randomized Trees (ExtraTrees) is a related method for building randomized decision trees. With ExtraTrees, when building a decision node, several candidate splits are created randomly instead of using the *Gini index* or *information gain* metric to calculate the optimal split [2]. The best split from all random splits is then chosen for the node. The methodology for ExtraTrees can be applied to a single decision tree or used in conjunction with Random Forests. scikit-learn implements ExtraTrees as an extension to random forests (`https://scikit-learn.org/stable/modules/ensemble.html#extremely-randomized-trees`).

In scikit-learn, the ExtraTrees implementation has the same hyperparameters as random forests.

Training random forests using scikit-learn

We'll now have a look at using random forests with scikit-learn.

In this example, we'll use the *Forest CoverType* dataset (https://archive.ics.uci.edu/ml/datasets/Covertype), which is available within scikit-learn (https://scikit-learn.org/stable/modules/generated/sklearn.datasets.fetch_covtype.html#sklearn.datasets.fetch_covtype). The dataset is a significant step up from the toy datasets we were using previously. The dataset consists of 581,012 samples and has a dimensionality (number of features) of 54. The features describe a 30x30m patch of forest in the US (for example, elevation, aspect, slope, and distances to hydrology). We must build a classifier to classify each patch into one of seven classes describing the forest cover type.

In addition to training a `RandomForestClassifier`, we'll train a standalone `DecisionTreeClassifier` and an `ExtraTreesClassifier` and compare the performance of the algorithms.

`RandomForestClassifier` and `ExtraTreesClassifier` live in the `sklearn.ensemble` package. In addition to our regular imports, we import the classifiers from there, like so:

```
from sklearn import datasets
from sklearn.tree import DecisionTreeClassifier
from sklearn.ensemble import RandomForestClassifier,
ExtraTreesClassifier
from sklearn.model_selection import train_test_split
from sklearn.metrics import f1_score
```

The scikit-learn datasets package provides the Forest Cover dataset. We can use scikit-learn to fetch the dataset and split it into our training and test sets, as follows:

```
dataset = datasets.fetch_covtype()
X_train, X_test, y_train, y_test = train_test_split(dataset.data,
dataset.target, random_state=179)
```

Finally, we can train our classifiers and evaluate each of them against the test set:

```
tree = DecisionTreeClassifier(random_state=179, min_samples_leaf=3,
min_samples_split=6)
tree = tree.fit(X_train, y_train)
print(f1_score(y_test, tree.predict(X_test), average="macro"))
forest = RandomForestClassifier(random_state=179, min_samples_leaf=1,
min_samples_split=2, n_estimators=140)
forest = forest.fit(X_train, y_train)
print(f1_score(y_test, forest.predict(X_test), average="macro"))
extra_tree = ExtraTreesClassifier(random_state=179, min_samples_
leaf=1, min_samples_split=2, n_estimators=180)
extra_tree = extra_tree.fit(X_train, y_train)
print(f1_score(y_test, extra_tree.predict(X_test), average="macro"))
```

We have set hyperparameters for the models that are appropriate to the problem. An additional step would be to optimize the algorithm hyperparameters to discover the best parameter values. Parameter optimization is discussed in detail in a later chapter.

Running the preceding code, we get the following F1 scores for each of the algorithms:

Model	F1 score
Decision Tree	0.8917
Random Forest	0.9209
ExtraTrees	0.9231

Table 2.1 – F1 scores for each of the algorithms on the Forest CoverType dataset

The ExtraTrees model slightly outperforms the random forest model, and both perform better than the decision tree classifier.

In this section, we gave an overview of bagging and random forests, a bagging-based decision tree ensemble learning method that provides some benefits over standard decision trees. The following section examines an alternative ensemble learning method: gradient boosting.

Gradient-boosted decision trees

Gradient boosting is an ensemble learning methodology that combines multiple models *sequentially* to produce a more robust ensemble model. Unlike bagging, where multiple *strong* models are used (in parallel), with boosting, multiple weak learners are trained, each learning from the mistakes of those before it to build a more accurate and robust ensemble model. Another distinct difference from bagging is that each model uses the entire dataset for training.

> **Note**
>
> As discussed next, gradient boosting always builds a series of regression trees to form part of the ensemble, regardless of whether a regression or classification problem is solved. Gradient boosting is also called **Multiple Additive Regression Trees (MART)**.

Abstractly, the boosting process starts with a weak base learner. In the case of decision trees, the base learner might have only a single split (also known as a decision stump). The error residuals (the difference between the predicted and actual targets) are then calculated. A new learner is then trained on the error residuals of the previous learner, looking to minimize the errors. The final prediction is a *summation* of the predictions from all the learners. The following diagram illustrates the iterative gradient-boosting process:

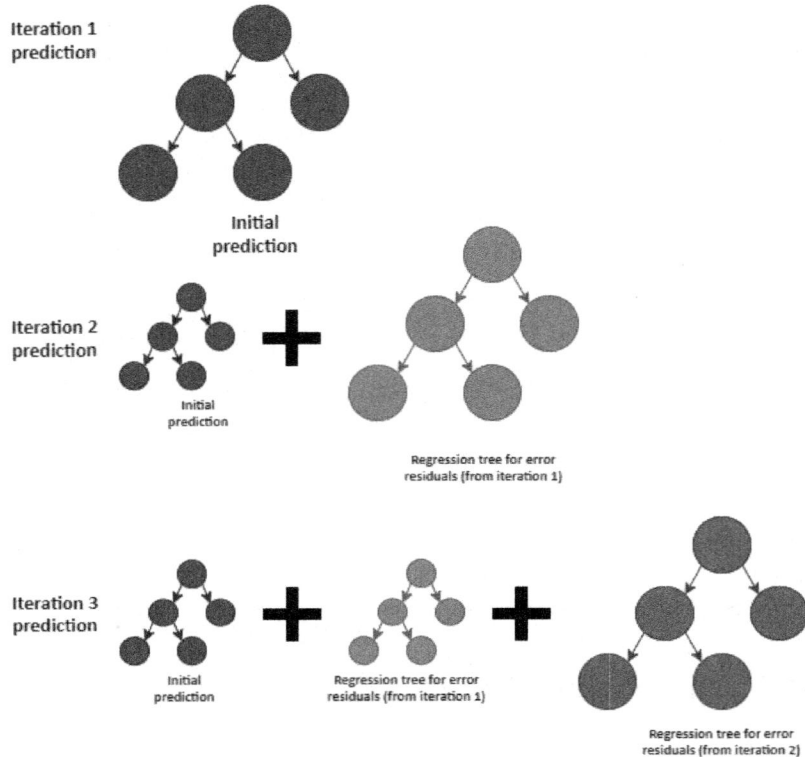

Figure 2.2 – Illustration of the gradient-boosting process; in each iteration, a new regression tree is added to compensate for the error residuals of the previous iteration

One of the critical questions relates to how we can determine the changes that reduce the error residuals. Gradient boosting solves the error minimization problem by applying a widely used optimization problem: gradient descent.

Gradient descent

Gradient descent is an optimization algorithm that attempts to find the optimal parameters to minimize a **loss function**. The parameters are updated iteratively by taking small steps in the direction of the negative gradient of the loss function (thereby decreasing the function value). A loss function is similar in concept to an error function but has two important properties, as outlined here:

- A loss function produces a numeric value that quantifies the model's performance or precisely how poorly a model is doing. A good loss function produces significantly different output for models with different performances. Some error functions can also be used as loss functions—for example, **mean squared error (MSE)**.

- The second property is that a loss function must be differentiable, specifically in the context of gradient descent. An example of an error function that's not differentiable is the F1 score. The F1 score may produce a numeric value of the model's performance, but it is not differentiable and cannot be used as a loss function.

The process for gradient descent can, then, be defined as follows. Suppose we have a loss function L defined for parameters x. For an initial set of parameters, the loss is calculated as $L(x_0)$. Gradient descent proceeds iteratively to minimize the loss function:

$$L(x_{n+1}) < L(x_n)$$

To update the parameters, *we take a step in the direction of the negative gradient of L*. We can specify the gradient descent update rule as follows:

$$x_{n+1} = x_n - \gamma_n \nabla L(x_n)$$

Here, γ_n is the **learning rate**, which defines the step size, and $\nabla L(x_n)$ is the gradient of L at x_n.

The graph in *Figure 2.3* illustrates the gradient descent process:

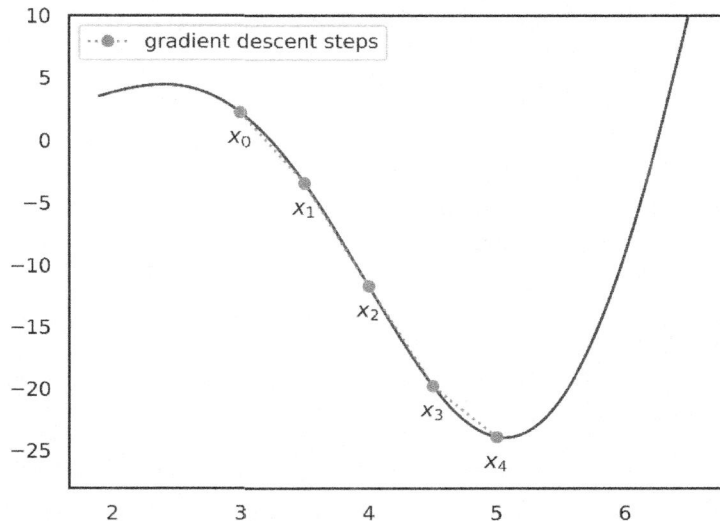

Figure 2.3 – Graph showing the gradient descent process to find the minimum of a function

Choosing an appropriate learning rate is critical to gradient descent's success. If the learning rate is too low, the optimization will be very slow, potentially not reaching a minimum in the allowed number of iterations. A small learning rate could also lead to the process getting stuck in a local minimum:

the step size being too small to escape. Conversely, suppose the learning rate is too large. In that case, we could step over the minimum and miss it entirely or get stuck oscillating around a minimum (constantly jumping back and forth but never descending to the optimal value).

Gradient boosting

Now that we understand how gradient descent works, we can see how it is applied in gradient boosting. We will work through the entire gradient-boosting algorithm in detail at the hand of a small example. In our example, we'll use a regression tree, as it is a bit easier to understand than the case for classification.

Gradient-boosting algorithm

The gradient-boosting algorithm is defined as follows, where M is the number of boosted trees [3]:

1. Given training data $\{(x_i, y_i)\}_{i=1}^n$, containing n training samples (defined by features x_i and target y_i) and a differentiable loss function $L(y_i, F(x))$, where $F(x)$ are the predictions from model F.

2. Initialize the model with a constant prediction value $F_0(X) = \underset{\gamma}{\mathrm{argmin}} \sum_{i=1}^n L(y_i, \gamma)$

3. For $m = 1 \ to \ M$:

    Compute pseudo residuals $r_{im} = - \left[\frac{\partial L(y_i, F(x_i))}{\partial F(x_i)} \right]_{F(X)=F_{m-1}(X)} for \ i = 1, \ldots, n$

    Fit a regression tree to the r_{im} values and create terminal regions $R_{jm} for \ j = 1 \ldots J_m$

    For $j = 1 \ldots J_m$ compute $\gamma_{jm} = \underset{\gamma}{\mathrm{argmin}} \sum_{x_i \in R_{ij}} L(y_i, F_{m-1}(x_i) + \gamma)$

    Update $F_m(x) = F_{m-1}(x) + v \sum_{j=1}^{J_m} \gamma_{jm} I(x \in R_{jm})$

4. Result: $F_M(x)$

Although the algorithm and especially the mathematics might look intimidating, it is practically much more straightforward than it appears. We'll go through the algorithm step by step. Consider the following toy dataset:

Gender	Fasting Blood Sugar	Waist Circumference	BMI	LDL Cholesterol
Male	105	110	29.3	170
Female	85	80	21	90
Male	95	93	26	113

Table 2.2 – Example dataset consisting of a patient's physical measurements and measured low-density lipoprotein (LDL) cholesterol

Given the physical measurements, we aim to predict a patient's LDL cholesterol.

The preceding table defines our training data $\{(x_i, y_i)\}_{i=1}^n$, where x is the features (blood sugar, waist circumference, BMI) and y is the target: LDL cholesterol.

We need a differentiable loss function, and to simplify some of the mathematical derivations in this example, we choose the following loss function, which is similar to the MSE function:

$$L = \frac{1}{2} \sum_{i=0}^{n} (y_i - \gamma_i)^2$$

We now work through each algorithm step in detail to see how the gradient-boosted tree is produced.

The first step is to find $F_0(x) = \mathrm{argmin}_\gamma \sum_{i=1}^{n} L(y_i, \gamma)$, where y_i is our target value and γ is our initial predicted value. *Our initial prediction is constant and is simply the average of the target values.* But let's see why.

The equation for $F_0(x)$ is stating that we need to find a value for γ that minimizes our loss function. To find the minimum, we take the derivative of the loss function with respect to gamma:

$$\frac{\partial L}{\partial \gamma} = \frac{2}{2} \left(\sum_{i=0}^{n} (y_i - \gamma) \right) \times -1$$

Then, set it to 0 and solve the following equation:

$$-\left(\sum_{i=0}^{n} (y_i - \gamma) \right) = 0$$

$$-\frac{1}{n} \sum_{i=0}^{n} y_i + \gamma = 0$$

$$\gamma = \frac{1}{n} \sum_{i=0}^{n} y_i$$

The equation simplifies to calculating the average of the target values.

Updating our table with the predictions, we have the following:

Gender	F. Blood Sugar	W. Circum.	BMI	LDL Cholesterol	PredictionF 0(x)
Male	105	110	29.3	170	125
Female	85	80	21	90	125
Male	95	93	26	113	125

Table 2.3 – Our initial prediction of LDL cholesterol predictions $\left(F_0(x) \right)$ for each patient is constant

We repeat the following M times, where M is the number of trees we choose to build.

We now need to calculate the pseudo residuals $r_{im} = -\left[\frac{\partial L(y_i, F(x_i))}{\partial F(x_i)} \right]_{F(X)=F_{m-1}(X)}$. This equation for r_{im} is stating that we use the negative of the partial derivative of the loss function, with respect to the predictions, to calculate the pseudo residuals. *This portion of the gradient-boosting algorithm relates to gradient descent: we are taking the negative of the gradient to minimize the residuals.* Fortunately, we have already calculated this derivative:

$$-\left[\frac{\partial L(y_i, F(x_i))}{\partial F(x_i)} \right] = -\frac{\partial}{\partial F(x_i)} \left(\frac{1}{2} (y_i - F(x_i))^2 \right) = \frac{2}{2}(y_i - F(x_i)) = \left(y_i - F(x_i) \right)$$

Here, $F(x_i)$ is the predicted value. In other words, *the equation simplifies the difference between the target and predicted values.* We can add the residuals to the table, as follows:

Gender	F. Blood Sugar	W. Circum.	BMI	LDL Cholesterol	Prediction F 0(x)	Residuals for F 0(x)
Male	105	110	29.3	170	125	45
Female	85	80	21	90	125	-35
Male	95	93	26	113	125	-12

Table 2.4 – Based on our initial prediction, we can calculate the residuals
for each patient, as shown in the Residuals for F 0(x) column

The next step is straightforward: we build a regression tree to predict the residuals. We do not use the predictions of the regression tree directly. Instead, we use the *terminal regions* to calculate our updated prediction. The terminal regions refer to the tree's leaf nodes.

For this example, we assume the following simple regression tree is built:

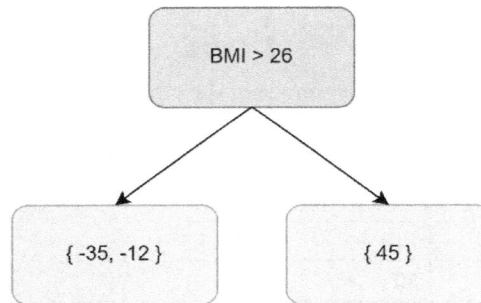

Figure 2.4 – Regression tree predicting the residuals

With our regression tree built and our leaf nodes defined, we can proceed with the next step. We need to compute γ_{jm} that minimizes our loss function, taking into account the previous predictions as per $\gamma_{jm} = \arg\min_{\gamma} \sum_{x_i \in R_{ij}} L\left(y_i, F_{m-1}(x_i) + \gamma\right)$. This is almost precisely what we did in *step 1*, where we showed that the equation simplifies taking the average of the predicted values due to our choice of the loss function. *Here, that means taking the average of the residuals in each leaf node.* Therefore, we have $\gamma_{1,1} = \frac{-35-12}{2} = -23.5$ and $\gamma_{2,1} = \frac{45}{1} = 45$.

Finally, we can now calculate our next prediction, $F_1(x)$, defined by: $F_m(x) = F_{m-1}(x) + v\sum_{j=1}^{J_m}\gamma_{jm}I\left(x \in R_{jm}\right)$, meaning our next prediction consists of the previous prediction plus the γ values calculated in *step 2.3*, weighed by a learning rate v. The summation here means that should a sample be part of multiple leaf nodes, we take the sum of the gamma values. Let's calculate $F_1(x)$ for the first sample in our dataset, using a learning rate of 0.1. According to the regression tree from *step 2.2*, our sample (which has a

BMI > 26) maps to $y_{2,1}$. Since it's only mapping to a single leaf, we don't need the summation part of the equation. Therefore, the equation looks like this:

$$F_1(x) = F_0(x) + vy_{2,1} = 125 + 0.1(45) = 129.5$$

As expected, our prediction has improved in the direction of our target values. Doing the same for the other samples, we have the following:

Gender	F. Blood Sugar	W. Circum.	BMI	LDL Cholesterol	Prediction F 0(x)	Residuals for F 0(x)	Prediction F 1(x)
Male	105	110	29.3	170	125	45	129.5
Female	85	80	21	90	125	-35	122,65
Male	95	93	26	113	125	-12	122,65

Table 2.5 – Following steps 2.1 to 2.4, we calculate a new prediction, F_1 (x), based on the initial prediction and the residuals

The purpose of the learning rate is to limit the impact each tree might have on the overall prediction: by improving our prediction with small steps, we end up with an overall more accurate model.

Step 2 is then repeated until we have a final prediction $F_M(x)$.

In summary, our gradient-boosting ensemble consists of a weighted (by the learning rate) summation of predictions made by a series of regression trees, each predicting the pseudo residuals (the error gradient, with respect to previous prediction) of previous predictions, thereby minimizing the error of previous predictions to produce an accurate final prediction.

Gradient boosting for classification

Our explanation of gradient boosting given previously used a regression problem as an example. We will not be going through a detailed example for classification as the algorithm is the same. However, instead of working with continuous predicted values, we use the same techniques as logistic regression (https://en.wikipedia.org/wiki/Logistic_regression). The individual trees, therefore, predict the probabilities of a sample belonging to the class. The probabilities are calculated by taking the log odds of a sample and converting them to a probability using the logistic function, as follows:

$$p(x) = \frac{1}{1 + e^{-(x-\mu)/s}}$$

The pseudo residuals are calculated as the difference between the observed value (1 or 0 for the class) and the predicted value (the probability from the logistic function). A final difference is the loss function. Instead of a function such as MSE, we can use cross-entropy for loss, as follows:

$$H_p(q) = -\frac{1}{N}\sum_{i=1}^{N} y_i \log(p(y_i)) + (1 - y_i)\log\left(1 - p(y_i)\right)$$

Gradient-boosted decision tree hyperparameters

In addition to the parameters for standard decision tree training, the following new hyperparameters are available in scikit-learn specific to gradient-boosted trees:

- `n_estimators`: Controls the number of trees in the ensemble. Generally, more trees are better. However, a point of diminishing returns is often reached, and overfitting occurs when there are too many trees.

- `learning_rate`: Controls the contribution of each tree to the ensemble. Lower learning rates lead to longer training times and may require more trees to be built (larger values for `n_estimators`). Setting `learning_rate` to a very large value may cause the optimization to miss optimum points and must be combined with fewer trees.

A complete list of scikit-learn gradient-boosting hyperparameters can be found at `https://scikit-learn.org/stable/modules/generated/sklearn.ensemble.GradientBoostingClassifier.html`.

Gradient boosting in scikit-learn

The details of gradient boosting are mathematical and complicated; fortunately, the algorithm is as accessible as any other via scikit-learn. The following is an example of a `GradientBoostingClassifier` class in scikit-learn, again using the *Forest CoverType* dataset we used earlier in the chapter to train a random forest classifier.

The classifier is also imported from the `ensemble` package, like so:

```
from sklearn.ensemble import GradientBoostingClassifier
```

We fetch and split the data as before and then fit the model, as follows:

```
dataset = datasets.fetch_covtype()

X_train, X_test, y_train, y_test = train_test_split(dataset.data,
dataset.target, random_state=179)
booster = GradientBoostingClassifier(random_state=179, min_samples_
leaf=3, min_samples_split=3, learning_rate=0.13, n_estimators=180)
booster = booster.fit(X_train, y_train)
print(f1_score(y_test, booster.predict(X_test), average="macro"))
```

Running the preceding code should produce an F1 score of 0.7119, a score that's significantly worse than even a standard decision tree. We can spend time optimizing our hyperparameters to improve performance. However, there is a more significant issue. The previous code takes very long to execute—in the order of 45 minutes on our hardware—compared to ExtraTrees, which takes approximately 3 minutes.

LightGBM addresses both issues we have with the gradient-boosted tree and builds a gradient-boosted tree with significantly better performance in a fraction of the time.

In the following section, we'll briefly cover an advanced algorithm related to gradient boosting: DART.

Advanced boosting algorithm – DART

DART is an extension of the standard GBDT algorithm discussed in the previous section [4]. DART employs **dropouts**, a technique from **deep learning** (**DL**), to avoid overfitting by the decision tree ensemble. The extension is straightforward and consists of two parts. First, when fitting the next prediction tree, $M_{n+1}(x)$, which consists of the scaled sum of all previous trees $M_n...M_1$, a random subset of the previous trees is instead used, with other trees dropped from the sum. The p_{drop} parameter controls the probability of a previous tree being included. The second part of the DART algorithm is to apply additional scaling of the contribution of the new tree. Let k be the number of trees dropped when the new tree, M_{n+1}, was calculated. Since M_{n+1} was calculated without the contribution of those k trees when updating our prediction, F_{n+1}, which includes all trees, the prediction overshoots. Therefore, the new tree is scaled by a factor of $\frac{1}{k}$ to compensate.

DART has been shown to outperform standard GBDTs while also significantly improving overfitting.

Scikit-learn does not implement DART for GBDTs, but DART is incorporated in LightGBM.

Summary

In conclusion, this chapter looked at the two most common methods of ensemble learning for decision trees: bagging and boosting. We looked at the Random Forests and ExtraTrees algorithms, which build decision tree ensembles using bagging.

This chapter also gave a detailed overview of boosting in decision trees by going through the GBDT algorithm step by step, illustrating how gradient boosting is applied. We covered practical examples of random forests, ExtraTrees, and GBDTs for scikit-learn.

Finally, we looked at how dropouts can be applied to GBDTs with the DART algorithm. We now thoroughly understand decision tree ensemble techniques and are ready to dive deep into LightGBM.

The next chapter introduces the LightGBM library in detail, both the theoretical advancements made by the library and the practical application thereof. We will also look at using LightGBM with Python to solve ML problems.

References

[1]   L. Breiman, "Random forests," Machine learning, vol. 45, p. 5-32, 2001.

[2]   P. Geurts, D. Ernst and L. Wehenkel, "Extremely randomized trees," Machine learning, vol. 63, p. 3-42, 2006.

[3]   J. H. Friedman, "Greedy function approximation: a gradient boosting machine," The Annals of Statistics, p. 1189-1232, 2001.

[4]   R. K. Vinayak and R. Gilad-Bachrach, "Dart: Dropouts meet multiple additive regression trees," in Artificial Intelligence and Statistics, 2015.

3

An Overview of LightGBM
in Python

In the previous chapter, we looked at ensemble learning methods for decision trees. Both **bootstrap aggregation** (**bagging**) and gradient boosting were discussed in detail, with practical examples of how to apply the techniques in scikit-learn. We also showed how **gradient-boosted decision trees** (**GBDTs**) are slow to train and may underperform on some problems.

This chapter introduces LightGBM, a gradient-boosting framework that uses tree-based learners. We look at the innovations and optimizations LightGBM makes to the ensemble learning methods. Further details and examples are given for using LightGBM practically via Python. Finally, the chapter includes a modeling example using LightGBM, incorporating more advanced techniques for model validation and parameter optimization.

By the end of the chapter, you will have a thorough understanding of the theoretical and practical properties of LightGBM, allowing us to dive deeper into using LightGBM for data science and production systems.

The main topics of this chapter are set out here:

- Introducing LightGBM
- Getting started with LightGBM in Python
- Building LightGBM models

Technical requirements

The chapter includes examples and code excerpts illustrating how to use LightGBM in Python. Complete examples and instructions for setting up a suitable environment for this chapter are available at `https://github.com/PacktPublishing/Practical-Machine-Learning-with-LightGBM-and-Python/tree/main/chapter-3`.

Introducing LightGBM

LightGBM is an open source, gradient-boosting framework for tree-based ensembles (`https://github.com/microsoft/LightGBM`). LightGBM focuses on efficiency in speed, memory usage, and improved accuracy, especially for problems with high dimensionality and large data sizes.

LightGBM was first introduced in the paper *LightGBM: A Highly Efficient Gradient Boosting Decision Tree* [1].

The efficiency and accuracy of LightGBM are achieved via several technical and theoretical optimizations to the standard ensemble learning methods, particularly GBDTs. Additionally, LightGBM supports distributed training of ensembles with optimizations in network communication and support for GPU-based training of tree ensembles.

LightGBM supports many **machine learning** (**ML**) applications: regression, binary and multiclass classification, cross-entropy loss functions, and ranking via LambdaRank.

The LightGBM algorithm is also very customizable via its hyperparameters. It supports many metrics and features, including **Dropouts meet Multiple Additive Regression Trees** (**DART**), bagging (random forests), continuous training, multiple metrics, and early stopping.

This section reviews the theoretical and practical optimizations LightGBM utilizes, including a detailed overview of the hyperparameters to control LightGBM features.

LightGBM optimizations

At its core, LightGBM implements the same ensemble algorithms we discussed in the previous chapter. However, LightGBM applies theoretical and technical optimizations to improve performance and accuracy while significantly reducing memory usage. Next, we discuss the most significant optimizations implemented in LightGBM.

Computational complexity in GBDTs

First, we must understand where the inefficiency in building GBDTs stems from to understand how LightGBM improves the efficiency of GBDTs. The most computationally complex part of the GBDT algorithm is training the regression tree for each iteration. More specifically, finding the optimal split is very expensive. Pre-sort-based algorithms are among the most popular methods for finding the best splits [2], [3]. A naïve approach requires the data to be sorted by feature for every decision node with algorithmic complexity $O(\#data \times \#feature)$. Pre-sort-based algorithms sort the data once before training, which reduces the complexity when building a decision node to $O(\#data)$ [2]. Even with pre-sorting, the complexity is too high for large datasets when finding splits for decision nodes.

Histogram-based sampling

An alternative approach to pre-sorting involves building histograms for continuous features [4]. The continuous values are added into discrete bins when building these **feature histograms**. Instead of using the data directly when calculating the splits for decision nodes, we can now use the histogram bins. Constructing the histograms has a complexity of $O(\#data)$. However, the complexity for building a decision node now reduces to $O(\#bins)$, and since the number of bins is much smaller than the amount of data, this significantly speeds up the process of building regression trees, as illustrated in the following diagram:

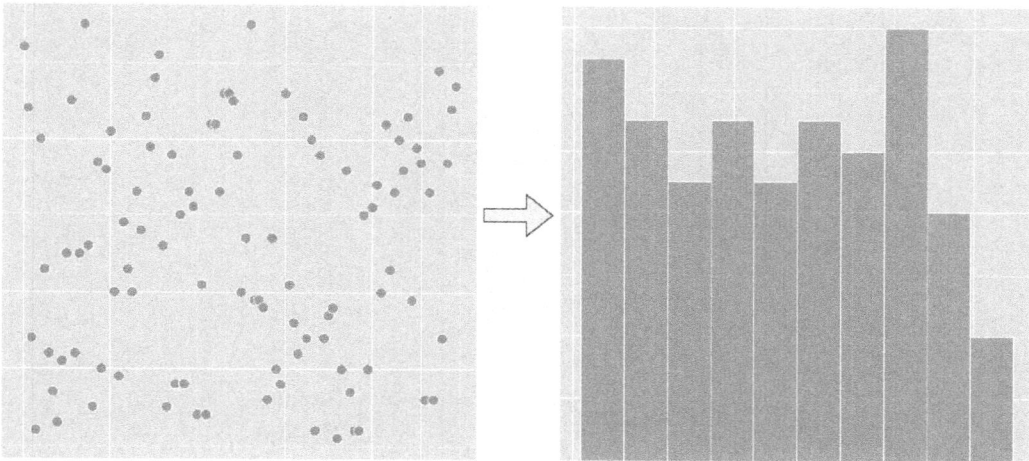

Figure 3.1 – Creating feature histograms from continuous features allows calculating splits for decision nodes using bin boundary values instead of having to sample each data point, significantly reducing the algorithm's complexity since #bins << #data

A secondary optimization that stems from using histograms is "histogram subtraction" for building the histograms for the leaves. Instead of calculating the histogram for each leaf, we can subtract the leaf's neighbor's histogram from the parent's histogram. Choosing the leaf with the smaller amount of data leads to a smaller $O(\#data)$ complexity for the first leaf and $O(\#bin)$ complexity for the second leaf due to histogram subtraction.

A third optimization that LightGBM applies using histograms is to reduce the memory cost. Feature pre-sorting requires a supporting data structure (a dictionary) for each feature. No such data structures are required when building histograms, reducing memory costs. Further, since #bins is small, a smaller data type, such as uint8_t, can store the training data, reducing memory usage.

Detailed information regarding the algorithms for building feature histograms is available in the paper *CLOUDS: A decision tree classifier for large datasets* [4].

Exclusive Feature Bundling

Exclusive Feature Bundling (**EFB**) is another data-based optimization that LightGBM applies when working with sparse data (sparse data is pervasive in high-dimensional datasets). When the feature data is sparse, it's common to find that many features are *mutually exclusive*, signifying they never present non-zero values simultaneously. Combining these features into a single one is generally safe, given this exclusivity. EFB is illustrated in the following diagram:

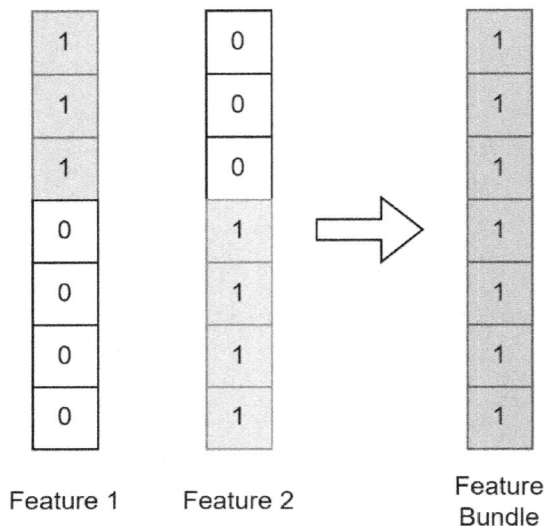

Feature 1   Feature 2   Feature
                                       Bundle

Figure 3.2 – Building a feature bundle from two mutually exclusive features

Bundling mutually exclusive features allows building the same feature histograms as from the individual features [1]. The optimization reduces the complexity of building feature histograms from $O(\#data \times \#feature)$ to $O(\#data \times \#bundle)$. For datasets where there are many mutually exclusive features, this dramatically improves performance since $\# bundle \ll \#feature$. Detailed algorithms for, and proof of the correctness of, EFB are available in [1].

Gradient-based One-Side Sampling

A final data-based optimization available in the LightGBM framework is **Gradient-based One-Side Sampling** (**GOSS**) [1]. GOSS is a method of discarding training data samples that no longer contribute significantly to the training process, effectively reducing the training data size and speeding up the process.

We can use the gradient calculation of each sample to determine its importance. If the gradient change is small, it implies that the training error was also small, and we can infer that the tree is well fitted to the specific data instance [1]. One option would be to discard all instances with small gradients. However, this changes the distribution of the training data, reducing the tree's ability to generalize. GOSS is a method for choosing which instances to keep in the training data.

To maintain the data distribution, GOSS is applied as follows:

1. The data samples are sorted by the absolute value of their gradients.

2. The top $a \times 100\%$ instances are then selected (instances with large gradients).

3. A random sample of $b \times 100\%$ instances is then taken from the rest of the data.

4. A factor is added to the loss function (for these instances) to amplify their influence: $\frac{1-a}{b}$, thereby compensating for the underrepresentation of data with small gradients.

Therefore, GOSS samples a large portion of instances with large gradients and a random portion of instances with small gradients and amplifies the influence of the small gradients when calculating information gain.

The downsampling enabled by GOSS can significantly reduce the amount of data processed during training (and the training time for the GBDTs), especially in the case of large datasets.

Best-first tree growth

The most common method for building decision trees is to grow the tree by level (that is, one level at a time). LightGBM uses an alternative approach and grows the tree leaf-wise or best-first. The leaf-wise approach selects an existing leaf with the most significant change in the loss of the tree and builds the tree from there. The downside of this approach is that if the dataset is small, the tree is likely to overfit the data. A maximum depth has to be set to counteract this. However, if the number of leaves to construct is fixed, leaf-wise tree building is shown to outperform level-wise algorithms [5].

L1 and L2 regularization

LightGBM supports both L1 and L2 regularization of the objective function when training the regression trees in the ensemble. From *Chapter 1, Introducing Machine Learning*, we recall that regularization is a way to control overfitting. In the case of decision trees, simpler, shallow trees overfit less.

To support L1 and L2 regularization, we extend the objective function with a regularization term, as follows:

$$obj = L(y, F(x)) + \Omega(w)$$

Here, $L(y, F(x))$ is the loss function discussed in *Chapter 2, Ensemble Learning – Bagging and Boosting*, and $\Omega(w)$ is the regularization function defined over w, the leaf scores (the leaf score is the output calculated from the leaf as per *step 2.3* in the GBDT algorithm defined in *Chapter 2, Ensemble Learning – Bagging and Boosting*).

The regularization term effectively adds a penalty to the objective function, where we aim to penalize more complex trees prone to overfitting.

There are multiple definitions for Ω. A typical implementation for the terms in decision trees is this:

$$\Omega(w) = \alpha \sum_i^n |w_i| + \lambda \sum_i^n w_i^2$$

Here, $\alpha \sum_i^n |w_i|$ is the L1 regularization term, controlled by the parameter α, $0 \leq \alpha \leq 1$, and $\lambda \sum_i^n w_i^2$ is the L2 regularization term, controlled by the parameter λ.

L1 regularization has the effect of driving leaf scores to zero by penalizing leaves with large absolute outputs. *Smaller leaf outputs have a smaller effect on the tree's prediction, effectively simplifying the tree.*

L2 regularization is similar but has an outsized effect on outliers' leaves due to taking the square of the output.

Finally, when larger trees are built (trees with more leaves, and therefore a large w vector), both sum terms for $\Omega(w)$ increase, increasing the objective function output. Therefore, *larger trees are penalized,* and overfitting is reduced.

Summary of LightGBM optimizations

In summary, LightGBM improves upon the standard ensemble algorithms by doing the following:

- Implementing histogram-based sampling of features to reduce the computational cost of finding optimal splits
- Calculating exclusive feature bundles to reduce the number of features in sparse datasets
- Applying GOSS to downsample the training data without losing accuracy
- Building trees leaf-wise to improve accuracy
- Overfitting can be controlled through L1 and L2 regularization and other control parameters

In conjunction, the optimizations improve the computational performance of LightGBM by **orders of magnitude (OOM)** over the standard GBDT algorithm. Additionally, LightGBM is implemented in C++ with a Python interface, which results in much faster code than Python-based GBDTs, such as in scikit-learn.

Finally, LightGBM also has support for improved data-parallel and feature-parallel distributed training. Distributed training and GPU support are discussed in a later *Chapter 11, Distributed and GPU-Based Learning with LightGBM.*

Hyperparameters

LightGBM exposes many parameters that can be used to customize the training process, goals, and performance. Next, we discuss the most notable parameters and how they may be used to control specific phenomena.

> **Note**
>
> The core LightGBM framework is developed in C++ but includes APIs to work with LightGBM in C, Python, and R. The parameters discussed in this section are the framework parameters and are exposed differently by each API. The following section discusses the parameters available when using Python.

The following are **core framework parameters** used to control the optimization process and goal:

- `objective`: LightGBM supports the following optimization objectives, among others—`regression` (including regression applications with other loss functions such as Huber and Fair), `binary` (classification), `multiclass` (classification), `cross-entropy`, and `lambdarank` for ranking problems.

- `boosting`: The boosting parameter controls the boosting type. By default, this is set to `gbdt`, the standard GBDT algorithm. The other options are `dart` and `rf` for random forests. The random forest mode does not perform boosting but instead builds a random forest.

- `num_iterations` (or `n_estimators`): Controls the number of boosting iterations and, therefore, the number of trees built.

- `num_leaves`: Controls the maximum number of leaves in a single tree.

- `learning_rate`: Controls the learning, or shrinkage rate, which is the contribution of each tree to the overall prediction.

LightGBM also provides many parameters to control the learning process. We'll discuss these parameters relative to how they may be used to tune specific aspects of training.

The following control parameters can be used to improve **accuracy**:

- `boosting`: Use `dart`, which has been shown to outperform standard GBDTs.

- `learning_rate`: The learning rate must be tuned alongside `num_iterations` for better accuracy. A small learning rate with a large value for `num_iterations` leads to better accuracy at the expense of optimization speed.

- `num_leaves`: A larger number of leaves improves accuracy but may lead to overfitting.

- `max_bin`: The maximum number of bins in which features are bucketed when constructing histograms. A larger `max_bin` size slows the training and uses more memory but may improve accuracy.

The following **learning control parameters** can be used to deal with **overfitting**:

- `bagging_fraction` and `bagging_freq`: Setting both parameters enables feature bagging. Bagging may be used in addition to boosting and doesn't force the use of a random forest. Enabling bagging reduces overfitting.

- `early_stopping_round`: Enables early stopping and controls the number of iterations used to determine whether training should be stopped. Training is stopped if no improvement is made to any metric in the iterations set by `early_stopping_round`.

- `min_data_in_leaf`: The minimum samples allowed in a leaf. Larger values reduce overfitting.

- `min_gain_to_split`: The minimum amount of information gain required to perform a split. Higher values reduce overfitting.

- `reg_alpha`: Controls L1 regularization. Higher values reduce overfitting.

- `reg_lambda`: Controls L2 regularization. Higher values reduce overfitting.

- `max_depth`: Controls the maximum depth of individual trees. Shallower trees reduce overfitting.

- `max_drop`: Controls the maximum number of dropped trees when using the DART algorithm (is only used when `boosting` is set to `dart`). A larger value reduces overfitting.

- `extra_trees`: Enables the **Extremely Randomized Trees (ExtraTrees)** algorithm. LightGBM then chooses a split threshold at random for each feature. Enabling Extra-Trees can reduce overfitting. The parameter can be used in conjunction with any boosting mode.

The parameters discussed here include only some of the parameters available in LightGBM and focus on improving accuracy and overfitting. A complete list of parameters is available at the following link: `https://lightgbm.readthedocs.io/en/latest/Parameters.html`.

Limitations of LightGBM

LightGBM is designed to be more efficient and effective than traditional methods. It is particularly well known for its ability to handle large datasets. However, as with any algorithm or framework, it also has its limitations and potential disadvantages, including the following:

- **Sensitive to overfitting**: LightGBM can be sensitive to overfitting, especially with small or noisy datasets. Care should be taken to monitor and control for overfitting when using LightGBM.

- **Optimal performance requires tuning**: As discussed previously, LightGBM has many hyperparameters that need to be properly tuned to get the best performance from the algorithm.

- **Lack of representation learning**: Unlike **deep learning (DL)** approaches, which excel at learning from raw data, LightGBM requires feature engineering to be applied to the data before learning. Feature engineering is a time-consuming process that requires domain knowledge.

- **Handling sequential data**: LightGBM is not inherently designed for working with sequential data such as time series. For LightGBM to be used with time-series data, feature engineering needs to be applied to create lagged features and capture temporal dependencies.

- **Complex interactions and non-linearities**: LightGBM is a decision-tree-driven approach that might be incapable of capturing complex feature interactions and non-linearities. Proper feature engineering needs to be applied to ensure the algorithm models these.

Although these are potential limitations of using the algorithm, they may not apply to all use cases. LightGBM is often a very effective tool in the right circumstances. As with any model, understanding the trade-offs is vital to making the right choice for your application.

In the next session, we look at getting started using the various LightGBM APIs with Python.

Getting started with LightGBM in Python

LightGBM is implemented in C++ but has official C, R, and Python APIs. This section discusses the Python APIs that are available for working with LightGBM. LightGBM provides three Python APIs: the standard **LightGBM** API, the **scikit-learn** API (which is fully compatible with other scikit-learn functionality), and a **Dask** API for working with Dask. Dask is a parallel computing library discussed in *Chapter 11, Distributed and GPU-Based Learning with LightGBM* (https://www.dask.org/).

Throughout the rest of the book, we mainly use the scikit-learn API for LightGBM, but let's first look at the standard Python API.

LightGBM Python API

The best way to dive into the Python API is with a hands-on example. The following are excerpts from a code listing that illustrates the use of the LightGBM Python API. The complete code example is available at https://github.com/PacktPublishing/Practical-Machine-Learning-with-LightGBM-and-Python/tree/main/chapter-3.

LightGBM needs to be imported. The import is often abbreviated as lgb:

```
import lightgbm as lgb
```

LightGBM provides a `Dataset` wrapper class to work with data. `Dataset` supports a variety of formats. Commonly, it is used to wrap a `numpy` array or a `pandas` DataFrame. `Dataset` also accepts a `Path` to a CSV, TSV, LIBSVM text file, or LightGBM `Dataset` binary file. When a path is supplied, LightGBM loads the data from the disk.

Here, we load our Forest Cover dataset from `sklearn` and wrap the `numpy` arrays in a LightGBM `Dataset`:

```
dataset = datasets.fetch_covtype()
X_train, X_test, y_train, y_test = train_test_split(dataset.data,
dataset.target, random_state=179)
training_set = lgb.Dataset(X_train, y_train - 1)
test_set = lgb.Dataset(X_test, y_test - 1)
```

We subtract 1 from the `y_train` and `y_test` arrays because the classes supplied by `sklearn` are labeled in the range [1, 7], whereas LightGBM expects zero-indexed class labels in the range [0, 7].

We cannot set up the parameters for training. We'll be using the following parameters:

```python
params = {
    'boosting_type': 'gbdt',
    'objective': 'multiclass',
    'num_classes': '7',
    'metric': {'auc_mu'},
    'num_leaves': 120,
    'learning_rate': 0.09,
    'force_row_wise': True,
    'verbose': 0
}
```

We are using the standard GBDT as a boosting type and setting the objective to multiclass classification for seven classes. During training, we are going to capture the auc_mu metric. AUC_μ is a multiclass adaptation of the **area under the receiver operating characteristic curve (AUC)**, as defined by Kleiman and Page [6].

We set num_leaves and learning_rate to reasonable values for the problem. Finally, we specify force_row_wise as True, a recommended setting for large datasets.

LightGBM's training function also supports **callbacks**. A callback is a hook into the training process that is executed each boosting iteration. To illustrate their purpose, we'll be using the following callbacks:

```python
metrics = {}
callbacks = [
    lgb.log_evaluation(period=15),
    lgb.record_evaluation(metrics),
    lgb.early_stopping(15),
    lgb.reset_parameter(learning_rate=learning_rate_decay(0.09,
0.999))
]
```

We use the log_evaluation callback with a period of 15, which logs (prints) our metrics to standard output every 15 boosting iterations. We also set a record_evaluation callback that captures our evaluation metrics in the metrics dictionary. We also specify an early_stopping callback, with stopping rounds set to 15. The early_stopping callback stops training if no validation metrics improve after the specified number of stopping rounds.

Finally, we also use the reset_parameter callback to implement **learning rate decay**. The decay function is defined as follows:

```python
def learning_rate_decay(initial_lr, decay_rate):
    def _decay(iteration):
        return initial_lr * (decay_rate ** iteration)
    return _decay
```

The reset_parameter callback takes a function as input. The function receives the current iteration and returns the parameter value. Learning rate decay is a technique where we decrease the value of the learning rate over time. Learning rate decay improved the overall accuracy achieved. Ideally, we want the initial trees to have a more significant impact on correcting the prediction errors. In contrast, later on, we want to reduce the impact of additional trees and have them make minor adjustments to the errors. We implement a slight exponential decay that reduces the learning rate from 0.09 to 0.078 throughout training.

Now, we are ready for training. We use lgb.train to train the model:

```
gbm = lgb.train(params, training_set, num_boost_round=150, valid_
sets=test_set, callbacks=callbacks)
```

We use 150 boosting rounds (or boosted trees). In conjunction with a lower learning rate, having many boosting rounds should improve accuracy.

After training, we can use lgb.predict to get predictions for our test set and calculate the F1 score:

```
y_pred = np.argmax(gbm.predict(X_test, num_iteration=gbm.best_
iteration), axis=1)
f1_score(y_test - 1, y_pred, average="macro")
```

The LightGBM predict function outputs an array of activations, one for each class. Therefore, we use np.argmax to choose the class with the highest activation as the predicted class. LightGBM also has support for some plotting functions. For instance, we can use plot_metric to plot our AUC_μ results as captured in the metrics:

```
lgb.plot_metric(metrics, 'auc_mu')
```

The results of this are shown in *Figure 3.3*.

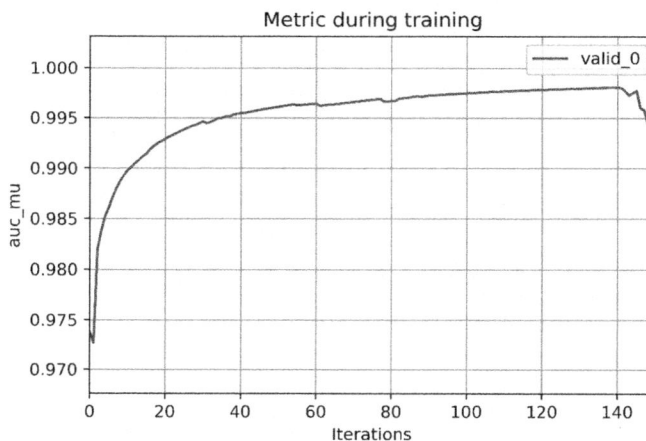

Figure 3.3 – A plot of the **AUC_μ** metric per training iteration created using lgb.plot_metric

Running the preceding code should produce a LightGBM GBDT tree with an F1 score of around 0.917, in line with the score the Random Forest and Extra-Trees algorithms achieved in *Chapter 2, Ensemble Learning – Bagging and Boosting*. However, LightGBM is significantly faster in reaching these accuracies. LightGBM completed the training in just 37 seconds on our hardware: this is 4.5 times faster than running Extra-Trees on the same problem and hardware and 60-70 times faster than scikit-learn's `GradientBoostingClassifier` in our testing.

LightGBM scikit-learn API

We now take a look at the scikit-learn Python API for LightGBM. The scikit-learn API provides four classes: `LGBMModel`, `LGBMClassifier`, `LGBMRegressor`, and `LGBMRanker`. Each of these provides the same functionality as the LightGBM Python API, but with the same convenient scikit-learn interfaces we have worked with before. Additionally, the scikit-learn classes are compatible and interoperable with the rest of the scikit-learn ecosystem.

Let's replicate the previous example using the scikit-learn API.

The dataset is loaded precisely as before. The scikit-learn API doesn't require wrapping the data in a `Dataset` object. We also don't have to zero-index our target classes, as scikit-learn supports any label for the classes:

```
dataset = datasets.fetch_covtype()
X_train, X_test, y_train, y_test = train_test_split(dataset.data,
dataset.target, random_state=179)
```

The scikit-learn API also supports LightGBM callbacks; as such, we use the same callbacks as before:

```
metrics = {}
callbacks = [
    lgb.log_evaluation(period=15),
    lgb.record_evaluation(metrics),
    lgb.early_stopping(15),
    lgb.reset_parameter(learning_rate=learning_rate_decay(0.09,
0.999))
]
```

We then create the `LGBMClassifier` exactly as we would any other scikit-learn model. When creating the classifier, we also set the parameters:

```
model = lgb.LGBMClassifier(
    boosting_type='gbdt',
    n_estimators=150,
    num_leaves=120,
    learning_rate=0.09,
    force_row_wise=True
)
```

Note that we do not have to specify the number of classes; scikit-learn infers this automatically. We then call `fit` on the model, passing the training and test data along with our callbacks:

```
model = model.fit(X_train, y_train, eval_set=(X_test, y_test), eval_
metric='auc_mu', callbacks=callbacks)
```

Finally, we evaluate our model with the F1 score. We don't have to use `np.argmax` on the predictions as this is done automatically with the scikit-learn API:

```
f1_score(y_test, model.predict(X_test), average="macro")
```

Overall, we can see that using LightGBM via the scikit-learn API is more straightforward than the standard Python API. The scikit-learn API was also approximately 40% faster than the LightGBM API on our hardware. This section examined the ins and outs of using the various Python APIs available for LightGBM. The following section looks at training LightGBM models using the scikit-learn API.

Building LightGBM models

This section provides an end-to-end example of solving a real-world problem using LightGBM. We provide a more detailed look at data preparation for a problem and explain how to find suitable parameters for our algorithms. We use multiple variants of LightGBM to explore relative performance and compare them against random forests.

Cross-validation

Before we delve into solving a problem, we need to discuss a better way of validating algorithm performance. Splitting the data into two or three subsets is standard practice when training a model. The training data is used to train the model, the validation data is a hold-out set used to validate the data during training, and the test data is used to validate the performance after training.

In previous examples, we have done this split only once, building a single training and test to train and validate the model. The issue with this approach is that our model could get "lucky." If, by chance, our test set closely matches the training data but is not representative of real-world data, we would report a good test error, even though we can't be confident of our model's performance.

An alternative is to do the dataset splitting multiple times and train the model multiple times, once for each split. This approach is called **cross-validation**.

The most common application of cross-validation is *k-fold cross-validation*. With k-fold cross-validation, we choose a value, *k*, and partition the (shuffled) dataset into *k* subsamples (or folds). We then repeat the training process *k* times, using a different subset as the validation data and all other subsets as training data. The model's performance is calculated as the mean (or median) score across all folds. The following diagram illustrates this process:

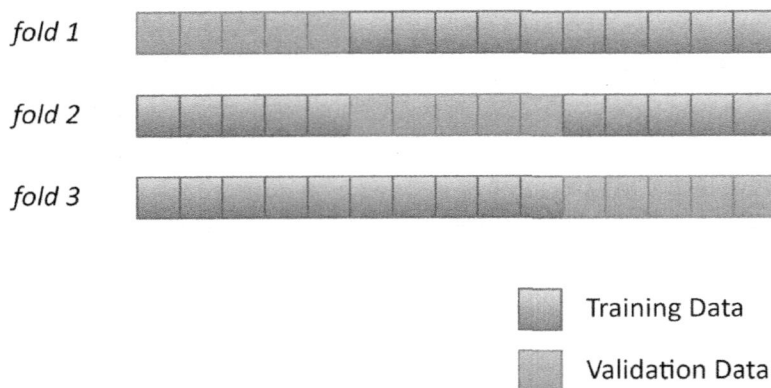

Figure 3.4 – k-fold cross-validation with k = 3; the original dataset is shuffled and split into 3 equal parts (or folds); training and validation are repeated for each combination of subsampled data, and the average performance is reported

Using a high value for k reduces the chance that the model coincidentally shows good performance and indicates how the model might perform in the real world. However, the entire training process is repeated for each fold, which could be computationally expensive and time-consuming. Therefore, we need to balance the resources available with the need to validate the model. A typical value for k is 5 (the default for scikit-learn), also called 5-fold cross-validation.

Stratified k-fold validation

A problem that might arise with k-fold cross-validation is that, due to chance, a fold may contain samples from only a single class. **Stratified sampling** solves this issue by preserving the percentage of samples for each class when creating folds. In this way, each fold has the same distribution of classes as the original dataset. When applied to cross-validation, this technique is called stratified k-fold cross-validation.

Parameter optimization

Parameter optimization, also called parameter tuning, is the process of finding good hyperparameters for the model and training process specific to the problem being solved. In the previous examples of training models, we have been setting the model and training algorithm's parameters based on intuition and minimal experimentation. There is no guarantee that the parameter choices were optimal for the optimization problem.

But how might we go about finding the best parameter choices? A naïve strategy is to try an extensive range of values for a parameter, find the best value, and then repeat the process for the following parameter. However, it is frequently the case that parameters are **co-dependent**. When we change one parameter, the optimal value for another might differ. An excellent example of co-dependence in GBDTs is the number of boosting rounds and the learning rate. Having a small learning rate necessitates more boosting rounds. Therefore, optimizing the learning rate and then, independently, the number of boosting rounds is unlikely to produce optimal results. *Both parameters must be optimized in unison.*

Grid search

An approach that accounts for parameter co-dependence is grid search. With grid search, a parameter grid is set up. The grid consists of a range of values to try for each parameter we are optimizing. An exhaustive search is then performed, training and validating the model on each possible combination of parameters.

Here is an example of a parameter grid for three parameters:

```
grid = {
    'learning_rate': [0.001, 0.01, 0.1, 0.2, 0,5],
    'num_rounds': [20, 40, 60, 80, 100],
    'num_leaves': [2, 16, 32, 64, 128, 256],
}
```

Each parameter is specified with a range of possible values. The previous grid would require 150 trails to search.

Since grid search is exhaustive, it has the advantage that it is guaranteed to find the best combination of parameters within the ranges specified. However, the downside to grid search is the cost. Trying each possible combination of parameters is very expensive and quickly becomes intractable for many parameters and large parameter ranges.

Scikit-learn provides a utility class to implement grid search and perform cross-validation at the same time. `GridSearchCV` takes a model, a parameter grid, and the number of cross-validation folds as parameters. `GridSearchCV` then proceeds to search the grid for the best parameters, using cross-validation to validate the performance for each combination of parameters. We'll illustrate the use of `GridSearchCV` in the next section.

Parameter optimization is a crucial part of the modeling process. Finding suitable parameters for a model could be the difference between a successful or failed process. However, as discussed previously, parameter optimization is also often enormously expensive regarding time and computational complexity, necessitating a trade-off between cost and performance.

Predicting student academic success

We now move on to our example. We build a model to predict students' dropout rate based on a range of social and economic factors using LightGBM [7] (`https://archive-beta.ics.uci.edu/dataset/697/predict+students+dropout+and+academic+success`). The data is available in CSV format. We start by exploring the data.

Exploratory data analysis

One of the most fundamental properties of any dataset is the shape: the rows and columns our data consists of. It's also an excellent way to validate that the data read succeeded. Here, our data consists of 4,424 rows and 35 columns. Taking a random sample of the data gives us a sense of the columns and their values:

```
df = pd.read_csv("students/data.csv", sep=";")
print(f"Shape: {df.shape}")
df.sample(10)
```

Next, we can run `df.info()` to see all the columns, their non-null counts, and their data types:

```
df.info()
<class 'pandas.core.frame.DataFrame'>
RangeIndex: 4424 entries, 0 to 4423
Data columns (total 35 columns):
 #    Column                                        Non-Null
Count  Dtype
---   ------                                        -------------
-    -----
 0    Marital status                                4424 non-
null    int64
 1    Application mode                              4424 non-
null    int64
 2    Application order                             4424 non-
null    int64
 ...
```

Running the preceding code shows us that most columns are integer types, except for the `Target` column, with a few floats in between. The `Target` column is listed as type `object`; if we look at the values in the sample, we can see the `Target` column consists of `Graduate`, `Dropout`, and `Enrolled` strings. LightGBM can't work with strings as targets, so we'll map these to integer values before training our models.

We can also run `df.describe()` to get a statistical description (mean, standard deviation, min, max, and percentiles) of the values in each column. Calculating descriptive statistics helps check the bounds of the data (not a big problem with working with decision tree models) and check for outliers. For this dataset, there aren't any data bounds or outlier concerns.

Next, we need to check for duplicated and missing values. We need to drop the rows containing missing values or impute appropriate substitutes if there are any missing values. We can check for missing values using the following code:

```
df.isnull().sum()
```

Running the preceding code shows us there are no missing values for this dataset.

To locate duplicates, we can run the following code:

```
df.loc[df.duplicated()]
```

There are also no duplicates in the dataset. If there were any duplicated data, we would drop the extra rows.

We also need to check the distribution of the target class to ensure it is balanced. Here, we show a histogram that indicates the target class distribution. We create the histogram using Seaborn's `countplot()` method, like so:

```
sns.countplot(data=df, x='Target')
```

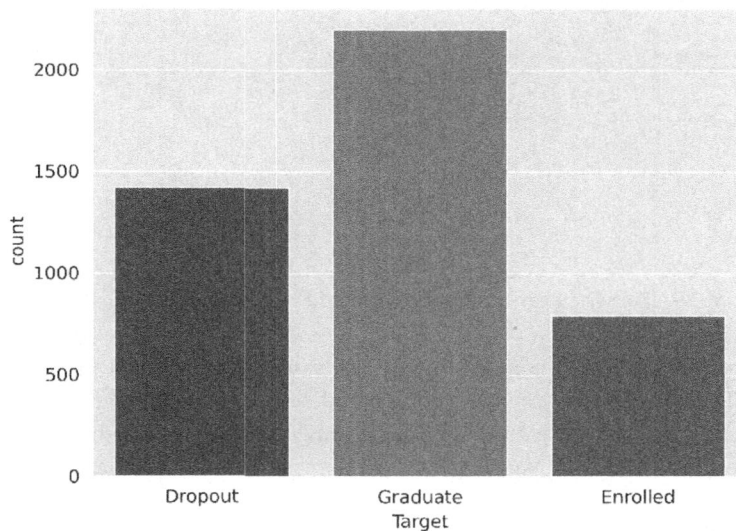

Figure 3.5 – Distribution of target class in the academic success dataset

Although not perfectly balanced, the target distribution is not overly skewed to any one class, and we don't have to perform any compensating action.

So far, we have found that our dataset is suitable for modeling (we still need to remap `Target`) and clean (it does not contain missing or duplicated values and is well balanced). We can now take a deeper look at some features, starting with feature correlation. The following code plots a correlation heatmap. Pairwise Pearson correlations are calculated using `df.corr()`. The screenshot that follows the snippet shows a correlation heatmap built using pairwise Pearson correlations:

```
sns.heatmap(df.corr(), cmap='coolwarm')
```

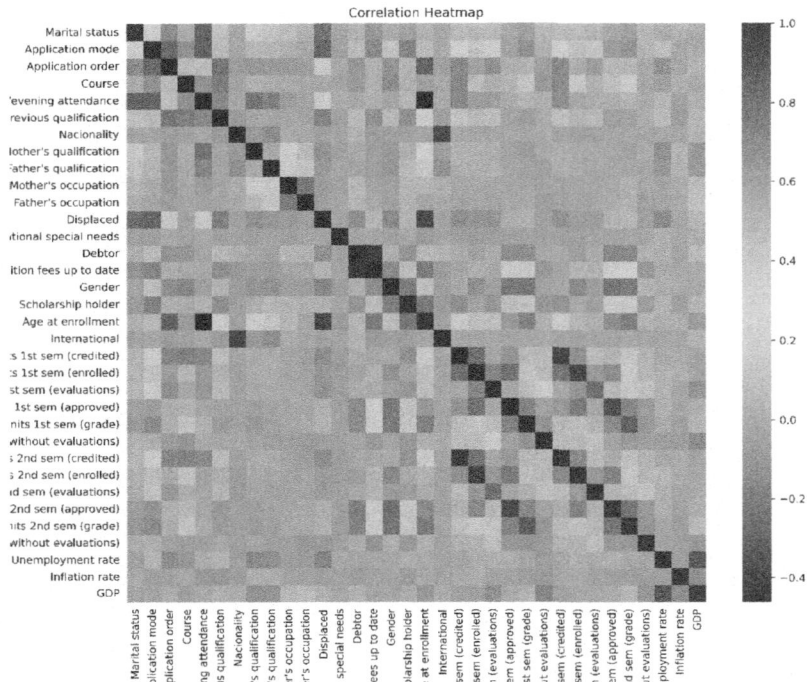

Figure 3.6 – Pairwise Pearson feature correlation of the academic success dataset

We can see three patterns of correlations: first-semester credits, enrollments, evaluations, and approvals are all correlated. First-semester and second-semester values for these are also correlated. These correlations imply that students tend to see through the year once enrolled instead of dropping out mid-semester. Although correlated, the correlations aren't strong enough to consider dropping any features.

The third correlation pattern is between `Nacionality` and `International`, which are strongly correlated.

> **Note**
>
> The word *Nacionality* refers to *nationality*. We have retained the spelling from the original dataset here too for the purpose of consistency.

A closer look at `Nacionality` shows that almost all rows have a single value: the country where the dataset was collected. The strong correlation implies the same for `International`:

```
nationalities = df.groupby(['Nacionality', 'Target']).size().reset_
index().pivot(columns='Target', index='Nacionality', values=0)
nationalities_total = nationalities.sum(axis=1)
nationalities_total = nationalities_total.sort_values(ascending=True)
nationalities.loc[nationalities_total.index].plot(kind='barh',
stacked=True)
```

The following screenshot shows a stacked bar plot of the nationalities:

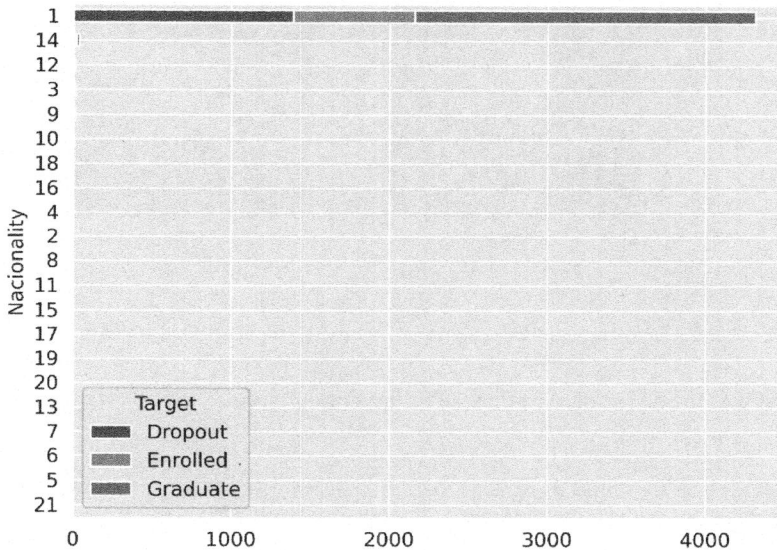

Figure 3.7 – Distribution of the 'Nacionality' feature, showing almost all
rows have a single value in the academic success dataset

The distribution of 'Nacionality' and 'International' means that they are not very informative (nearly all rows have the same value), so we can drop them from the dataset.

Finally, we notice the 'Gender' feature. When working with gender, it's always good to check for bias. We can visualize the distribution of the 'Gender' feature relative to the target classes using a histogram. The results are shown in the screenshot that follows this code snippet:

```
sns.countplot(data=df, x='Gender', hue='Target', hue_order=['Dropout',
'Enrolled', 'Graduate'])
plt.xticks(ticks=[0,1], labels=['Female','Male'])
```

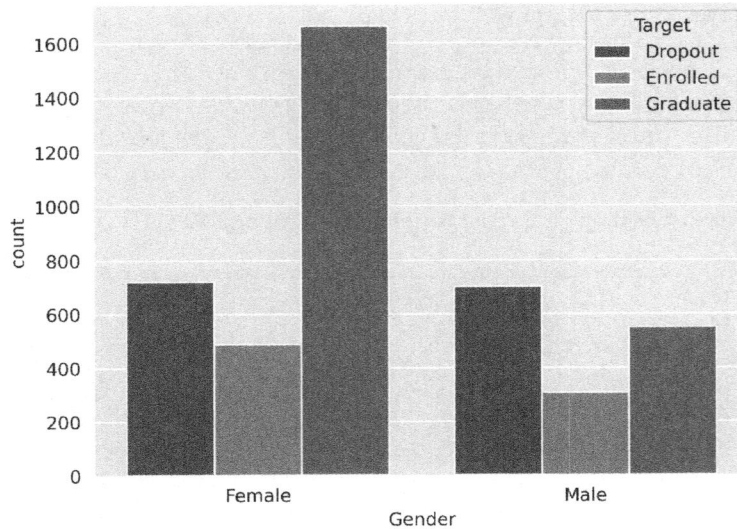

Figure 3.8 – Distribution of the 'Gender' feature in the academic success dataset

There is a slight bias toward female students, but not enough to warrant concern.

Modeling

We can now prepare our dataset for modeling. We must map our `Target` values to integers and drop the `Nacionality` and `International` features. We also need to remove the spaces in the feature names. LightGBM cannot work with spaces in the names; we can replace them with underscores:

```
df.columns = df.columns.str.strip().str.replace(' ', '_')
df = df.drop(columns=["Nacionality", "International"], axis=1)
df["Target"]=df["Target"].map({
    "Dropout":0,
    "Enrolled":1,
    "Graduate":2
})
X = df.drop(columns=["Target"], axis=1)
y = df["Target"]
```

We train and compare four models: a LightGBM GBDT, a LightGBM DART tree, a LightGBM DART tree with GOSS, and a scikit-learn random forest.

We'll perform parameter optimization with 5-fold cross-validation using `GridSearchCV` to ensure good performance for the models.

The following code sets up the parameter optimization for the GBDT. A similar pattern is followed for the other models, which can be seen in the source code:

```
def gbdt_parameter_optimization():
    params = {
        "max_depth": [-1, 32, 128],
        "n_estimators": [50, 100, 150],
        "min_child_samples": [10, 20, 30],
        "learning_rate": [0.001, 0.01, 0.1],
        "num_leaves": [32, 64, 128]
    }
    model = lgb.LGBMClassifier(force_row_wise=True, boosting_
type="gbdt", verbose=-1)
    grid_search = GridSearchCV(estimator=model, param_grid=params,
cv=5, verbose=10)
    grid_search.fit(X, y)
    return grid_search
results = gbdt_parameter_optimization()
print(results.best_params_)
print(results.best_score_)
```

Running the preceding code takes some time, but once completed, it prints the best parameters found along with the score of the best model.

After all the models are trained, we can evaluate each using F1-scoring, taking the mean of 5-fold cross-validation, using the best parameters found. The following code illustrates how to do this for the GBDT model:

```
model = lgb.LGBMClassifier(force_row_wise=True, boosting_type="gbdt",
learning_rate=0.1, max_depth=-1, min_child_samples=10, n_
estimators=100, num_leaves=32, verbose=-1)
scores = cross_val_score(model, X, y, scoring="f1_macro")
scores.mean()
```

Jupyter notebooks for the parameter optimization for each model are available in the GitHub repository: https://github.com/PacktPublishing/Practical-Machine-Learning-with-LightGBM-and-Python/tree/main/chapter-3.

The following table summarizes the best parameter values found and the cross-validated F1 scores for each model:

Model	Learning Rate	Max Depth	Min Child Samples	N Estimators	Num Leaves	Min Samples Leaf	Min Samples Split	F1 score
GBDT	0.1	-	10	100	32	N/A	N/A	0.716
DART	0.1	128	30	150	128	N/A	N/A	0.703
DART (GOSS)	0.1	128	30	150	128	N/A	N/A	0.703
Random Forest	N/A	N/A	N/A	150	N/A	10	20	0.665

Table 3.1 – Summary of best parameters found for each model with the corresponding F1 scores

As we can see from the table, the LightGBM models performed much better than the scikit-learn random forest. Both DART models achieved nearly the same F1 score, with GOSS having a slightly lower F1 score (the table values are rounded to 3 digits).

This concludes our end-to-end example of exploring a dataset and building an optimized model for the dataset (using parameter grid search). We look at more complicated datasets in the coming chapters and delve deeper into analyzing model performance.

Summary

This chapter introduced LightGBM as a library to train boosted machines efficiently. We looked at where the complexity of building GBDTs comes from and the features in LightGBM that address them, such as histogram-based sampling, feature bundling, and GOSS. We also reviewed LightGBM's most important hyperparameters.

We also gave a detailed overview of using LightGBM in Python, covering both the LightGBM Python API and the scikit-learn API. We then built our first tuned models using LightGBM to predict student academic performance, utilizing cross-validation and grid-search-based parameter optimization.

In the next chapter, we compare LightGBM against another popular gradient-boosting library, XGBoost, and DL techniques for tabular data.

References

[1]   G. Ke, Q. Meng, T. Finley, T. Wang, W. Chen, W. Ma, Q. Ye and T.-Y. Liu, "LightGBM: A Highly Efficient Gradient Boosting Decision Tree," in Advances in Neural Information Processing Systems, 2017.

[2]   M. Mehta, R. Agrawal and J. Rissanen, "SLIQ: A fast scalable classifier for data mining," in Advances in Database Technology—EDBT'96: 5th International Conference on Extending Database Technology Avignon, France, March 25-29, 1996 Proceedings 5, 1996.

[3]   J. Shafer, R. Agrawal, M. Mehta and others, "SPRINT: A scalable parallel classifier for data mining," in Vldb, 1996.

[4]   S. Ranka and V. Singh, "CLOUDS: A decision tree classifier for large datasets," in Proceedings of the 4th Knowledge Discovery and Data Mining Conference, 1998.

[5]   H. Shi, "Best-first decision tree learning," 2007.

[6]   R. Kleiman and D. Page, "Aucµ: A performance metric for multi-class machine learning models," in International Conference on Machine Learning, 2019.

[7]   V. Realinho, J. Machado, L. Baptista and M. V. Martins, Predicting student dropout and academic success, Zenodo, 2021.

4

Comparing LightGBM, XGBoost, and Deep Learning

The previous chapter introduced LightGBM for building **gradient-boosted decision trees** (**GBDTs**). In this chapter, we compare LightGBM against two other methods for modeling tabular data: XGBoost, another library for building gradient-boosted trees, and **deep neural networks** (**DNNs**), a state-of-the-art machine learning technique.

We compare LightGBM, XGBoost, and DNNs on two datasets, focusing on complexity, dataset preparation, model performance, and training time.

This chapter is aimed at advanced readers, and some understanding of deep learning is required. However, the primary purpose of the chapter is not to understand XGBoost or DNNs in detail (neither technique is used in subsequent chapters). Instead, by the end of the chapter, you should have some understanding of how competitive LightGBM is within the machine-learning landscape.

The main topics are as follows:

- An overview of XGBoost
- Deep learning and TabTransformers
- Comparing LightGBM, XGBoost, and TabTransformers

Technical requirements

The chapter includes examples and code excerpts illustrating how to train LightGBM, XGBoost, and TabTransformer models in Python. Complete examples and instructions for setting up a suitable environment for this chapter are available at https://github.com/PacktPublishing/Practical-Machine-Learning-with-LightGBM-and-Python/tree/main/chapter-4.

An overview of XGBoost

XGBoost, short for **eXtreme Gradient Boosting**, is a widely popular open source gradient boosting library with similar goals and functionality to LightGBM. XGBoost is older than LightGBM and was developed by Tianqi Chen and initially released in 2014 *[1]*.

At its core, XGBoost implements GBDTs and supports building them highly efficiently. Some of the main features of XGBoost are as follows:

- **Regularization**: XGBoost incorporates both L1 and L2 regularization to avoid overfitting
- **Sparsity awareness**: XGBoost efficiently handles sparse data and missing values, automatically learning the best imputation strategy during training
- **Parallelization**: The library employs parallel and distributed computing techniques to train multiple trees simultaneously, significantly reducing training time
- **Early stopping**: XGBoost provides an option to halt the training process if there is no significant improvement in the model's performance, improving performance and preventing overfitting
- **Cross-platform compatibility**: XGBoost is available for many programming languages, including Python, R, Java, and Scala, making it accessible to a diverse user base

Over the years, XGBoost has gained popularity in the machine learning community due to its support for various applications and the library's ease of use and efficiency.

Comparing XGBoost and LightGBM

There is considerable overlap in functionality between XGBoost and LightGBM. Both libraries implement GBDTs and DART and support building random forests. Both have similar techniques to avoid overfitting and handle missing values and sparse data automatically.

However, some of the differences between XGBoost and LightGBM are as follows:

- **Tree-growing strategy**: XGBoost employs a level-wise tree growth approach, where trees are built level by level, while LightGBM uses a leaf-wise tree growth strategy that focuses on growing the tree by choosing the leaf with the highest delta loss. This difference in growth strategy generally makes LightGBM faster, especially for large datasets.
- **Speed and scalability**: LightGBM is designed to be more efficient regarding memory usage and computation time, making it a better choice for large-scale datasets or when training time is critical. However, this speed advantage can sometimes come at the cost of higher variance in model predictions.
- **Handling categorical features**: LightGBM has built-in support for categorical features, meaning it can handle them directly without needing one-hot encoding or other preprocessing techniques. XGBoost, on the other hand, requires the user to preprocess categorical features before feeding them into the model.

- **Early stopping**: XGBoost provides an option to halt the training process if there is no significant improvement in the model's performance. LightGBM does not have this feature built in, although it can be implemented manually using callbacks, as seen in earlier chapters.

In summary, LightGBM and XGBoost provide similar functionality. LightGBM performs better on large datasets with many features, whereas XGBoost may provide more stable and accurate results on smaller or medium-sized datasets.

Python XGBoost example

XGBoost provides a scikit-learn-based interface for building models. The following example shows how to use XGBoost on the Forest Cover dataset:

```
from xgboost import XGBClassifier
...
dataset = datasets.fetch_covtype()

X_train, X_test, y_train, y_test = train_test_split(
    dataset.data, dataset.target, random_state=179
    )
y_train = y_train - 1
y_test = y_test - 1
xgb = XGBClassifier(
    n_estimators=150, max_leaves=120, learning_rate=0.09
    )
xgb = xgb.fit(X_train, y_train)
f1_score(y_test, xgb.predict(X_test), average="macro")
```

The scikit-learn interface should be familiar to you at this stage. The preceding code shows that XGBoost supports similar hyperparameters as we used to train LightGBM-based models. A full list of parameters is available at `https://xgboost.readthedocs.io/en/stable/parameter.html`.

XGBoost represents a direct alternative to LightGBM as another gradient-boosting library. In the next section, we look at deep learning, a wholly different but extremely popular learning technique, and how it compares to gradient boosting on tabular learning problems.

Deep learning and TabTransformers

We now look at an approach to solving tabular-based data problems using deep learning. Deep learning has gained immense popularity in recent years due to the performance of deep-learning-based models. Deep-learning-based techniques such as AlphaZero, Stable Diffusion, and the GPT series of language models have achieved human or superhuman performance in gameplay, art generation, and language-based reasoning.

What is deep learning?

Deep learning is a subfield of the broader machine learning field of artificial neural networks. Artificial neural networks are mathematical mimics of the human brain and consist of interconnected layers of nodes (or "neurons" in biological parlance) that process and transmit information.

Simple artificial neural networks consist of only a few layers. The term "deep" in deep learning refers to using neural networks of many more layers, each with potentially thousands of neurons. These layers are organized hierarchically, with *input* layers at the bottom, *output* at the top, and *hidden* between. Each layer extracts and refines features as data passes through the network, allowing the model to learn complex patterns and representations.

The following diagram depicts a simple neural network called a multilayer perceptron with a single hidden layer.

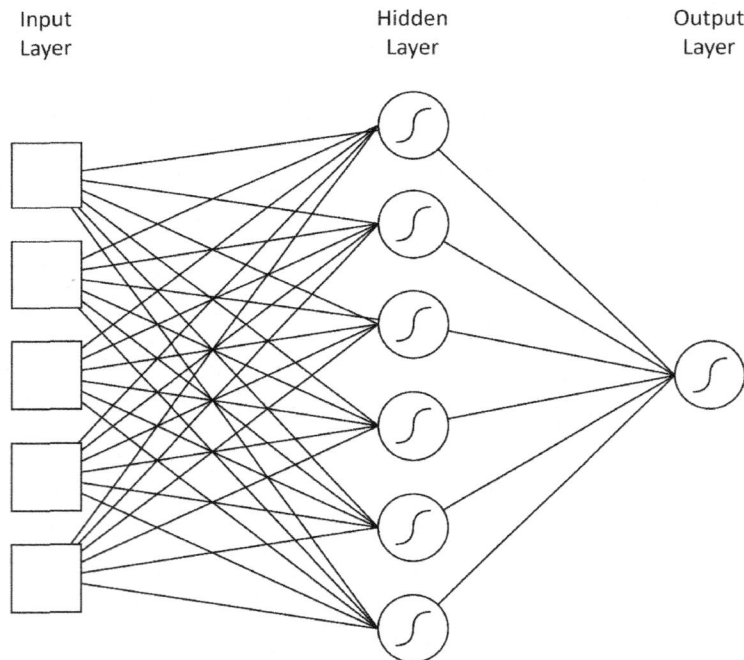

Figure 4.1 – A multilayer perceptron with a single hidden layer
and an output layer. The layers are fully connected

Each neuron receives input from other neurons, performs a mathematical operation, and then passes the result to the next layer of neurons.

The mathematical operation involves two main steps – weighted sum and activation function:

1. **Weighted sum**: The neuron takes the inputs (input data or outputs from previous neurons), multiplies each input by its corresponding weight, and then adds them together. A bias term is often added to the weighted sum for better control over the neuron's output. Mathematically, this can be represented as follows:

$$z_j = \sum_i \left(w_{ij} x_i \right) + b_j$$

   Here, x_i represents all inputs to the neuron, w_{ij} is the weight associated with the ith input, and b_j is the bias for the neuron.

2. **Activation function**: The weighted sum is then passed through an activation function, determining the neuron's output. The purpose of the activation function is to introduce non-linearity into the mathematical operation. The non-linearity allows the neural network to model non-linear and, therefore, complex relationships between inputs and outputs. There are various activation functions, such as **sigmoid** (logistic function), **hyperbolic tangent (tanh)**, and **Rectified Linear Unit (ReLU)**, each with its own properties and use cases. This can be represented as:

$$a_j = \sigma \left(z_j \right)$$

   where a_j is the neuron output and σ is the activation function.

Combining these two steps, a neuron in a neural network processes the input data, allowing the network to learn and model complex patterns.

Neural networks are trained by adjusting the weights associated with the neurons. The algorithm can be summarized as follows:

1. Weights are initialized to small, random values.

2. A **forward pass** is performed: for each example in a batch, the input features are passed through the entire network (calculating the sum and activation at each neuron) to produce a prediction at the output layer.

3. The loss is then calculated by comparing the output against the actual output for each example in a batch. Like GBDTs, the loss function has to be differentiable, and standard loss functions include the MSE and cross-entropy loss.

4. **Backpropagation** is performed: the gradient of the loss function with respect to the weights is calculated using the calculus chain rule. The process is started at the output layer and works backward through the network.

5. The weights are then updated using gradient descent or one of the modern variants, such as Adam, based on the backpropagated gradients.

6. The process is repeated for a set number of epochs (each epoch running through the entire dataset) to minimize the loss function.

A unique property of neural networks is that neural networks have been proven to be **universal function approximators**. DNNs have the theoretical capability to approximate any continuous function to a desired level of accuracy, given a sufficient number of hidden neurons and an appropriate activation function. This property is based on the **Universal Approximation Theorem**, which has been proven for various types of neural networks.

This means that a neural network can learn to represent complex relationships between input and output data, no matter how intricate or non-linear these relationships might be. This capability is one of the reasons why neural networks, especially DNNs, have successfully solved a wide range of problems across different domains. However, this guarantee is theoretical. In practice, finding the correct network architecture, hyperparameters, and training techniques to achieve the desired level of approximation can be challenging. The process often requires experimentation, expertise, and prohibitive computational resources.

Advantages and disadvantages of deep learning

Given the capabilities of DNNs, we might believe that they should be our first port of call for all machine learning problems. The primary advantage of using DNNs is their high accuracy in very complex domains: the current state-of-the-art performance on a wide range of complex tasks, natural language processing, generative AI, image recognition, and speech recognition are all achieved by DNNs due to their ability to learn complex and hidden patterns in large datasets.

Another advantage is automatic feature extraction. With the correct architecture, a DNN can extract complex or higher-order features automatically, alleviating the need for a data scientist to perform feature engineering.

Finally, DNNs can also transfer learning: pre-trained deep learning models can be fine-tuned on a smaller dataset for a specific task, leveraging the knowledge acquired during the initial training. Transfer learning can significantly reduce training time and data requirements for new tasks.

However, deep learning is not a panacea to all machine learning problems. Some of the disadvantages of using DNNs include the following:

- **Computational resources**: Deep learning models often require significant computing power and memory for training, especially when dealing with large datasets and complex architectures.

- **Large datasets**: DNNs usually perform well when trained on large datasets, but their performance can degrade when trained on smaller datasets. When a dataset is too small, the DNN overfits the training data and cannot generalize to unseen data.

- **Interpretability**: DNNs are often considered "black boxes" due to their complex architectures and the large number of parameters involved. The complexity can make understanding how the model makes decisions difficult, which may be a concern for applications requiring transparency or regulatory compliance.

- **Hyperparameter tuning**: DNNs involve numerous hyperparameters, such as network architecture, learning rate, and activation functions. Coupled with longer training times and resource needs, finding the optimal combination of these hyperparameters can be expensive and time-consuming.

Introducing TabTransformers

We want to apply deep learning to tabular data, as most practical machine learning problems have tabular data. To this end, we use a new deep learning architecture called **TabTransformer**: a deep neural network model designed to handle tabular data specifically.

Like the GPT family of DNNs, TabTransformer is based on the transformer architecture originally introduced by Vaswani et al. *[2]*. TabTransformer adapts the transformer architecture to work effectively with tabular data, providing an alternative to other machine learning models such as decision trees and gradient boosting machines for such data *[3]*.

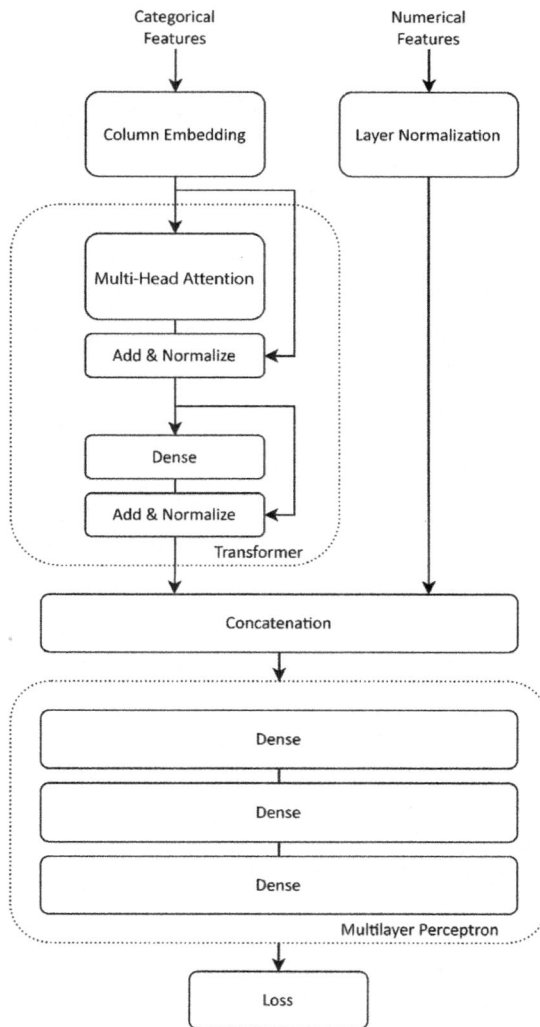

Figure 4.2 – The TabTransformer architecture as implemented in Keras [3]

The model architecture for TabTransformer is shown in *Figure 4.2*. With TabTransformer, each feature in the tabular data is treated as a token, similar to how words are treated as tokens in natural language processing. The model applies self-attention mechanisms to learn complex interactions and dependencies between features in the input data. The token embedding and attention mechanism allows the model to capture global and local relationships between features.

The TabTransformer model has several key components: token embedding, positional encoding, transformer layers, pooling, and output layers. The token embedding converts each feature value into a continuous vector representation, combined with positional information through positional encoding.

Moving through the layers, shown in *Figure 4.2*, we can see that the categorical and numerical features are split.

The categorical features first go through an embedding layer, as implemented by `layers.Embedding` in Keras, and are then passed along to the transformer blocks. A variable number of transformer blocks can be implemented (as set using a hyperparameter), but each consists of a `layers.MultiHeadAttention` layer and a `layers.Dense` layer with `Dropout`. The output values are added and normalized after passing through the attention and dense layers.

Due to their performance, the transformer feedforward layer uses the **Gaussian error linear unit (GELU)** activation function in our implementation. However, other activation functions may be used *[5]*.

The numerical features are passed through a normalization layer (normalizing the numerical input ranges) and then concatenated with output from the transformers.

The concatenated results are passed through a **multilayer perceptron (MLP)** block consisting of a variable number of dense layers, each with `Dropout`. Our implementation uses **scaled exponential linear unit (SELU)**, which causes the activations to self-normalize *[6]*.

Finally, the output from the MLP block is passed to the loss function, the implementation of which depends on the learning problem (classification or regression).

TabTransformers are much more complex to implement and train than gradient-boosted trees. Like other DNNs, TabTransformers require more data preparation and computational power than gradient-boosted trees.

In addition to TabTransformers, this section introduced deep learning alongside its advantages and disadvantages. In the next section, we use a practical example to compare the different approaches, including the complexity of working with TabTransformers.

Comparing LightGBM, XGBoost, and TabTransformers

In this section, we compare the performance of LightGBM, XGBoost, and TabTransformers on two different datasets. We also look at more data preparation techniques for unbalanced classes, missing values, and categorical data.

Predicting census income

The first dataset we use is the Census Income dataset, which predicts whether personal income will exceed $50,000 based on attributes such as education, marital status, occupation, and others *[4]*. The dataset has 48,842 instances, and as we'll see, some missing values and unbalanced classes.

The dataset is available from the following URL: `https://archive.ics.uci.edu/ml/machine-learning-databases/adult/adult.data`. The data has already been split into a training set and a test set. Once loaded, we can sample the data:

```
train_data.sample(5)[["age", "education", "marital_status", "hours_per_week", "income_bracket"]]
```

The data sample for the selected columns is shown in *Table 4.1*.

	age	education	marital_status	hours_per_week	income_bracket
12390	34	Some-college	Never-married	40	<=50K
20169	41	Assoc-acdm	Married-civ-spouse	45	>50K
17134	35	Doctorate	Never-married	60	>50K
23452	49	HS-grad	Married-civ-spouse	40	>50K
22372	31	HS-grad	Separated	45	<=50K

Table 4.1 – Sample data from the Census Income dataset

Table 4.1 shows that we have mixed data types: some features are numeric, and others are text. Notably, some columns in the dataset are **categorical features**: string-based features with a fixed set of values. Next, we look at encoding these features for use in machine learning.

Encoding categorical features

Most machine learning algorithms need string-based features to be encoded to numbers; in some cases, this can be done automatically. We discuss automatic encoding for LightGBM in *Chapter 6, Solving Real-World Data Science Problems with LightGBM*. In this example, we encode the features to understand what this entails.

We need to map each categorical value to a unique number; therefore, we first build a vocabulary of all values for each feature:

```
CATEGORICAL_FEATURES_WITH_VOCABULARY = {
    "workclass": sort_none_last(list(train_data["workclass"].
unique())),
    "education": sort_none_last(list(train_data["education"].
unique())),
    "marital_status": sort_none_last(list(train_data["marital_
status"].unique())),
```

```
    "occupation": sort_none_last(list(train_data["occupation"].
unique())),
    "relationship": sort_none_last(list(train_data["relationship"].
unique())),
    "race": sort_none_last(list(train_data["race"].unique())),
    "gender": sort_none_last(list(train_data["gender"].unique())),
    "native_country": sort_none_last(list(train_data["native_
country"].unique())),
    "income_bracket": sort_none_last(list(train_data["income_
bracket"].unique())),
}
```

The preceding code extracts unique values for each column into a list and sorts the list, putting `null` values last. When working with pandas DataFrames, it's also useful to explicitly set the data type for categorical columns to `category`:

```
for c in CATEGORICAL_FEATURES_WITH_VOCABULARY.keys():
    for dataset in [train_data, test_data]:
        dataset[c] = dataset[c].astype('category')
        dataset[c] = dataset[c].astype('category')
```

Using our vocabulary, we can now update the values in each column to numbers representing their category (using the index in the vocabulary list as the numeric value):

```
def map_to_index(val, vocab):
    if val is None:
        return None
    return vocab.index(val)


for dataset in (train_data, test_data):
    for feature, vocab in CATEGORICAL_FEATURES_WITH_VOCABULARY.
items():
        dataset[feature] = dataset[feature].map(lambda val: map_to_
index(val, vocab))
```

The result is a DataFrame where all features are now numeric:

	age	education	marital_status	hours_per_week	income_bracket
18545	37	11	2	40	0
26110	51	14	0	60	1
21905	36	11	5	32	0
1496	32	1	0	43	1
3148	47	15	2	40	0

Table 4.2 – Encoded categorical data from the Census Income dataset

Our categorical features are now encoded, and we can proceed with further data cleaning.

Missing values and duplicates

We need to check for missing values, duplicates, and outliers. We can use the following code:

```
train_data.isnull().sum()
train_data.drop_duplicates(inplace=True)
train_data.describe()
```

We drop the duplicate data, and reviewing the output of `describe` shows us there are no significant outliers. However, there are **missing values** in the dataset. LightGBM and XGBoost can deal with missing values automatically, a significant advantage of tree-based algorithms. However, for TabTransformers, we need to implement particular logic to deal with the missing values, as we'll see next.

Unbalanced data

The dataset is also skewed: the number of examples of each class is not balanced. We can calculate the skew using the following code:

```
counts = np.bincount(train_data["income_bracket"])
class_weight = {
    0: counts[0] / train_data.shape[0],
    1: counts[1] / train_data.shape[0]
}
```

The output shows a roughly 75%/25% skew toward the negative (0) class. One of the simplest ways of dealing with unbalanced classes (if we have binary classes) is to weigh the positive class more strongly than the negative class. Therefore, when calculating the loss, a prediction that misses the positive class has a more significant impact.

LightGBM and XGBoost both support this through the `scale_pos_weight` parameter, which can be calculated as follows:

```
scale_pos_weight = class_weight[0]/class_weight[1]
```

Training LightGBM and XGBoost models

With the data cleaned and prepared, we can now train our models. Training the LightGBM and XGBoost models is straightforward. For LightGBM, we have the following:

```
model = lgb.LGBMClassifier(force_row_wise=True, boosting_type="gbdt",
scale_pos_weight=scale_pos_weight)
model = model.fit(X_train, y_train)
```

And for XGBoost, we can run the following code:

```
model = xgb.XGBClassifier(scale_pos_weight=scale_pos_weight)
model = model.fit(X_train, y_train)
```

The preceding code highlights the simplicity of working with both libraries.

Training a TabTransformer model

We'll now build a TabTransformer model. We'll use **TensorFlow's Keras** to define the model based on the example code: `https://keras.io/examples/structured_data/tabtransformer/`.

Our dataset preparation remains mostly the same, with two key differences: we don't encode the categorical features and must handle the missing values explicitly.

We don't encode the categorical features because Keras provides a special layer to perform string lookup and conversion to a numerical value. However, we must still supply the vocabulary. The following code illustrates creating a lookup layer:

```
lookup = layers.StringLookup(
            vocabulary=vocabulary,
            mask_token=None,
            num_oov_indices=0,
            output_mode="int",
        )
```

The `num_oov_indices` parameter is set to 0, meaning no indices are used if an **out-of-vocabulary** (**OOV**) value is encountered. Since our vocabulary is exhaustive, this is not needed. The `mask_token` parameter is also set to `None`, as we aren't masking any string inputs.

We need to supply a default value for each column in the dataset to handle missing values. Our strategy is to replace string values with a default string value, NA. We use the statistical mean for the numeric columns to fill in the missing value. The following code creates a list of the default values:

```
train_data_description = train_data.describe()
COLUMN_DEFAULTS = [
    train_data_description[feature_name]["mean"] if feature_name in
NUMERIC_FEATURE_NAMES else ["NA"]
    for feature_name in HEADERS
]
```

The Keras code for implementing a TabTransformer model is roughly 100 lines long and is available in our GitHub repository: `https://github.com/PacktPublishing/Practical-Machine-Learning-with-LightGBM-and-Python/blob/main/chapter-4/tabtransformer-census-income.ipynb`.

The following code sets up the gradient optimizer and data that we can use with the TabTransformer model:

```
optimizer = tfa.optimizers.AdamW(
    learning_rate=learning_rate,
    weight_decay=weight_decay
)
model.compile(
    optimizer=optimizer,
    loss=keras.losses.BinaryCrossentropy(),
    metrics=[keras.metrics.BinaryAccuracy(name="accuracy"),
             f1_metric,
             precision_metric,
             recall_metric],
)
train_dataset = get_dataset_from_csv(
    train_data_file, batch_size, shuffle=True
)
validation_dataset = get_dataset_from_csv(
    test_data_file, batch_size
)
```

We use an `AdamW` optimizer with weight decay *[7]* with a binary cross-entropy loss function to fit the binary classification problem. We can then train and evaluate our model with the following code:

```
callback = keras.callbacks.EarlyStopping(
    monitor='loss', patience=3
)
history = model.fit(
    train_dataset,
    epochs=num_epochs,
    validation_data=validation_dataset,
    class_weight=class_weight,
    callbacks=[callback]
)

model.evaluate(validation_dataset, verbose=0)
```

We also add early stopping via the Keras callback with a patience of 3 epochs. During training and for validation, we track the accuracy and F1 score.

Training takes significantly longer than either gradient-boosting framework and requires a GPU (training on a CPU is technically possible but takes an inordinate amount of time).

We can now look at the results of the three algorithms on the Census Income dataset.

Results

Parameter optimization was performed for all three algorithms using the grid search technique discussed in the previous chapter. The learning rate, bin size, and number of trees were optimized for the two boosting algorithms. For the TabTransformer, both parameters and aspects of the architecture must be optimized. In terms of parameters, the learning rate, weight decay, and dropout rate were optimized, while for the architecture, the number of transformer blocks and hidden layers (in the MLP) had to be chosen. The optimized parameters are available in the source code.

The following table shows the results of the validation set for the algorithms.

Model	Training Time	Accuracy	F1 score
LightGBM GBDT	1.05s	84.46%	0.71
XGBoost GBDT	5.5s	84.44%	0.72
TabTransformer	113.63s	77.00%	0.64

Table 4.3 – Results from training the three models on the Census Income dataset

XGBoost and LightGBM performed similarly on the dataset, reaching an accuracy of 84% and an F1 score of 0.7. The TabTransformer model performed worse, with a lower accuracy and F1 score.

Regarding training time, LightGBM was much faster than the other approaches. The LightGBM model was trained 5.23 times faster than XGBoost and 108.22 times faster than the TabTransformer. The TabTransformer was trained for 15 epochs on an 8-core P4000 GPU.

For another point of comparison and to illustrate how the TabTransformer architecture can be adapted when categorical features aren't present, we look at solving a second problem using the three algorithms.

Detecting credit card fraud

Our second task is detecting fraudulent transactions in a credit card transaction dataset [8]. The dataset is available at https://www.kaggle.com/datasets/mlg-ulb/creditcardfraud. The task is a binary classification problem, with the training data transactions labeled non-fraudulent (0) and fraudulent (1). The dataset consists only of numerical features that have been anonymized for confidentiality. Notably, the dataset is highly unbalanced, with fraudulent transactions making up only 0.17% of the data.

Training LightGBM and XGBoost models

Since the values are all numeric, very little data preparation is required for the gradient-boosting models. To counteract the imbalance in the dataset, we again calculate scale_pos_weight and pass it to the model as a parameter. We perform a grid search with cross-validation to find good hyperparameters for both the LightGBM and XGBoost models. For LightGBM, both DART and a GBDT model were tried, with DART performing better. Unlike the Census Income dataset, the credit cards dataset is not pre-split into a training and test set. We, therefore, apply five-fold cross-validation to measure performance on unseen data. The following code trains the LightGBM model, with the XGBoost code being very similar:

```
model = lgb.LGBMClassifier(force_row_wise=True, boosting_type="dart",
learning_rate=0.0023, max_bin=384, n_estimators=300, scale_pos_
weight=scale_pos_weight, verbose=-1)
scores = cross_val_score(model, X, y, scoring="f1_macro")
print(f"Mean F1-score: {scores.mean()}")
```

The results for both LightGBM and XGBoost are shown in *Table 4.4* alongside the TabTransformer results.

Training a TabTransformer model

Without categorical features, the TabTransformer architecture can be significantly simplified. Let's look at the architecture as shown in *Figure 4.2*. We can see that the embedding and attention layers are no longer required. Indeed, *the model simplifies to a regular MLP* (it is disingenuous to still call the model a transformer as the attention layers are not used at all).

Besides removing the unneeded layers, the rest of the architecture and process remain the same as for the Census Income problem. AdamW is again used as the optimizer, and we perform grid search optimization of the hyperparameters and the number of hidden layers in the model. As with the gradient-boosting models, five-fold cross-validation is performed to measure the performance.

Results

Although the accuracy is also reported next, it is essential to note that it is not a good performance indicator with unbalanced data. In the dataset, 99.82% of the samples are of one class, and a model that predicts only that class will have a 99.82% accuracy and be completely pointless. The F1 score is unaffected by the class imbalance and remains a good performance indicator for classification performance in unbalanced datasets. The following table shows the results for all three algorithms with five-fold cross-validation.

Model	Training Time	Accuracy	F1 score
LightGBM GBDT	113s	99.88%	0.80
XGBoost GBDT	351s	98.41%	0.82
TabTransformer	528.59s	93.37%	0.05

Table 4.4 – Results from training the three models on the Credit Card Fraud
dataset. Training time includes five-fold cross-validation

XGBoost and LightGBM performed very similarly on the dataset, obtaining F1 scores of 0.82 and 0.80, respectively. The DNN struggles significantly with the problem, obtaining an F1 score of only 0.05 even using class weights to compensate for the imbalanced dataset.

Debugging performance issues in DNNs are notoriously tricky. Due to the complexity and opaqueness of building and training DNN models, small changes can have a significant effect.

Possible reasons for the poor performance include the following:

- **Inadequate model architecture**: This is the most likely cause. The architecture is not well suited to the problem. Further experimentation with the architecture, the size of layers, or even the type of neural network is needed.

- **Insufficient training**: The model might not be trained long enough. Increasing the training epochs can improve performance. However, in our experiments, the loss stagnated after 10 epochs (while training continued to 15).

- **Inappropriate loss function**: We applied a `BinaryCrossentropy` loss function with class weights. However, a more advanced loss function, such as a focal loss, may be tried *[9]*.

In terms of the training and validation time, it is a similar story as with the Census Income dataset. The LightGBM model was trained and validated significantly faster than the other approaches: 3.1 times faster than the XGBoost and 4.62 times faster than the DNN.

Summary

In this chapter, we discussed two additional algorithms that may be used to solve tabular learning problems: XGBoost, another gradient-boosting framework, and TabTransformer, a deep learning approach.

We showed how to set up and train both XGBoost models and TabTransformer on two datasets. We also showed how to encode categorical features for tree-based and neural network models. Both datasets also had imbalanced classes, which we had to compensate for during training.

We found that LightGBM and XGBoost produced similarly accurate models but that LightGBM trained models much faster and more efficiently. We also saw the complexity of training DNNs and the lackluster performance on these problems. Deep learning is an extremely powerful technique, but tree-based approaches are often more applicable when working with tabular datasets.

In the next chapter, we focus on more effective parameter optimization with LightGBM using a framework called **Optuna**.

References

[1]   T. Chen and C. Guestrin, "XGBoost," in Proceedings of the 22nd ACM SIGKDD International Conference on Knowledge Discovery and Data Mining, 2016.

[2]   A. Vaswani, N. Shazeer, N. Parmar, J. Uszkoreit, L. Jones, A. N. Gomez, L. Kaiser, and I. Polosukhin, Attention Is All You Need, 2017.

[3]   X. Huang, A. Khetan, M. Cvitkovic, and Z. Karnin, TabTransformer: Tabular Data Modeling Using Contextual Embeddings, 2020.

[4]   R. Becker, Adult, UCI Machine Learning Repository, 1996.

[5]   D. Hendrycks and K. Gimpel, Gaussian Error Linear Units (GELUs), 2020.

[6]   G. Klambauer, T. Unterthiner, A. Mayr and S. Hochreiter, Self-Normalizing Neural Networks, 2017.

[7]   I. Loshchilov and F. Hutter, Decoupled Weight Decay Regularization, 2019.

[8]   A. Dal Pozzolo, O. Caelen, R. Johnson and G. Bontempi, "Calibrating Probability with Undersampling for Unbalanced Classification," 2015.

[9]   T.-Y. Lin, P. Goyal, R. Girshick, K. He and P. Dollár, Focal Loss for Dense Object Detection, 2018.

Part 2: Practical Machine Learning with LightGBM

Part 2 delves into the intricate processes that underpin practical machine learning engineering, starting with a look at efficient hyperparameter optimization via a framework called **Optuna**. We will then transition into a comprehensive exploration of the data science lifecycle, illustrating the rigorous steps from problem definition and data handling to practical data science modeling applications. Concluding this part, the focus will shift to automated machine learning, spotlighting the FLAML library, which aims to simplify and streamline model selection and tuning. Throughout this part, a blend of case studies and hands-on examples will provide a clear roadmap to harnessing the full potential of these advanced tools, underscoring the themes of efficiency and optimization.

This part will include the following chapters:

- *Chapter 5, LightGBM Parameter Optimization with Optuna*

- *Chapter 6, Solving Real-World Data Science Problems with LightGBM*

- *Chapter 7, AutoML with LightGBM and FLAML*

LightGBM Parameter Optimization with Optuna

Previous chapters have discussed the LightGBM hyperparameters and their effect on building models. A fundamental problem when building a new model is finding the optimal hyperparameters to achieve the best performance.

This chapter focuses on the parameter optimization process using a framework called Optuna. Different optimization algorithms are discussed alongside the pruning of the hyperparameter space. A practical example shows how to apply Optuna to find optimal parameters for LightGBM. Advanced use cases for Optuna are also shown.

The chapter's main topics are as follows:

- Optuna and optimization algorithms
- Optimizing LightGBM with Optuna

Technical requirements

The chapter includes examples and code excerpts illustrating how to perform parameter optimization studies for LightGBM using Optuna. Complete examples and instructions for setting up a suitable environment for this chapter are available at `https://github.com/PacktPublishing/Practical-Machine-Learning-with-LightGBM-and-Python/tree/main/chapter-5`.

Optuna and optimization algorithms

Examples from previous chapters have shown that choosing the best hyperparameters for a problem is critical in solving a machine learning problem. The hyperparameters significantly impact the algorithm's performance and generalization capability. The optimal parameters are also specific to the model used and the learning problem being solved.

Other issues complicating hyperparameter optimization are as follows:

- **Cost**: For each unique set of hyperparameters (of which there can be many), an entire training run, often with cross-validation, must be performed. This is highly time-consuming and computationally expensive.

- **High-dimensional search spaces**: Each parameter can have a vast range of potential values, making testing each value impossible.

- **Parameter interaction**: Optimizing each parameter in isolation is often impossible, as some parameters' values interact with others' values. A good example is the learning rate and the number of estimators in LightGBM: fewer estimators necessitate a larger learning rate, and vice versa. This phenomenon is shown in *Figure 5.1*.

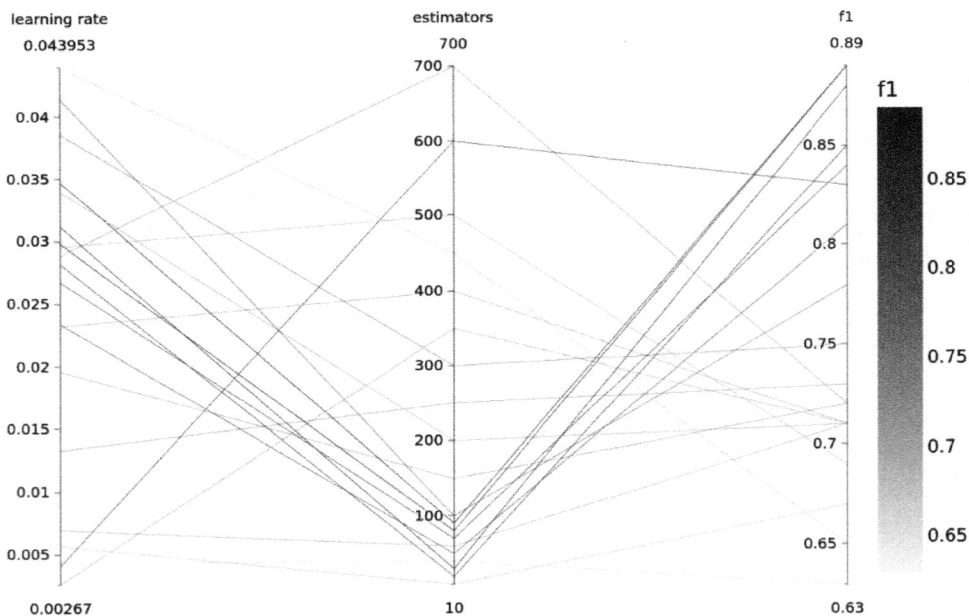

Figure 5.1 – A parallel coordinate plot showing a parameter interaction between the learning rate and the number of estimators: having more estimators requires a lower learning rate, and vice versa

Figure 5.1 visualizes parameter interactions using a technique called a **parallel coordinate plot**. Parallel coordinate plots are a visualization tool designed to represent high-dimensional data, making them especially useful for visualizing the results of hyperparameter optimization. Each dimension (in this context, a hyperparameter) is portrayed as a vertical axis arranged in parallel. The range of each axis mirrors the range of values that the hyperparameter can assume. Every individual configuration of hyperparameters is depicted as a line crossing all these axes, with the intersection point on each axis indicating the value of that hyperparameter for the given configuration. Lines can also be color-coded based on performance metrics, such as validation accuracy, to discern which hyperparameter combinations yield superior outcomes.

The beauty of parallel coordinate plots lies in their ability to illustrate relationships between multiple hyperparameters and their cumulative impact on performance, such as the parameter interaction shown in *Figure 5.1*. Observing the lines' clustering or similarities in their color allows us to glean trends and intricate interdependencies between hyperparameters. This ability to visualize multidimensional patterns helps data scientists pinpoint which hyperparameter values or combinations are most conducive to optimal model performance.

Given the challenges and complications of hyperparameter optimization, a naive approach to finding the optimal parameters is manual optimization. With manual optimization, a human practitioner selects parameters based on intuitive understanding and experience. A model is trained with these parameters, and the process is repeated until satisfactory parameters are found. Manual optimization is simple to implement but is very time-consuming due to the human-in-the-loop nature of the process. Human intuition is also fallible, and good parameter combinations can easily be missed.

> **Note**
>
> The process of finding optimal parameters is often called a parameter **study**. Each configuration (combination of parameters) tested in the study is referred to as a **trial**.

In the previous chapters' examples, the approach we used thus far was **grid search**. With grid search, we set up a parameter grid consisting of each parameter and a range of potential values and exhaustively tested each possible combination to find the optimal values.

Grid search solves the parameter interaction problem well: since each possible combination is tested, each interaction is accounted for.

However, the downside of using grid search is the cost. Since we exhaustively test each parameter combination, the number of trials quickly becomes prohibitive, especially if more parameters are added. For example, consider the following grid:

```
params = {"learning_rate": [0.001, 0.01, 0.1],
          "num_leaves": [10, 20, 50, 100],
          "num_estimators": [100, 200, 500]}
```

An optimization study for this grid would require 36 trials. Adding just one additional parameter with two possible values doubles the cost of the study.

What's needed is an algorithm and framework that can intelligently optimize the parameters within a limited number of trials that we control. Several frameworks exist for this purpose, including SHERPA, a Python library for tuning machine learning models; Hyperopt, another Python library for parameter optimization over complex search spaces; and Talos, a tool specifically tailored for Keras. However, in the next section, and for the rest of the chapter, we look at **Optuna**, a framework designed to automate tuning machine learning models.

Introducing Optuna

Optuna is an open source **hyperparameter optimization** (**HPO**) framework designed to automate finding the best hyperparameters for machine learning models (https://optuna.org/). It is written in Python and can be easily integrated with various machine learning libraries, including LightGBM.

Optuna provides efficient optimization algorithms to search hyperparameter spaces more effectively. In addition to the optimization algorithms, Optuna also provides pruning strategies to save computational resources and time by pruning poorly performing trials.

Besides optimization and pruning algorithms, Optuna also provides an easy-to-use API for defining parameter types (integer, float, or categorical), creating and automating resumable optimization studies, and visualizing the results of optimization runs. Later in the chapter, we see how to use the API practically.

Optimization algorithms

Optuna provides several efficient optimization algorithms. In this section, we focus on two of the available algorithms: a **Tree-Structured Parzen Estimator** (**TPE**) and a **Covariance Matrix Adaptation Evolution Strategy** (**CMA-ES**) algorithm.

TPE

To understand TPE, we must first know what a Parzen estimator is.

A Parzen estimator, or **Kernel Density Estimator** (**KDE**), is a technique used to estimate the probability distribution of a set of data points. It's a non-parametric method, meaning it doesn't assume any specific underlying distribution for the data. Instead, it tries to "learn" the distribution based on the observed data points.

Imagine you have data points and want to know how the data is distributed. One way to do this is by placing small "hills" (kernel functions) over each data point. These "hills" can have different shapes, such as Gaussian (bell-shaped) or uniform (box-shaped). The height of the "hill" at any point represents the likelihood that a new data point would fall at that location. The Parzen estimator works by adding up all these "hills" to create a smooth landscape representing the estimated probability distribution of the data.

In the case of TPE, the data points we care about are the parameter combinations, and the probability distribution is the likelihood of a set of parameters being good or bad [1], [2].

TPE starts by sampling a few random combinations of hyperparameters and evaluating the model's performance for each. Based on these initial results, TPE divides the hyperparameter combinations into two groups: good (those that lead to better performance) and bad (those that lead to worse performance):

- $l(x)$: The probability density function of good configurations
- $g(x)$: The probability density function of bad configurations

TPE then estimates the probability distributions of hyperparameter combinations for both good and bad groups using the Parzen estimator technique.

With estimations of the probability distributions available, TPE calculates the **Expected Improvement** (**EI**) of hyperparameter configurations. EI can be calculated as the ratio between the two densities: $\frac{l(x)}{g(x)}$. With each trail, the algorithm samples new hyperparameter configurations that maximize the EI.

The tree structure in TPE comes from the algorithm's ability to handle parameter interaction within the hyperparameter search space, where specific hyperparameters' relevance depends on others' values. To handle this, TPE builds a hierarchical structure that captures the relationships between different hyperparameters and adapts the sampling process accordingly.

In summary, TPE estimates the distributions of good and bad parameters and uses them to find optimal parameters by maximizing new trials' expected improvement. TPE is cost-effective since it approximates the distributions and can search for better parameters optimally (in a non-exhaustive way). TPE also handles parameter interactions.

An alternative algorithm provided by Optuna is the CMA-ES algorithm, which we discuss next.

CMA-ES

CMA-ES is another optimization algorithm that can be used to find optimal hyperparameters [3]. Compared to TPE, CMA-ES is well suited to cases that involve continuous variables and when the search space is non-linear and non-convex.

CMA-ES is an example of an **evolutionary algorithm** (**EA**). An EA is a type of optimization algorithm inspired by the process of natural evolution. It aims to find the best solution to a problem by mimicking how nature evolves species through selection, reproduction, mutation, and inheritance. Evolutionary algorithms start with a population of candidate solutions and modify the candidates with each subsequent *generation* to adapt more closely to the best solution. This generational process is illustrated in *Figure 5.2*.

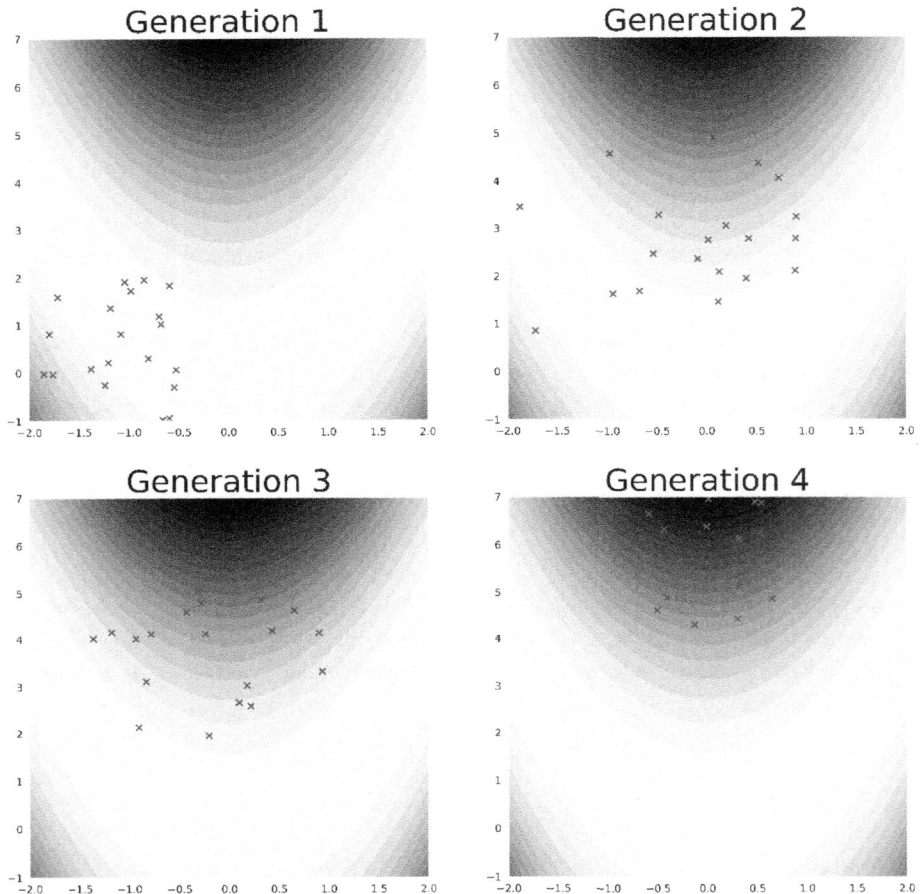

Figure 5.2 – A two-dimensional illustration of candidate solutions (red x marks) evolving with each subsequent generation to approximate the global optimum (located at the top and center of each landscape). In the context of CMA-ES, each candidate solution represents a combination of hyperparameter values, and the algorithm's performance determines the optimum

Central to the evolutionary process of CMA-ES is the covariance matrix. A covariance matrix is a square, symmetric matrix representing the covariance between pairs of variables (in the case of CMA-ES, the hyperparameters), providing insight into their relationships. The diagonal elements of the matrix represent the variances of individual variables, while the off-diagonal elements represent the covariances between pairs of variables. When there's a positive covariance, it signals that the variables usually move in the same direction, either increasing or decreasing. Conversely, a negative covariance points to a relationship where, as one variable rises, the other tends to fall, and vice versa. A covariance of zero suggests no linear relationship between the variables.

CMA-ES applies the evolutionary principles as follows when optimizing hyperparameters:

1. Within the hyperparameter search space, initialize the mean and the covariance matrix.

2. Repeat the evolutionary process:

   I. Generate a population of candidates from the search space using the mean and the covariance matrix. Each candidate represents a combination of hyperparameter values.

   II. Evaluate the fitness of the candidates. **Fitness** refers to the quality of a candidate or how well it solves the optimization problem. With CMA-ES, this means training the model on the dataset using the candidate hyperparameters and evaluating the performance on the validation set.

   III. Select the best candidates from the population.

   IV. Update the mean and the covariance matrix from the best candidates.

   V. Repeat for a maximum number of trials or until no improvement is seen in the population's fitness.

CMA-ES performs well in complex search spaces and intelligently samples the search space, guided by the covariance matrix. It is beneficial when the hyperparameter search space is complex and non-linear or when the evaluation of the validation data is noisy (for instance, when a metric is an inconsistent performance indicator).

Both TPE and CMA-ES address the issues associated with hyperparameter optimization: both algorithms effectively search a high-dimensional search space. Both algorithms capture parameter interaction. Both algorithms give us control of the cost: we can decide our optimization budget and limit our search to that.

The main differences between TPE and CMA-ES lie in their overall approach. TPE is a probabilistic model with a sequential search strategy, compared to CMA-ES, which is population-based and evaluates solutions in parallel. This often means TPE is more exploitative in its search, while CMA-ES balances exploration and exploitation using population control mechanisms. However, TPE is typically more efficient than CMA-ES, especially for a small number of parameters.

Optuna provides further optimization to the search process in pruning ineffective trials. We'll discuss some pruning strategies next.

Pruning strategies

Pruning strategies refer to methods that avoid spending optimization time on unpromising trials by pruning these trials from the study. Pruning occurs synchronously with the model training process: the validation error is checked during training, and the training is stopped if the algorithm is underperforming. In this way, pruning is similar to *early stopping*.

Median pruning

Optuna provides several pruning strategies, one of the simplest being **median pruning**. With median pruning, each trial reports an intermediate result after n steps. The median of the intermediate results is then taken, and any trials below the median of previous trials at the same step are stopped.

Successive halving and Hyperband

A more sophisticated strategy is called **successive halving** [4]. This takes a more global approach and assigns a small, equal budget of training steps to all trials. Successive halving then proceeds iteratively: at each iteration, the performance of each trial is evaluated, and the top half of the candidates are selected for the next round, with the bottom half pruned away. The training budget is doubled for the next iteration, and the process is repeated. This way, the optimization budget is spent on the most promising candidates. As a result, a small optimization budget is spent on eliminating the underperforming candidates, and more resources are spent on finding the best parameters.

Hyperband is another pruning technique that extends successive halving by incorporating random search and a multi-bracket resource allocation strategy [5]. While successive halving efficiently narrows down a set of candidate configurations by iteratively pruning underperforming ones and allocating more resources to the remaining promising ones, it relies on a fixed initial set of configurations and a single resource allocation scheme.

Hyperband instead uses a multi-bracket resource allocation strategy, which divides the total computational budget into several brackets, each representing a different level of resource allocation. Within each bracket, successive halving is applied to iteratively eliminate underperforming configurations and allocate more resources to the remaining promising ones. At the beginning of each bracket, a new set of hyperparameter configurations is sampled using random search, which allows Hyperband to explore the hyperparameter space more broadly and reduce the risk of missing good configurations. This concurrent process enables Hyperband to adaptively balance exploration and exploitation in the search process, ultimately leading to more efficient and effective hyperparameter tuning.

Optuna has performed empirical studies of optimization algorithms and corresponding pruning strategies (https://github.com/optuna/optuna/wiki/Benchmarks-with-Kurobako). *Empirically, they found that Hyperband is the best TPE or CMA-ES optimization strategy.*

This section gave an overview of the theory and algorithms powering Optuna, focusing on TPE, CMA-ES, and advanced pruning strategies. In the next section, we'll practically apply Optuna to a machine learning problem with LightGBM.

Optimizing LightGBM with Optuna

We'll walk through applying Optuna using a classification example. The problem we'll be modeling is to predict customer churn (*Yes/No*) for a telecommunications provider. The dataset is available from https://github.com/IBM/telco-customer-churn-on-icp4d/tree/master/data.

The data describes each customer using data available to the provider – for example, gender, whether the customer is paying for internet service, has paperless billing, pays for tech support, and their monthly charges. The data consists of both numeric and categorical features. The data has already been cleaned and is balanced, allowing us to focus on the parameter optimization study.

We start by defining the objective of our parameter study. The `objective` function is called once for each trial. In this case, we want to train a LightGBM model on the data and calculate the F1 score. Optuna passes a `trial` object to the `objective` function, which we can use to set up the parameters for the specific trial. The following is an example code snippet that shows how to define an `objective` function with parameters:

```
def objective(trial):
        boosting_type = trial.suggest_categorical(
            "boosting_type", ["dart", "gbdt"])
        lambda_l1= trial.suggest_float(
            'lambda_l1', 1e-8, 10.0, log=True),
    ...

        min_child_samples= trial.suggest_int(
            'min_child_samples', 5, 100),
        learning_rate = trial.suggest_float(
            "learning_rate", 0.0001, 0.5, log=True),
        max_bin = trial.suggest_int(
            "max_bin", 128, 512, 32)
        n_estimators =  trial.suggest_int(
            "n_estimators", 40, 400, 20)
```

Here, we can see how we use the methods provided by `trial` to set up the hyperparameters. For each parameter, a value is suggested by the optimization algorithm within the range specified. We can suggest categorical variables using `trial.suggest_categorical` (as can be seen for the `boosting` type), and `int` and `float` parameters using `suggest_int` and `suggest_float`, respectively. When suggesting floats or integers, a range and, optionally, a step size are specified:

```
n_estimators =  trial.suggest_int(
            name="n_estimators", low=40, high=400, step=20)
```

Setting a step size means the optimization algorithm does not suggest any arbitrary value in the range but limits suggestions to the steps between the lower and upper bound (40, 60, 80, 100, …, 400).

We also have the option to log scale the range of possible values by passing `log=True` for numeric parameters. Log scaling the parameter range has the effect that more values are tested close to the range's lower bound and (logarithmically) fewer values towards the upper bound. Log scaling is particularly well suited to the learning rate where we want to focus on smaller values and exponentially increase tested values until the upper bound.

To apply pruning when training LightGBM models, Optuna provides a purpose-built callback that integrates with the optimization process:

```
pruning_callback = optuna.integration.LightGBMPruningCallback(trial,
"binary")
```

We must specify an error metric when creating the callback, and, in our case, we specify `"binary"` for the binary error.

With the hyperparameters set up, we can fit as we usually do, passing the parameters and the callback as we would normally:

```
model = lgb.LGBMClassifier(
    force_row_wise=True,
    boosting_type=boosting_type,
    n_estimators=n_estimators,
    lambda_l1=lambda_l1,
    lambda_l2=lambda_l2,
    num_leaves=num_leaves,
    feature_fraction=feature_fraction,
    bagging_fraction=bagging_fraction,
    bagging_freq=bagging_freq,
    min_child_samples=min_child_samples,
    learning_rate=learning_rate,
    max_bin=max_bin,
    callbacks=[pruning_callback],
    verbose=-1)
scores = cross_val_score(model, X, y, scoring="f1_macro")
return scores.mean()
```

We train the model using five-fold cross-validation with the F1 macro score for scoring. Finally, the `objective` function returns the mean of the F1 scores as the trial evaluation.

We are ready to start an optimization study with the defined `objective` function. We create a sampler, pruner, and the study itself and then call `optimize` with our `objective` function:

```
sampler = optuna.samplers.TPESampler()
pruner = optuna.pruners.HyperbandPruner(
    min_resource=10, max_resource=400, reduction_factor=3)

study = optuna.create_study(
    direction='maximize', sampler=sampler,
    pruner=pruner
)
study.optimize(objective(), n_trials=100, gc_after_trial=True, n_
jobs=-1)
```

We use the TPE optimization algorithm as a sampler alongside Hyperband pruning. The minimum and maximum resources specified for the Hyperband pruner control the minimum and the maximum number of iterations (or estimators) trained per trial. When applying pruning, the reduction factor controls how many trials are promoted in each halving round.

The study is created by specifying the optimization direction (`maximize` or `minimize`). Here, we are optimizing the F1 score, so we want to maximize the value.

We then call `study.optimize` and set our optimization budget: `n_trials=100`. We also perform a memory optimization setting, `gc_after_trial=True`. Performing **garbage collection (GC)** helps ensure the memory is cleaned up after each trial, avoiding out-of-memory or memory leak errors. Optuna studies can run trials in parallel. Setting `n_jobs=-1` runs as many trials as there are CPU cores in parallel.

After running the optimization, we can get the best trial and parameters by calling the following:

```
print(study.best_trial)
```

The preceding example shows how to apply Optuna to find LightGBM hyperparameters effectively. Next, we look at some advanced features of the Optuna framework.

Advanced Optuna features

When optimizing hyperparameters for large machine learning problems, the optimization process may run for days or weeks. In these cases, saving an optimization study and resuming it later is helpful to guard against data loss or migrating the study between different machines.

Saving and resuming an optimization study

Optuna supports saving and resuming an optimization study in two ways: **in memory** and using a **remote database (RDB)**.

When a study is run in memory, the standard Python methods for serializing an object can be applied. For example, either `joblib` or `pickle` may be used. We use `joblib` to save a study:

```
joblib.dump(study, "lgbm-optuna-study.pkl")
```

To restore and resume the study, we deserialize the `study` object and continue with optimization:

```
study = joblib.load("lgbm-optuna-study.pkl")
study.optimize(objective(), n_trials=20, gc_after_trial=True, n_jobs=-1)
```

The alternative to running the study in memory is to use an RDB. When using an RDB, the study's intermediate (trial) and final results are persisted in a SQL database backend. The RDB can be hosted on a separate machine. Any of the SQL databases supported by SQL Alchemy may be used (`https://docs.sqlalchemy.org/en/20/core/engines.html#database-urls`).

In our example, we use a SQLite database as an RDB:

```
study_name = "lgbm-tpe-rdb-study"
storage_name = f"sqlite:///{study_name}.db"
study = optuna.create_study(
    study_name=study_name,
    storage=storage_name,
    load_if_exists=False,
    sampler=sampler,
    pruner=pruner)
```

Optuna manages the connection to the RDB and the persistence of the results. After setting up the connection, optimization can proceed as usual.

Restoring the study from an RDB backend is straightforward; we specify the same storage and set load_if_exists to True:

```
study = optuna.create_study(study_name=study_name, storage=storage_
name, load_if_exists=True)
```

Understanding parameter effects

In many cases, it's also valuable to better understand the effects of hyperparameters when solving a specific problem. For example, the n_estimators parameter directly affects the computational complexity of a model. If we know the parameter to be less important, we can choose smaller values to improve our model's runtime performance. Optuna provides several visualizations to dive deeper into the results of a study and gain insight into hyperparameters.

A straightforward visualization plots the *importance of each parameter*: how much each affected the training outcome. We can create an importance plot as follows:

```
fig = optuna.visualization.plot_param_importances(study)
fig.show()
```

The importance plot for our study is shown here:

Hyperparameter Importances

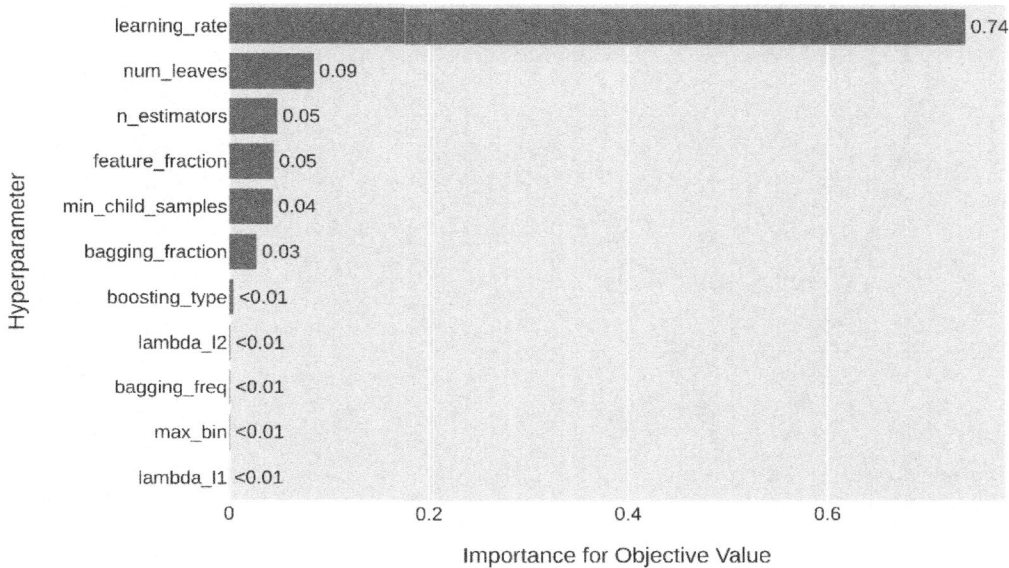

Figure 5.3 – A parameter importance plot showing the importance of
each hyperparameter to the object values (F1 score)

In *Figure 5.3*, we can see that the learning rate is by far the most critical parameter affecting the success of a trial. The number of leaves and estimators follows this. Using this information, we may decide to focus more heavily on finding an optimal learning rate in future studies.

We create a parallel coordinate plot as follows, specifying the parameters it should contain. The plot helps us visualize the interaction between hyperparameters:

```
fig = optuna.visualization.plot_parallel_coordinate(study,
params=["boosting_type", "feature_fraction", "learning_rate", "n_
estimators"])
fig.show()
```

Here is the resulting plot:

Parallel Coordinate Plot

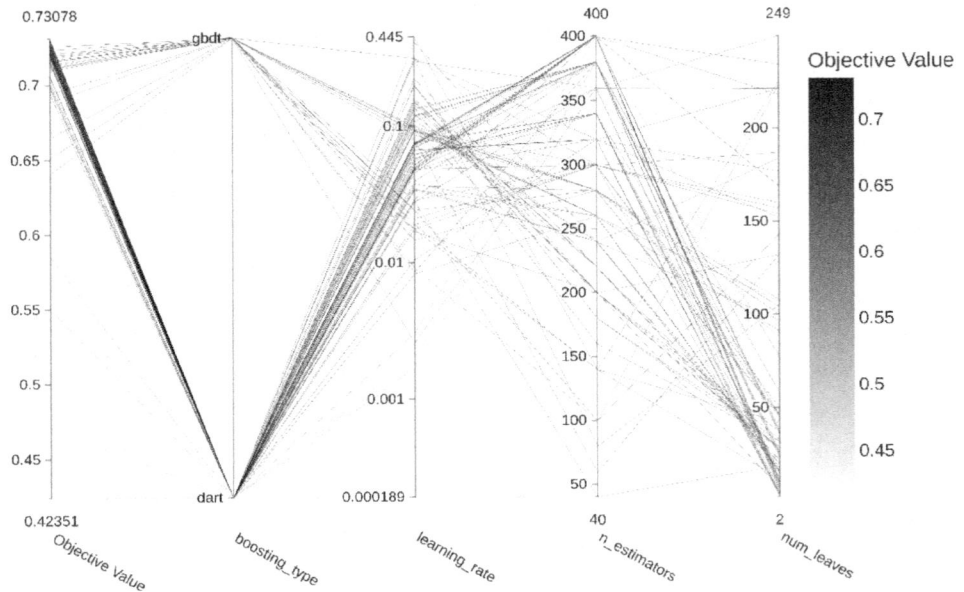

Figure 5.4 – A parallel coordinate plot for our study. Each horizontal line is the configuration for a single trial. Darker lines indicate more successful trials (higher F1 scores)

The parallel coordinate plot shows that the best trials all used DART as the boosting type and have a learning rate of just below 0.1 and more than 200 estimators. We can also visually see some parameter interactions: GBDT models correlate with slightly higher learning rates. Far fewer leaf nodes are required when there is a large number of estimators because having many estimators and large numbers of leaf nodes leads to overfitting.

Multi-objective optimization

In the optimization studies shown previously, we focused on a single optimization objective: maximizing our F1 score. However, in some instances, we would like to optimize two potentially competing objectives. For example, say we want to create the smallest GBDTs possible (fewest leaves) while obtaining a good F1 score. Reducing the number of leaves can potentially negatively impact our performance, so a trade-off exists.

Optuna supports solving this type of problem by using **multi-objective optimization (MOO)**. When optimizing multiple objectives, we return two evaluations from our `objective` function and specify the optimization directions.

As an example, consider the trade-off between the learning rate and performance. We want to train our model as fast as possible, which requires a high learning rate. However, we know the best performance is achieved using a small learning rate and many iterations.

We can use Optuna to optimize this trade-off. We define a new `objective` function, fixing all other parameters to the optimal values found earlier. We return two evaluations: the learning and the cross-validated F1-score. We want to maximize both values:

```
def moo_objective(trial):
    learning_rate = trial.suggest_float("learning_rate", 0.0001, 0.5,
log=True),

    model = lgb.LGBMClassifier(
        force_row_wise=True,
        boosting_type='gbdt',
        n_estimators=200,
        num_leaves=6,
        bagging_freq=7,
        learning_rate=learning_rate,
        max_bin=320,
    )
    scores = cross_val_score(model, X, y, scoring="f1_macro")
    return learning_rate[0], scores.mean()
```

When calling `optimize`, we then set the direction for the optimization of both evaluations:

```
study = optuna.create_study(directions=["maximize", "maximize"])
study.optimize(moo_objective, n_trials=100)
```

When performing MOO, there isn't always a single best result: a trade-off often exists between the objectives. Therefore, we want to visualize the study results to explore the trade-off and select parameter values that perform well with both objectives. This type of visualization is called a **Pareto front** and can be created as follows:

Pareto Front Plot

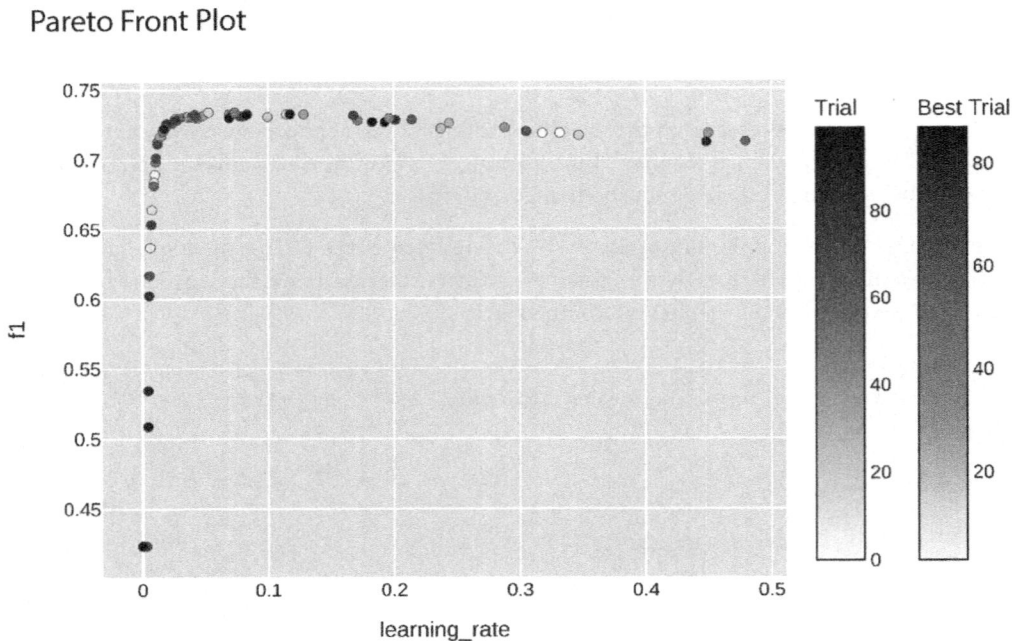

Figure 5.5 – A scatter plot showing the Pareto front for a MOO study

As shown in *Figure 5.5*, the F1 score is poor if the learning rate is too low and picks up quickly as the learning rate gets to 0.01. The F1 score peaks at 0.12 and slowly trails off as the learning rate increases. We now have the necessary information to decide on our trade-off: we can choose a higher learning rate for faster training, sacrificing the minimum amount of classification performance.

Summary

This chapter introduced Optuna as a framework for HPO. We discussed the problems of finding optimal hyperparameters and how HPO algorithms may be used to find suitable parameters efficiently.

We discussed two optimization algorithms available in Optuna: TPE and CMA-ES. Both algorithms allow a user to set a specific budget for optimization (the number of trials to perform) and proceed to find suitable parameters within the constraints. Further, we discussed the pruning of unpromising optimization trials to save additional resources and time. Median pruning and the more complex but effective pruning techniques of successive halving and Hyperband were discussed.

We then proceeded to show how to perform HPO studies for LightGBM in a practical example. We also showed advanced features of Optuna that can be used to save and resume studies, understand the effects of parameters, and perform MOO.

The next chapter focuses on two case studies using LightGBM, where the data science process is discussed and applied in detail.

References

[1]   J. Bergstra, R. Bardenet, Y. Bengio, and B. Kégl, *"Algorithms for Hyper-Parameter Optimization,"* in *Advances in Neural Information Processing Systems*, 2011.

[2]   J. Bergstra, D. Yamins, and D. Cox, *"Making a Science of Model Search: Hyperparameter Optimization in Hundreds of Dimensions for Vision Architectures,"* in *Proceedings of the 30th International Conference on Machine Learning, Atlanta*, 2013.

[3]   N. Hansen and A. Ostermeier, *"Adapting arbitrary normal mutation distributions in evolution strategies: the covariance matrix adaptation,"* in *Proceedings of IEEE International Conference on Evolutionary Computation*, 1996.

[4]   K. Jamieson and A. Talwalkar, *Non-stochastic Best Arm Identification and Hyperparameter Optimization*, 2015.

[5]   L. Li, K. Jamieson, G. DeSalvo, A. Rostamizadeh, and A. Talwalkar, *Hyperband: A Novel Bandit-Based Approach to Hyperparameter Optimization*, 2018.

6

Solving Real-World Data Science Problems with LightGBM

With the preceding chapters, we have slowly been building out a toolset for us to be able to solve machine learning problems. We've seen examples of examining our data, addressing data issues, and creating models. This chapter formally defines and applies the data science process to two case studies.

The chapter gives a detailed overview of the data science life cycle and all the steps it encompasses. The concepts of problem definition, data exploration, data cleaning, modeling, and reporting are discussed in a regression and classification problem context. We also look at preparing data for modeling and building optimized LightGBM models using our learned techniques. Finally, we look deeper at utilizing a trained model as an introduction to **machine learning operations** (**MLOps**).

The main topics of this chapter are as follows:

- The data science life cycle

- Predicting wind turbine power generation with LightGBM

- Classifying individual credit scores with LightGBM

Technical requirements

The chapter includes examples and code excerpts illustrating how to perform parameter optimization studies for LightGBM using Optuna. Complete examples and instructions for setting up a suitable environment for this chapter are available at `https://github.com/PacktPublishing/Practical-Machine-Learning-with-LightGBM-and-Python/tree/main/chapter-6`.

The data science life cycle

Data science has emerged as a critical discipline, enabling organizations to derive valuable insights from their data and drive better decision-making. At the heart of data science lies the data science life cycle, a systematic, iterative process that guides data-driven problem-solving across various industries and domains. This life cycle outlines a series of steps that data scientists follow to ensure they address the right problem and deliver actionable insights that create real-world impact.

The first stage of the data science life cycle involves defining the problem, which entails understanding the business context, articulating objectives, and formulating hypotheses. This crucial stage establishes the entire project's foundation by establishing a clear direction and scope. Subsequent stages in the life cycle focus on data collection, preparation, and exploration, collectively involving gathering relevant data, cleaning and preprocessing it, and conducting exploratory data analysis to unveil patterns and trends.

Once the data is analyzed, the data science life cycle progresses to model selection, training, evaluation, and tuning. These stages are central to developing accurate and reliable predictive or descriptive models by choosing the most appropriate algorithms, training them on the preprocessed data, and optimizing their performance. The goal is to build a robust model that generalizes well to unseen data and addresses the problem at hand effectively.

Lastly, the data science life cycle emphasizes the importance of deploying the final model into a production environment, monitoring its performance, and maintaining it to ensure its ongoing relevance and accuracy. Equally important is the communication of results and insights to stakeholders, which is vital for driving informed decision-making and realizing the full potential of data science. By following the data science life cycle, organizations can systematically extract value from their data and unlock new opportunities for growth and innovation.

With previous examples, we followed a loose recipe of steps for working with data and creating models. In the next section, we formally define and discuss the steps of the data science life cycle.

Defining the data science life cycle

The following are the key steps broadly applied in the data science life cycle. The steps are also shown in *Figure 6.1*, which illustrates the cyclical nature of the life cycle.

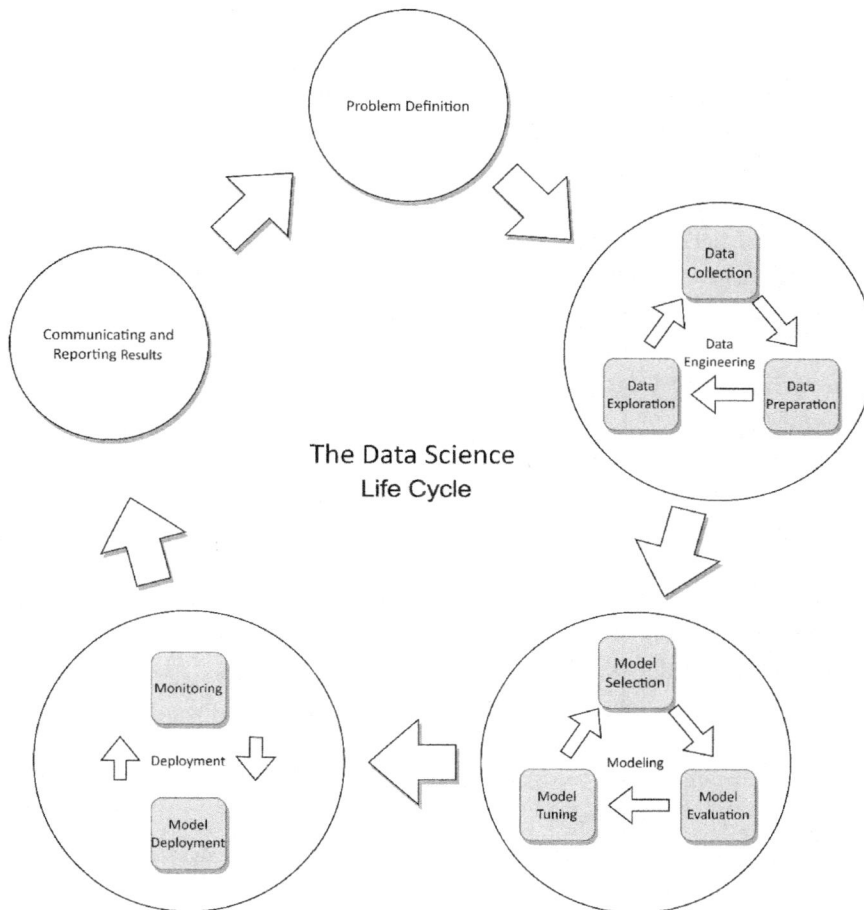

Figure 6.1 – Diagram depicting the data science life cycle

These are the key steps:

1. **Define the problem**: Clearly articulate the business problem, goals, and objectives. This stage involves understanding stakeholder requirements, formulating hypotheses, and determining the project's scope. Defining the problem also sets the stage for data collection and can determine how we'll utilize our models.

2. **Data collection**: Gather the required data from various sources, such as databases, APIs, web scraping, or third-party data providers. Ensure the data is representative, accurate, and relevant to the problem. It is important to document where data originates and how it is moved around to establish the **data lineage**. Further, build a **data dictionary** that documents the data's format, structure, content, and meaning. Importantly, validate any potential bias in the collection or sampling of data.

3. **Data preparation**: Clean and preprocess the data to make it suitable for analysis. This stage includes tasks such as **data cleansing** (e.g., handling missing values and removing duplicates), **data transformation** (e.g., normalization and encoding categorical variables), and **feature engineering** (e.g., creating new variables or aggregating existing ones). Moving and joining the data to where it can be analyzed and modeled might also be necessary.

4. **Data exploration**: Conduct **exploratory data analysis (EDA)** to gain insights into the data. This step involves visualizing data distributions, identifying trends and patterns, detecting outliers and anomalies, and checking for relationships and correlations between features.

5. **Model selection**: Choose the most appropriate data modeling techniques based on the problem type (e.g., regression, classification, or clustering) and the data characteristics. It's important to choose multiple model algorithms to validate performance on the data set.

6. **Model training**: Train the selected models using the prepared data. This step involves splitting the data into training and validation sets, setting model parameters (hyperparameters), and fitting the models to the data.

7. **Model evaluation**: Assess the performance of the trained models using appropriate evaluation metrics (e.g., accuracy, precision, recall, F1-score, **Area under the ROC Curve (AUC-ROC)**, or **root mean square error (RMSE)**) and compare them to select the best-performing model(s). Perform cross-validation or use holdout test sets to ensure an unbiased evaluation.

8. **Model tuning**: Fine-tune the selected model by optimizing hyperparameters, feature selection, or incorporating domain knowledge. This step aims to improve the model's performance and generalization to unseen data. It might also be appropriate to tune the model for the specific problem; for instance, when recognizing faces, a higher precision is more appropriate than a high recall.

9. **Model deployment**: If the model is to be part of a more extensive software system, deploy the final model into a production environment, where it can be used to make predictions or inform decision-making. Deployment may involve integrating the model into existing systems, creating APIs, or setting up monitoring and maintenance procedures.

10. **Model monitoring and maintenance**: Continuously monitor the model's performance and update it as necessary to ensure it remains accurate and relevant. Techniques such as detecting model and data drift should be used to ensure model performance. Model maintenance may involve retraining the model with new data, updating features, or refining the problem definition.

11. **Communicate results**: Share insights and results with stakeholders, including any recommendations or actions based on the analysis. Communicating the results may involve creating visualizations, dashboards, or reports to communicate the findings effectively.

We now examine two case studies to see how the data science life cycle is applied practically to real-world data. We look at a regression problem, predicting wind turbine power generation, and a classification problem, classifying individual credit scores.

Predicting wind turbine power generation with LightGBM

Our first case study is a problem where we aim to predict the power generation of wind turbines. The dataset for the problem is available from `https://www.kaggle.com/datasets/mukund23/hackerearth-machine-learning-challenge`.

We work through the problem using the steps defined in the previous section, articulating the details involved in each step alongside code snippets. The complete end-to-end solution is available at `https://github.com/PacktPublishing/Practical-Machine-Learning-with-LightGBM-and-Python/tree/main/chapter-6/wind-turbine-power-output.ipynb`.

Problem definition

The dataset consists of power generation (in kW/h) measurements of wind turbines taken at a specific date and time. Alongside each measurement are the parameters of the wind turbine, which include physical measurements of the windmill (including windmill height, blade breadth, and length), operating measurements for the turbine (including resistance in ohms, motor torque, generator temperature, and rotor torque) and atmospheric conditions (including wind speed, temperature, and pressure).

Given the set of parameters, we must build a regression model to predict the generated power in kW/h. Therefore, we employ regression modeling. The quality of the model is measured using the **mean squared error** (MSE) and the coefficient of determination (R^2). We must also determine which factors have the most significant impact on power generation.

Data collection

The dataset comprises 22,800 samples collected within 11 months, from October 2018 to September 2019. The data is available as CSV files and is released as public domain data. No additional data is collected.

Data preparation

We can now look at preparing the data for cleaning and exploration. The dataset consists of 18 numerical features, 2 categorical features, and the date feature, as we can see by getting the information from our pandas DataFrame:

```
train_df.info()
 #   Column                          Non-Null Count   Dtype
---  ------                          --------------   -----
 0   tracking_id                     28200 non-null   object
 1   datetime                        28200 non-null   object
 2   wind_speed(m/s)                 27927 non-null   float64
 3   atmospheric_temperature(°C)     24750 non-null   float64
 4   shaft_temperature(°C)           28198 non-null   float64
```

```
...
 20   windmill_height(m)                  27657 non-null   float64
 21   windmill_generated_power(kW/h)      27993 non-null   float64
```

We can immediately see that the dataset has missing values, with some features having fewer than 28,200 values. We can get a better sense of the data distribution by calculating the statistical description:

```
train_df.describe().T.style.bar(subset=['mean'])
```

This prints out the following:

Feature	count	mean	std	min	max
wind_speed(m/s)	27927	69.04	76.28	-496.21	601.46
atmospheric_temperature(°C)	24750	0.38	44.28	-99.00	80.22
shaft_temperature(°C)	28198	40.09	27.20	-99.00	169.82
blades_angle(°)	27984	-9.65	47.92	-146.26	165.93
gearbox_temperature(°C)	28199	41.03	43.66	-244.97	999.00
engine_temperature(°C)	28188	42.61	6.12	3.17	50.00
motor_torque(N-m)	28176	1710	827	500	3000.00
generator_temperature(°C)	28188	65.03	19.82	33.89	100.00
atmospheric_pressure(Pascal)	25493	53185	187504	-1188624	1272552
area_temperature(°C)	28200	32.74	7.70	-30.00	55.00
windmill_body_temperature(°C)	25837	20.80	54.36	-999.00	323.00
wind_direction(°)	23097	306.89	134.06	0.00	569.97
resistance(ohm)	28199	1575.6	483.33	-1005.22	4693.48
rotor_torque(N-m)	27628	25.85	32.42	-136.73	236.88
blade_length(m)	23107	2.25	11.28	-99.00	18.21
blade_breadth(m)	28200	0.40	0.06	0.20	0.50
windmill_height(m)	27657	25.89	7.77	-30.30	78.35
windmill_generated_power (kW/h)	27993	6.13	2.70	0.96	20.18

Table 6.1 – Statistical description of numerical features in the Wind Turbine dataset

Looking at the statistical description of the features in *Table 6.1*, we can see the following irregularities:

- **Many features have outliers**: Generally, a standard deviation larger than the mean may indicate outlying values. Examples include wind speed, atmospheric temperature, and atmospheric pressure. Similarly, a minimum or maximum far away from the mean may indicate outliers in the data. We can further verify this by visualizing the data distribution using a histogram.

- **Physical impossibilities**: The data shows impossibilities in the data of some of the measurements: lengths (in meters) less than 0 (e.g., blade length) and temperatures outside of natural ranges (a body temperature of -999).

- **Repeated values**: The values -99.0 and -999.0 repeat for a few features. It's improbable that these values occur naturally across features. We can infer that these indicate missing or erroneous measurements in the sample.

We can visualize the distribution of features to investigate the outlying values. For example, for atmospheric temperature, we have the following:

```
sns.histplot(train_df["atmospheric_temperature(°C)"], bins=30)
```

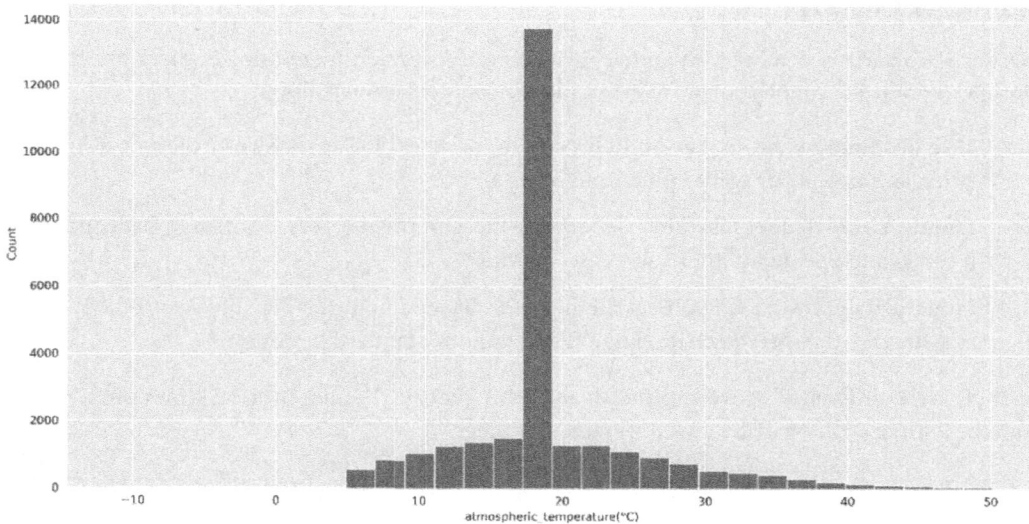

Figure 6.2 – Histogram showing atmospheric temperature in Celsius

Figure 6.2 illustrates two of the issues found in the data: a high frequency of measurements with a value of precisely -99.0, indicating an error. A few outlying values are also far removed from the mean.

Finally, we can check for duplicate data using the following:

```
train_df[train_df.duplicated()]
```

No rows are returned, indicating no duplicates in the dataset.

Data cleaning

We have identified multiple issues in the dataset that we need to address as part of the *data cleaning* step:

- **Outliers**: Many features have outlier values that skew the distribution of values for the feature.
- **Measurement errors**: Some features have values that fall out of the bounds of physical impossibilities (lengths smaller than 0 or temperatures in impossible ranges).
- **Missing values**: Many of the features have missing values. There are also particular values (-99.0 and -999.0) that we consider missing.

We first address the outliers and measurement errors, as this impacts how we handle the missing values.

Dealing with outliers

There are two parts to dealing with outliers in a dataset: accurately identifying outliers and choosing appropriate values for replacement. Ways to identify outliers are as follows:

- **Visualization**: As shown previously, histograms or other plots that visualize the data distribution (such as box plots or scatter plots) can be used
- **Domain knowledge**: Like how we identify measurement errors, domain knowledge can be leveraged to decide whether values are outlying
- **Statistical analysis**: Two popular methods for determining whether values are outlying using statistics are the **interquartile range** (**IQR**) and the standard deviation.

The IQR is the difference between the 25th and 75th quartiles. Values over 1.5 times the IQR away from the 25th or 75th quartiles are considered outlying.

Alternatively, we can leverage the standard deviation: we calculate the mean and standard deviation of the dataset. Any values over two or three times removed from the mean are outlying. Setting bounds to twice or three times the standard deviation depends on the underlying data. Using twice the standard deviation could lead to many false positives, but it is appropriate if a lot of data is centered around the mean. Using three times the standard deviation is more conservative and only marks values very far from the mean as outlying.

When the outlying values are detected, we must do something about them. Generally, our options are as follows:

- **Remove**: If an outlier results from an error in data entry, measurement, or collection, it may be reasonable to remove it from the dataset. However, this should be done cautiously, as removing too many data points can lead to a loss of information and biased results. Removing instances with outliers in our dataset would result in close to 70% data loss and isn't an option.

- **Impute**: Similar to missing values, replace the outlier value with a more representative value, such as the mean, median, or mode of the variable, or use more sophisticated imputation methods such as **k-nearest neighbors** or **regression-based imputation**.

- **Cap or truncate**: Set a threshold (either upper or lower) and cap or truncate the outlier values at that threshold. This method retains the data's original structure while reducing the influence of extreme values.

For the Wind Turbine dataset, we detect the outliers using bounds set to three times the standard deviation and map the values to np.nan, so we may replace them later:

```
column_data = frame[feature]
column_data = column_data[~np.isnan(column_data)]
mean, std = np.mean(column_data), np.std(column_data)
lower_bound = mean - std * 3
upper_bound = mean + std * 3
frame.loc[((frame[feature] < lower_bound) | (frame[feature] > upper_
bound))] = np.nan
```

Handling measurement errors

The values detected as types of measurement errors could also be considered outliers, although not in the statistical sense of the word. However, we can handle these values slightly differently than with the statistical outliers.

We apply our domain knowledge and some research surrounding the weather to identify appropriate ranges for these features. We then cap the erroneous values to these ranges:

```
frame.loc[frame["wind_speed(m/s)"] < 0, "wind_speed(m/s)"] = 0
frame.loc[frame["wind_speed(m/s)"] > 113, "wind_speed(m/s)"] = 113
frame.loc[frame["blade_length(m)"] < 0, "blade_length(m)"] = 0
frame.loc[frame["windmill_height(m)"] < 0, "windmill_height(m)"] = 0
frame.loc[frame["resistance(ohm)"] < 0, "resistance(ohm)"] = 0
```

Here, we set any negative lengths, heights, and electrical resistance to 0. We also cap the windspeed to 113 m/s, the maximum gust speed on record.

Finally, we can deal with the missing values in the dataset.

Handling missing values

We have discussed working with missing values in earlier chapters. To summarize here, some of the potential approaches we can take are as follows:

- Remove instances with missing values

- Impute the missing values using descriptive statistics (the mean, median, or mode)

- Use other machine learning algorithms, typically unsupervised techniques such as clustering, to calculate more robust statistics

Removing the missing values would discard a significant portion of our dataset. Here, we decide to replace missing values using descriptive statistics to retain as much data as possible.

First, we mark the -99.0 and -999.0 values as missing:

```
df.loc[frame[f] == -99.0, f] = np.nan
df.loc[frame[f] == 99.0, f] = np.nan
df.loc[frame[f] == -999.0, f] = np.nan
df.loc[frame[f] == 999.0, f] = np.nan
```

We then replace missing numerical values with the mean and categorical values with the mode:

```
if f in numerical_columns:
    frame[f].fillna(frame[f].mean(), inplace=True)
else:
    frame[f].fillna(frame[f].mode()[0], inplace=True)
```

Usually, we would have to be careful when using the mean since the mean is affected by outliers. However, since we have already marked the outlier values as np.nan, they are excluded when calculating the mean. An additional caveat comes into play when replacing missing values in the test set: since the test set should be treated as unseen data, we must use the mean from the training dataset to replace missing values in the test set.

This concludes the necessary data cleaning for our dataset. We should validate our work by rechecking for missing values and recalculating the descriptive statistics and data histograms.

With the dataset clean, we can move to the next data preparation step: feature engineering.

Feature engineering

Feature engineering refers to the process of creating new features or modifying existing ones to improve the performance of a machine learning model. In essence, feature engineering is using domain knowledge and data understanding to create features that make machine learning algorithms work more effectively. It's an art as much as a science, requiring creativity, intuition, and a deep understanding of the problem.

The feature engineering process often starts with exploring the data to understand its characteristics, distributions, and relationships between variables. This exploration phase can reveal potential opportunities for feature creation, such as interaction terms, aggregate features, or temporal features; for example, if you're working with a dataset containing customer transaction data, you might engineer features that capture the frequency of transactions, the average transaction value, or the time since the last transaction.

There are also several standard techniques used in feature engineering. These include encoding categorical variables, normalizing numerical variables, creating polynomial features, and binning continuous variables. For instance, categorical variables are often encoded into numerical formats (such as one-hot or ordinal encoding) to be used in mathematical models. Similarly, numerical variables are often normalized (such as min-max scaling or standardization) to ensure they're on a comparable scale and to prevent certain variables from dominating others simply because of their scale.

However, feature engineering is not a one-size-fits-all process. The appropriate features for a model can depend heavily on the specific problem, the algorithm used, and the nature of the data. Therefore, feature engineering often requires iterative experimentation and evaluation. Despite its challenges, effective feature engineering can significantly enhance model performance.

> **Note**
>
> As you may have noticed, feature engineering requires understanding and exploration of the data, which depends on the engineered features' availability. This highlights the cyclical process within the data science life cycle: we iterate between data preparation and exploration.

For example, a feature suitable for further engineering in our data is the datetime field. The specific date and time a measurement was taken are not informative to the model for future predictions.

However, suppose we extract the year, month, day of the month, and hour of the day into new features. In that case, the model can capture potential relationships between the power generated and different time cycles. The date decomposition allows questions such as: Does the time of year, seasons, specific months, and so on influence the power generated? Or does the time of day, morning, noon, or night have any impact?

We can decompose the date into new features as follows:

```
frame["date_year"] = train_df["datetime"].dt.year
frame["date_month"] = train_df["datetime"].dt.month
frame["date_day"] = train_df["datetime"].dt.day
frame["date_hour"] = train_df["datetime"].dt.hour
frame = frame.drop(columns=["tracking_id", "datetime"], axis=1)
```

If, after modeling, we find these features to be uninformative, we can do further work with the time fields to assist in modeling. Future directions to explore are aggregations based on specific periods or creating a time series by ordering measurements to study trends in power generation over time.

We now proceed to our case study's EDA portion to visualize and better understand our data.

EDA

We have already done some EDA to find missing values and outliers in our dataset. There is no fixed methodology for performing EDA on a dataset; some experience and creativity are required to guide the process.

Besides gaining insight and understanding of the data, the main goal is to attempt to identify patterns and relationships within the data. Here, we start with a correlation heatmap to explore any direct correlations between features:

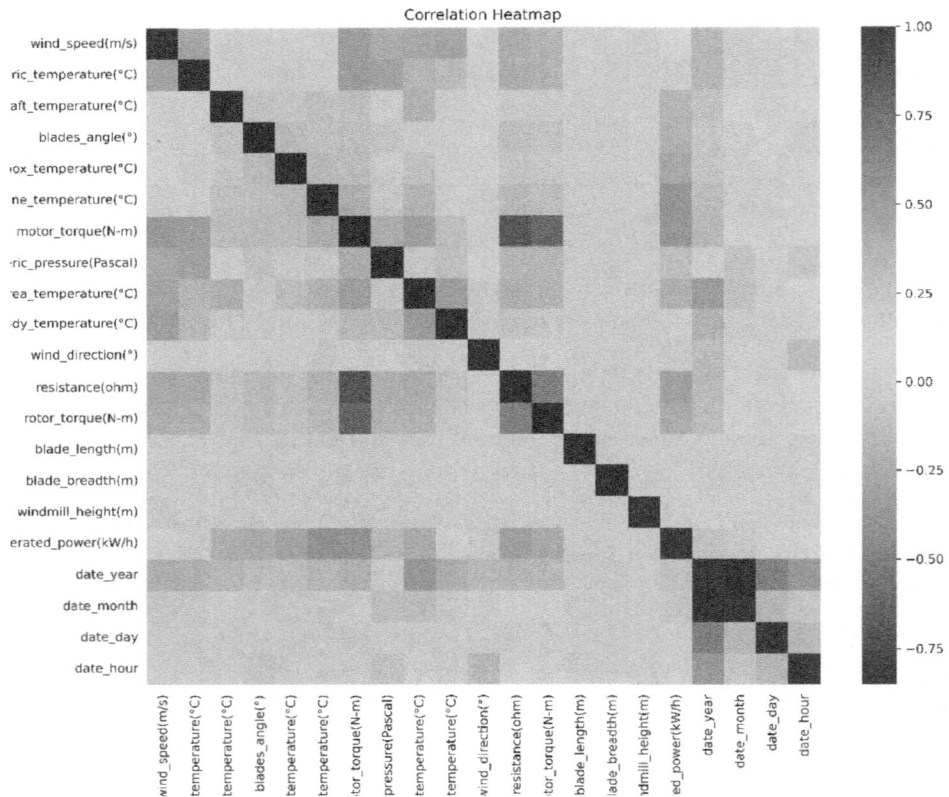

Figure 6.3 – Correlation heatmap for the Wind Turbine dataset

The correlation heatmap in *Figure 6.3* shows a few notable correlations between wind speed and atmospheric temperature, engine metrics such as engine temperature, generator temperature, and motor torque, and weaker correlations between our date features and atmospheric conditions.

Notably, a very strong correlation exists between motor torque and generator temperature. Intuitively, this makes sense: if the motor produces more torque, it will produce more heat. Since torque is the causative feature, we can consider dropping the generator temperature for modeling.

We can also see correlations between power generation and engine metrics, including electrical resistance and wind direction. We can anticipate that these features will have a significant impact on the model's performance.

We can also explore correlations between the categorical features and the power generated. The turbine status has seemingly little effect (in isolation) on the power generated. However, the cloud level has a significant impact. Plotting the cloud level against power generated, we have the following:

```
train_df.groupby("cloud_level")["windmill_generated_power(kW/h)"].
mean().plot.bar()
```

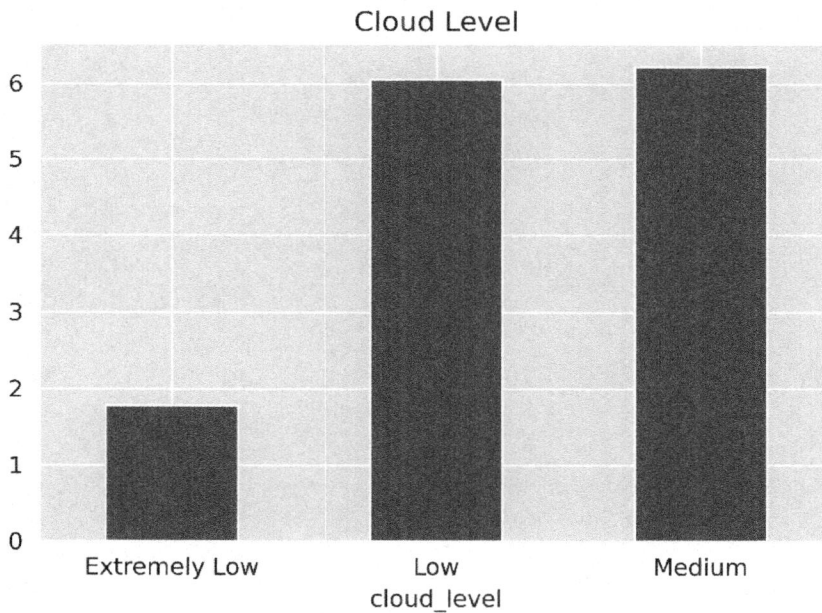

Figure 6.4 – Average power generated under the various cloud levels

As shown in *Figure 6.4*, extremely low clouds strongly correlate with reduced power generation. In further exploration of the data, it is helpful to control for cloud level to ensure the effect of the cloud level doesn't dominate any emergent patterns.

Another helpful visualization to see the effect of various features is the scatterplot. Plotting each value makes it straightforward to spot features by visually identifying patterns and clusters in the data.

Next, we provide examples of scatterplots that reveal patterns within our data.

To investigate any effect the blade angle might have on power generation, we can create a scatterplot as follows:

```
sns.scatterplot(x='blades_angle(°)', y='windmill_generated_
power(kW/h)', hue='cloud_level', data=train_df)
```

In the scatterplot, we also add hue differentiation for the cloud level so we can visually verify that any effect isn't stemming from the cloud level alone:

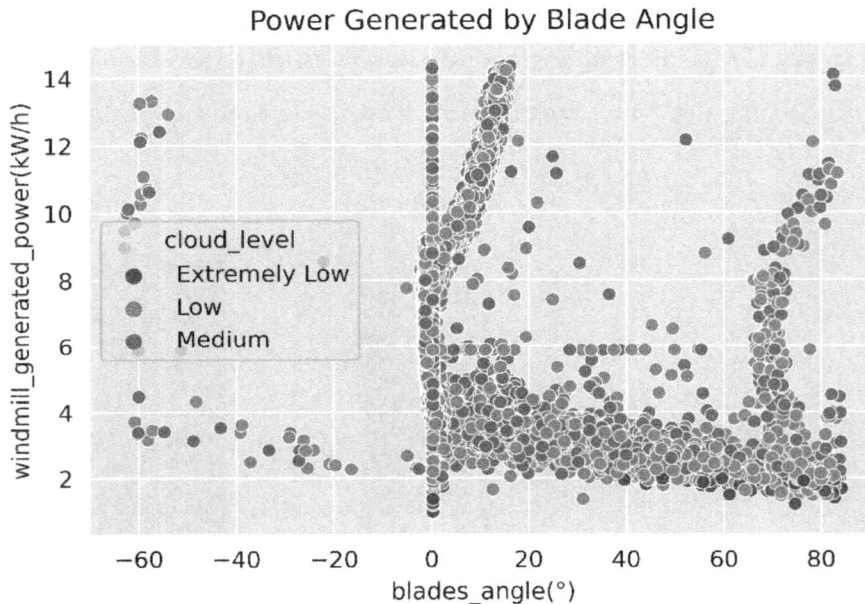

Figure 6.5 – Scatterplot of power generated (y axis) against the blade angle (x axis)

The blade angle scatterplot is shown in *Figure 6.5*. The scatterplot indicates that specific blade angle ranges correlate with increased power generated: [0, 10] degrees and [65, 75] degrees (both reciprocated in the other direction). Tree-based algorithms model correlations such as these as well.

Another example that illustrates the power of our feature engineering is a scatterplot of the month against the power generated. We again control for the cloud level via a different hue for those points:

```
sns.scatterplot(x='date_month',y='windmill_generated_power(kW/
h)',hue='cloud_level',data=train_df)
```

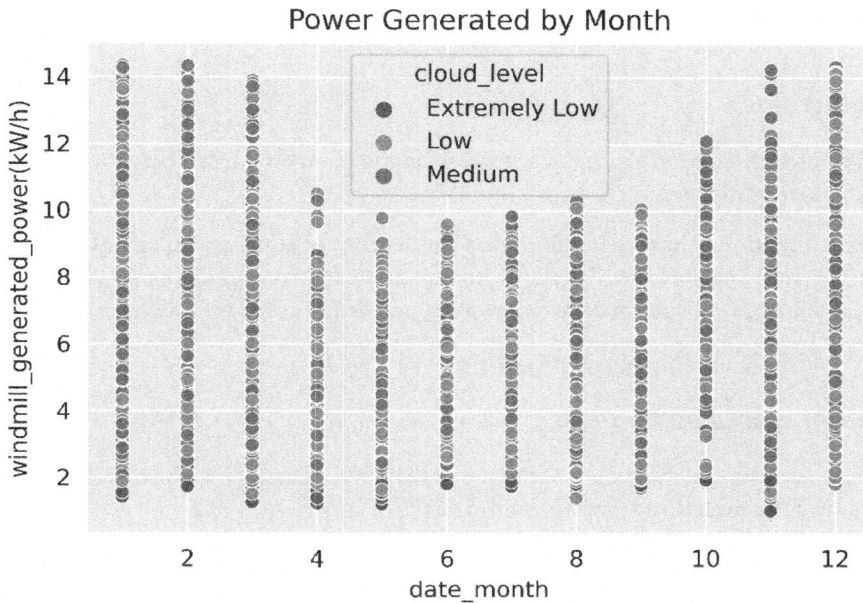

Figure 6.6 – Scatterplot of power generated (y axis) by month (x axis)

Figure 6.6 shows that April to September is correlated with a significant decrease in power generated. We could conclude that the wind turbines' location isn't particularly windy these months, and other sources would have to supplement the lack of power generation. By decomposing our date feature, we enable our learning algorithm to exploit this correlation.

There is no definitive end goal with EDA. For large, complex datasets, the analysis can go deeper and deeper into the data, iteratively exploring further facets and nuances almost indefinitely. However, two sanity checks that are useful in determining whether data has been explored sufficiently are as follows:

- Do we sufficiently understand the meaning of each feature and the potential effect on the model's output?
- Is the data well prepared for modeling? To the best of our knowledge, are the features informative, the data clean and unbiased, and formatted so that the model can be trained on it?

We now move on to modeling the data, leveraging the techniques of previous chapters to build a well-optimized model.

Modeling

The first step of modeling is model selection. It's best practice to first model the data using a straightforward algorithm to validate our data preparation and establish a baseline. If the modeling fails with a simple algorithm, it's easier to debug what might be going wrong or isolate data instances that may be causing the issue.

Model selection

For our wind turbine data, we use a linear regression model to establish a baseline and validate the data's suitability for modeling.

We also train a random forest regression model as a point of comparison against our LightGBM model. It's also good practice, if budget allows, to train more than one model using a different learning algorithm, as specific problems may be better suited to particular algorithms.

Finally, we train a LightGBM regressor as our primary model.

Model training and evaluation

From the EDA, we saw that the generator temperature is redundant (due to the correlation with motor torque). As such, we exclude it from the training data:

```
X = train_df.drop(columns=["windmill_generated_power(kW/h)", axis=1)
y = train_df["windmill_generated_power(kW/h)"]
```

Unlike LightGBM, neither linear regression nor scikit-learn's random forest regressor can automatically deal with categorical features.

We, therefore, use get_dummies from pandas to encode the features for training. The get_dummies operation performs a process known as **one-hot encoding**. The categorical value is decomposed into as many binary (0 or 1) columns as there are unique values. The corresponding value is marked with 1 (one-hot) for each pattern, and other values are marked with 0. For example, consider the cloud level feature: there are three categories (medium, low, and extremely low). A row in our dataset with a medium cloud level would be encoded as 100 (three separate columns). Similarly, a low cloud level is encoded as 010, and so on.

Performing one-hot encoding allows algorithms, such as linear regression, that only support numerical columns to model the data at the cost of increased memory usage for the additional columns.

As stated in the problem definition, we'll use two metrics to evaluate the models: the coefficient of determination and the MSE. Both are calculated using five-fold cross-validation.

We can now proceed to train our linear, random forest, and LightGBM regressors:

```
X_dummies = pd.get_dummies(X)
linear = LinearRegression()
scores = cross_val_score(linear, X_dummies, y)
scores = cross_val_score(linear, X_dummies, y, scoring="neg_mean_
squared_error")
forest = RandomForestRegressor()
```

```
X_dummies = pd.get_dummies(X)
scores = cross_val_score(forest, X_dummies, y)
scores = cross_val_score(forest, X_dummies, y, scoring="neg_mean_
squared_error")
lgbm = lgb.LGBMRegressor(force_row_wise=True, verbose = -1)
scores = cross_val_score(lgbm, X, y)
scores = cross_val_score(lgbm, X_dummies, y, scoring="neg_mean_
squared_error")
```

The following table summarizes the performance of each model:

Algorithm	$R2$	*MSE*
Linear Regression	0.558	2.261
Random Forest	0.956	0.222
LightGBM	0.956	0.222

Table 6.2 – Five-fold cross-validated performance metrics on the Wind Turbine dataset

The LightGBM and random forest regressors show almost identical performance with the same rounded R^2 and MSE scores. Both algorithms significantly outperformed linear regression.

Our model performs very well, with an absolute error of around 471 W/h. However, there's a problem that's easy to spot if we plot the feature importance of our trained model.

Figure 6.7 shows each feature's relative importance for our LightGBM model.

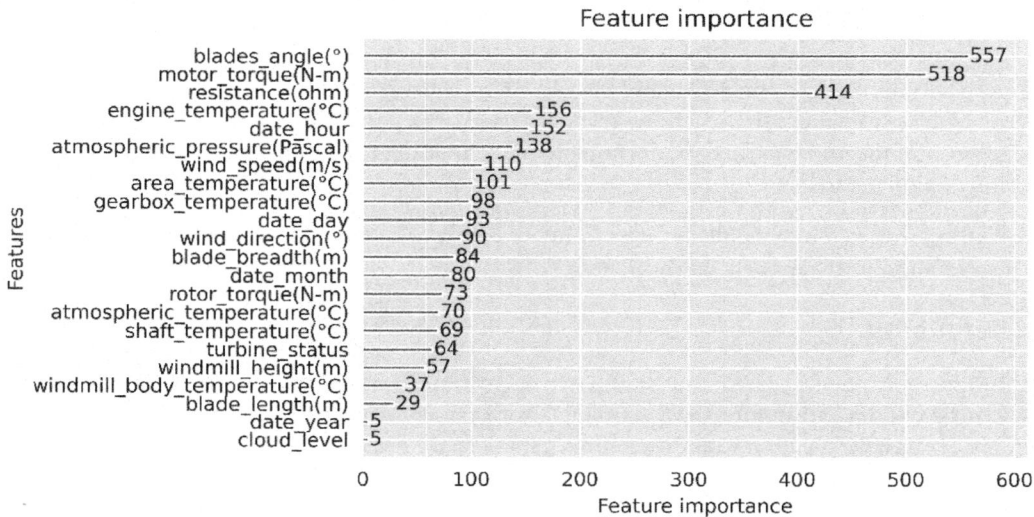

Figure 6.7 – Relative feature importance of each feature to our LightGBM model

As we can see from the features' importance, three features stand out: `blades_angle`, `motor_torque`, and `resistance`. However, for two of the features, `motor_torque` and `resistance`, we could ask: Do these features lead to improved generated power, or do they result from an increase in the power generated? These features are examples of **target leakage**, as explained next.

Target leakage

Target leakage, often called "leakage," is a common pitfall in designing and training machine learning models. It occurs when the model is inadvertently given access to the target variable (or some proxy of the target variable) during the training process. As a result, the model's performance during training may seem impressive, but it performs poorly on new, unseen data because it has effectively "cheated" during training.

Some common examples of how leakage can occur are as follows:

- **Time-based leakage**: Suppose you're trying to predict stock prices for tomorrow. If you include data from tomorrow in your training set (maybe accidentally), that would cause leakage. Similarly, data only available after the fact (such as aggregate data over all stocks) is another example of time-based leakage.

- **Preprocessing mistakes**: These happen when you perform a specific operation, such as scaling or normalizing, using statistics that include both the training and test set.

- **Incorrect data splits**: For time-series data, using a simple random split might result in future data being present in the training set.

- **Contaminated validation sets**: Sometimes, when creating validation or test sets, some data might overlap or be very closely related to the training data, causing optimistic and unrepresentative validation scores.

In our example, `motor_torque` and `resistance` are examples of time-based leakage: both metrics can only be measured after power is generated, which is what we are trying to predict. This also illustrates the importance of performing baseline training tests, as problems like these may not be easily found beforehand.

We fix this error by removing the features from our dataset. We can then proceed with model tuning to further improve the model's performance.

Model tuning

We utilize Optuna to perform our parameter optimization study. We'll leverage Optuna's **Tree-structured Parzen Estimator** (**TPE**) sampling algorithm with Hyperband pruning for efficiency. We define our objective function with the required parameters, a pruning callback, and measure the MSE:

```
def objective(trial):
    boosting_type = trial.suggest_categorical("boosting_type",
["dart", "gbdt"])
    lambda_l1 = trial.suggest_float(
```

```
        'lambda_l1', 1e-8, 10.0, log=True),
...

    pruning_callback = optuna.integration.
LightGBMPruningCallback(trial, "mean_squared_error")

    model = lgb.LGBMRegressor(
...

        callbacks=[pruning_callback],
        verbose=-1)
    scores = cross_val_score(model, X, y, scoring="neg_mean_squared_
error")
    return scores.mean()
```

We then create our Optuna study with a TPE sampler, Hyperband pruning, and an optimization budget of 200 trails:

```
sampler = optuna.samplers.TPESampler()
pruner = optuna.pruners.HyperbandPruner(
    min_resource=20, max_resource=400, reduction_factor=3)

study = optuna.create_study(
    direction='maximize', sampler=sampler,
    pruner=pruner
)
study.optimize(objective, n_trials=200, gc_after_trial=True, n_jobs=-
1)
```

Using the optimized parameters found through Optuna, we further improve the performance of the LightGBM model to an R^2 of 0.93 and an MSE of 0.21 in our run. Your results may differ slightly due to the stochastic nature of Optuna studies.

With an optimized model trained, we can proceed to the next phases of the data science process: deployment and reporting.

Model deployment

We can now use our trained model to make predictions on unseen data. The coming chapters focus on various ways to deploy and monitor models as part of the MLOps process.

However, the simplest way of using our model is to save the model and write a simple script that loads the model and makes the prediction.

We can save our model using standard Python serialization or the LightGBM API. Here, we illustrate using standard Python tooling:

```
joblib.dump(model, "wind_turbine_model.pkl")
```

A simple script to load the model and make predictions would be as follows:

```
def make_predictions(data):
    model = joblib.load("wind_turbine_model.pkl")
    return model.predict(data)


if __name__ == '__main__':
    make_predictions(prepare_data(pd.read_csv("wind-turbine/test.
csv")))
```

Importantly, we must repeat the data preparation for any data we want to predict to add engineered features and drop columns that aren't used.

Communicating results

The final step of the data science process is to communicate results. A data scientist typically compiles a report with salient findings and visualizations to present the results to stakeholders.

A report would look similar to the write-up of this case study. We might present the correlations found between our features, for example, the correlation between the month and the power generated. We would also highlight problems in the data, such as the outliers and missing values, to improve future data collection efforts.

We would further highlight features important to the model, such that wind turbines can be optimized to maximize the power generated.

Focus on the quality of the report. Use well-designed and detailed visualizations and other supporting material instead of solely relying on text. An infographic or interactive chart can be more helpful than a detailed write-up. Check your writing for errors, and be sure to have the report proofread before sending it out.

The content of a report should address the problem as defined by the problem statement. Any hypothesis that was tested must be answered in the report. But, the report also strongly depends on and should be tailored to your audience. For example, if your audience is business executives, include content that's understandable to them and answers questions they could have, which would be centered around the business impact of your findings.

We now look at a case study for a classification problem. We show that, though each dataset is unique and has specific challenges, the overall data science process remains the same.

Classifying individual credit scores with LightGBM

Our second case study is a problem of credit score classification for individuals. The dataset is available from https://www.kaggle.com/datasets/parisrohan/credit-score-classification?datasetId=2289007.

The dataset is significantly larger than the previous problem and has unique data formatting problems. For brevity, we will not go through the solution in as much detail as with the previous problem (as much of the work is the same), but the end-to-end solution is available at https://github.com/ PacktPublishing/Practical-Machine-Learning-with-LightGBM-and-Python/ tree/main/chapter-6/credit-score-classification.ipynb.

Problem definition

The dataset consists of 100,000 rows and 27 columns representing individuals' demographic and financial information, including a credit score rating. The data includes information regarding individual income, number of loans, payment behavior, and investments. The credit score may be rated as good, standard, or poor.

Our task is to analyze the data and build a model that accurately classifies the credit scores of unseen individuals. The quality of predictions is measured using classification accuracy and the F1-score.

Data collection

The data is collected from the database of customers of a US financial institution. Individuals aged 14 to 65 form part of the dataset. There is no documented bias toward sampling specific demographics (low-income brackets, age, or racial groups), but this must be validated. No additional data is collected.

Data preparation

As before, we start with simple data exploration tasks to determine the cleanliness of the data. We first check the data structure and types:

```
train_df.info()
 #   Column                  Non-Null Count   Dtype
---   ------                  --------------   -----
 0   ID                      100000 non-null  object
 1   Customer_ID             100000 non-null  object
 2   Month                   100000 non-null  object
 3   Name                    90015 non-null   object
 4   Age                     100000 non-null  object
 5   SSN                     100000 non-null  object
 ...
25   Payment_Behaviour       100000 non-null  object
26   Monthly_Balance         98800 non-null   object
27   Credit_Score            100000 non-null  object
```

We notice that there are missing values for some features. Also, many of the features we expect to be numeric (annual income, number of loans, and others) are interpreted as objects instead of integers or floats. These features have to be coerced into numeric features.

We also check the descriptive statistics of the features and for duplicated rows. Two features are found to have outlier values, age and the number of bank accounts, and need to be cleaned.

Notably, the `Type_of_Loan` field has a comma-separated list, including conjunctions, of the types of loans for each individual. For example "`student_loan, mortgage_loan, and personal_loan`". The modeling algorithm could not extract the loan types as part of a string. We have to engineer new fields to enable effective modeling.

Data cleaning

We can now proceed with cleaning the data. In summary, the following issues have to be addressed:

- Coercing object columns to numeric columns where appropriate
- Handling outliers in the age, number of bank accounts, and monthly balance columns
- Engineering new features for the types of loans
- Handling missing values and duplicate rows

Coercing to numeric columns

One of the main issues with the dataset is the mixed types found in columns that are supposed to be numeric, but due to error values, pandas interprets them as objects. For example, the `Annual_Income` column contains values such as `100000.0_`, which is then interpreted as a string.

To clean and convert the features to numbers, we first remove character symbols using a regular expression:

```
frame[col] = frame[col].astype(str).str.replace(r'[^\d\.]', '',
regex=True)
```

This allows us to use pandas to coerce the column to a numeric feature, turning any errors (empty values) into `np.nan` values:

```
frame[col] = pd.to_numeric(frame[col], errors="coerce")
```

The `Credit_History_Age` feature requires more work from our side. The age is specified using natural language such as "12 years and 3 months." Here, we use Python string processing to convert the years and months to a floating-point number:

```
def clean_credit_age(age):
    if age == 'nan':
        return np.nan
    if not "Years" in age:
        return age
    years, months = age.split(" Years and ")
    months = months.replace(" Months", "")
    return int(years) + int(months) / 12
```

Splitting delimiter-separated strings

As mentioned previously, the `Type_of_Loan` feature is a comma-separated list of the types of loans the individual has. Although we could approach the problem in multiple ways, the most helpful technique is to parse the fields and build a Boolean array of columns indicating which loans an individual has.

There are eight unique types of loans and a specific category if the loan type is unspecified. These are `Auto Loan`, `Credit-Builder Loan`, `Debt Consolidation Loan`, `Home Equity Loan`, `Mortgage Loan`, `Payday Loan`, `Personal Loan`, and `Student Loan`.

Our encoding strategy would then process the feature as follows. We create nine new columns (one per loan type and unspecified) and set the column to true if the individual has that loan type. For example, here we have three conjoined loan descriptions:

```
"Home Equity Loan, and Payday Loan"
"Payday Loan, Personal Loan"
"Student Loan, Auto Loan, and Debt Consolidation Loan"
```

Table 6.3 shows the encoding results for these examples, where a true flag is set if the individual has that type of loan.

Auto	Credit-Builder	Debt Cons.	Home Equity	Mortgage	Payday	Personal	Student	Unspecified
F	F	F	T	F	T	F	F	F
F	F	F	F	F	T	T	F	F
T	F	T	F	F	F	F	T	F

Table 6.3 – Loan type columns encode customers' types of loans

We can utilize pandas' String utilities to accomplish the preceding encoding, as in this example:

```
frame["auto_loan"] = frame["Type_of_Loan"].str.lower().str.
contains("auto loan").astype(bool)
```

Outliers and missing values

We follow the same general strategy as before: we impute missing values using descriptive statistics and, where able, set outlier values to boundaries we define using domain knowledge.

Duplicate rows are dropped.

In terms of outliers, the age, number of bank accounts, and monthly balance features have outlying values (which we confirm using the mean and standard deviation and distribution plots). We set the outlying values to the upper bound for these features:

```
frame.loc[frame["Age"] > 65, "Age"] = 65
frame.loc[frame["Num_Bank_Accounts"] > 1000, "Num_Bank_Accounts"] =
1000
frame.loc[frame["Monthly_Balance"] > 1e6, "Monthly_Balance"] = np.nan
```

After our data cleaning, we can verify that all features have the correct type and that missing values have been handled:

```
train_df.info()
train_df.isnull().sum()
train_df[train_df.duplicated()]
```

We can proceed with a more thorough exploratory analysis with the clean dataset.

EDA

Next, we highlight some of the patterns found during our EDA.

As described in the problem description, we need to validate whether any potential bias exists in the data.

We start by visualizing the customers' ages:

```
sns.histplot(train_df["Age"], bins=20)
```

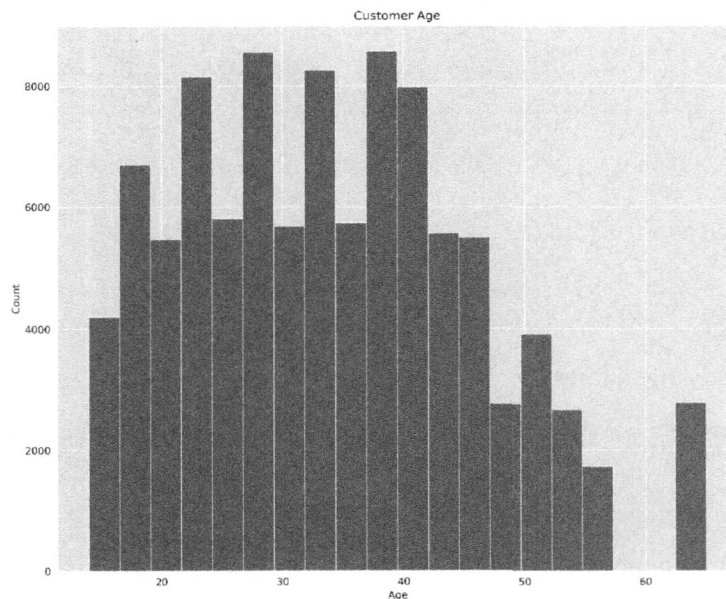

Figure 6.8 – Histogram showing the count of customers by age

Figure 6.8 shows that all age groups are represented, with data mainly normally distributed around the middle-aged.

We also check monthly income. A lack of data in lower income brackets could indicate that minorities were excluded:

```
sns.histplot(train_df["Monthly_Inhand_Salary"], bins=30)
```

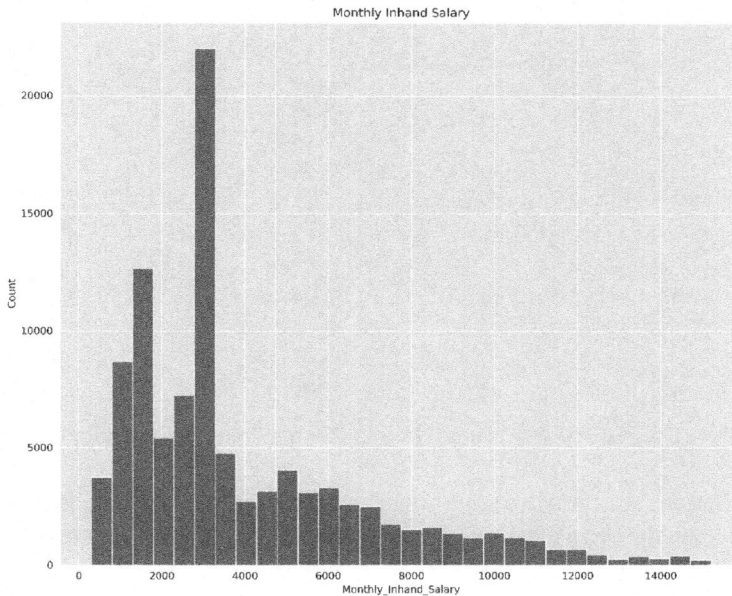

Figure 6.9 – Histogram showing the count of customers by monthly in-hand salary

As seen in *Figure 6.9*, monthly income follows an expected distribution and lower income brackets are well represented.

We again visualize the correlation heatmap for the numeric features to highlight and direct correlations:

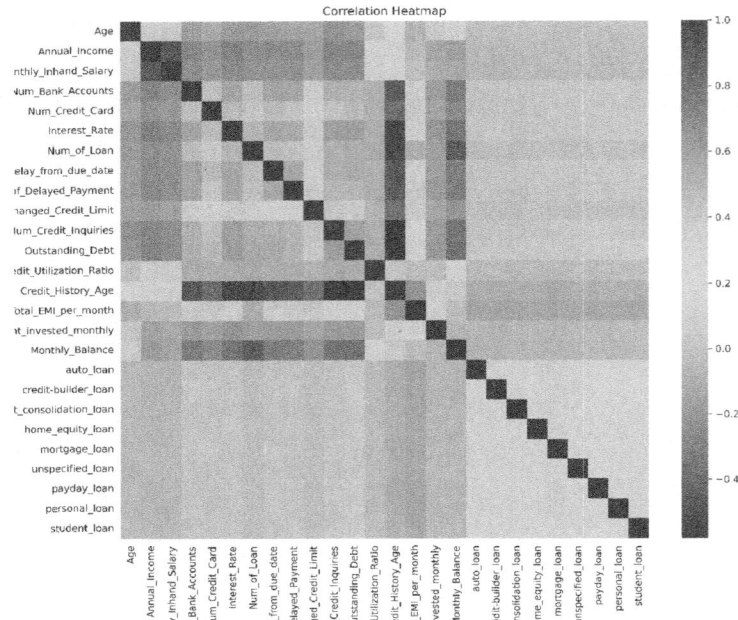

Figure 6.10 – Correlation heatmap for the Credit Score dataset

Two strong correlations are notable: monthly balance and monthly salary, and outstanding debt and delay in due date. Further visualization of these correlations indicates that a customer's monthly balance increases with salary and that poor credit scores are associated with lower balances and salaries.

A similar correlation exists between outstanding debt and credit score: an increase in debt is associated with poor credit scores, and vice versa. The analysis confirms that our model should be able to capture both of these correlations.

Finally, and importantly, we also have to check the class distribution for the dataset:

```
sns.histplot(train_df["Credit_Score"], bins=30)
```

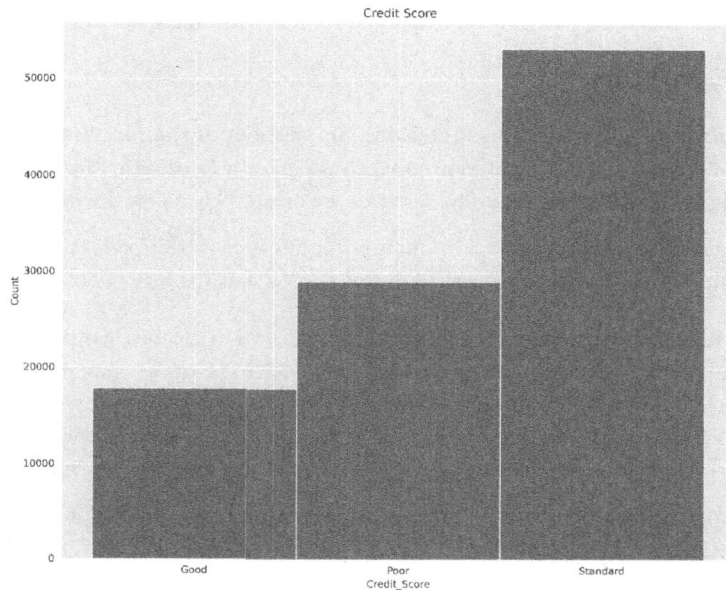

Figure 6.11 – Histogram of the class distribution for the credit scoring dataset

The class distribution for our dataset is shown in *Figure 6.11*. As we can see in the figure, there is a significant class imbalance. The imbalance has to be addressed before we can proceed with modeling.

Modeling

As before, we proceed with model selection first.

Model selection

Due to the dataset's size and complexity, a linear model is not expected to perform very well. As such, we use a regular decision tree as a baseline model and include a random forest for comparison.

Model training and evaluation

We are almost ready to train our models, but one issue remains: we must address the class imbalance.

Handling class imbalance

Class imbalance potentially biases any trained models to the majority class or classes. Although tree-based algorithms are better at dealing with imbalanced classes than most other learning algorithms, it's still best practice to address class imbalance before modeling.

Generally, the following strategies may be employed to deal with imbalanced classes:

- **Resampling techniques**:

  - **Oversampling**: This involves increasing the number of samples in the minority class to match the majority class. One common technique is the **Synthetic Minority Over-sampling Technique (SMOTE)**, where new samples are created based on the existing ones.

  - **Undersampling**: This involves reducing the number of samples in the majority class to match the minority class. One risk with this approach is the loss of potentially valuable data.

- **Cost-sensitive learning**: This method assigns higher costs to the misclassification of the minority class during the training process. The idea is to make the model pay more attention to the minority class. LightGBM supports this through the `class_weight` (for multi-class) and `scale_pos_weight` (for binary classes) parameters. Examples of applying these parameters are given in *Chapter 4, Comparing LightGBM, XGBoost, and Deep Learning*.

- **Data augmentation**: This involves creating new instances in the dataset by adding small perturbations to existing instances. This method is prevalent in image classification tasks.

- **Use of appropriate evaluation metrics**: Accuracy is often misleading in class imbalance. Instead, metrics such as precision, recall, F1-score, **Area under the ROC Curve (AUC-ROC)**, and confusion matrix can provide a more comprehensive view of model performance.

In our case study, we are already employing robust evaluation metrics against imbalanced classes. For this problem, we use SMOTE, an oversampling technique, to balance our classes while preserving our data.

SMOTE

SMOTE was developed to overcome some of the shortcomings of simple oversampling of the minority class, which can lead to overfitting due to the exact duplication of instances [1]. Instead of simply duplicating minority samples, SMOTE creates synthetic, or "fake," samples that are similar, but not identical, to existing samples in the minority class.

The SMOTE algorithm proceeds as follows. New sample points, called synthetic samples, are synthesized by choosing points between samples close to minority class samples. Specifically, for each minority class sample, SMOTE calculates the k-nearest neighbors, chooses one of these neighbors, and then multiplies the difference between the feature vectors of the sample and its chosen neighbor by a random number between 0 and 1, adding this to the original sample to create a new, synthetic sample.

By creating synthetic examples, SMOTE presents a more robust solution to the imbalance problem, encouraging the model to draw more generalizable decision boundaries. It's important to note, however, that while SMOTE can improve the performance of models on imbalanced datasets, it's not always the best choice. For instance, it can introduce noise if the minority samples are not sufficiently close in the feature space, leading to overlapping classes. As with all sampling techniques, it's essential to use cross-validation or a separate validation set to carefully evaluate the impact of SMOTE on your model's performance.

SMOTE over-sampling is implemented in the `imblearn` Python library. We can fit and resample our data as follows:

```
X = train_df.drop(columns=["Credit_Score"], axis=1)
X_dummies = pd.get_dummies(X)
y = train_df["Credit_Score"]
smote = SMOTE(sampling_strategy='auto')
return smote.fit_resample(X_dummies, y)
```

Figure 6.12 shows the class distribution for the dataset after resampling with SMOTE. As shown in the figure, the classes are now perfectly balanced.

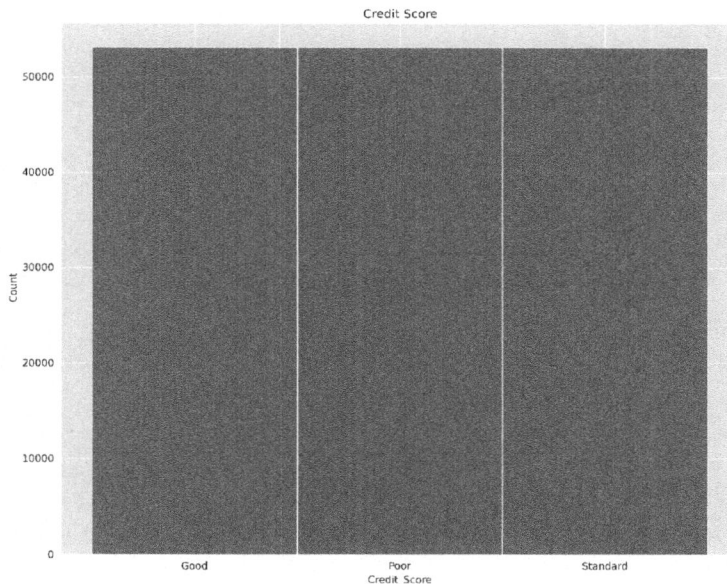

Figure 6.12 – Histogram of the class distribution for the Credit Score dataset
after resampling the data using SMOTE; classes are now balanced

Training and evaluation

We can now proceed with the modeling. The following table shows the results of our run from the decision tree classifier, random forest, and LightGBM models using default parameters.

Algorithm	Accuracy	F1 score
Decision tree	59.87%	0.57
Random forest	69.35%	0.67
LightGBM	70.00%	0.68

Table 6.4 – Five-fold cross-validated performance metrics on the Credit Score dataset

As shown in *Table 6.4*, the LightGBM model performs the best, slightly outperforming the random forest model accuracy. Both algorithms perform better than the decision tree baseline. The LightGBM model also trained the fastest, more than seven times faster than the random forest model.

We now proceed with parameter optimization of the LightGBM model.

Model tuning

Similar to the previous case study, we use Optuna for parameter optimization. We again use the TPE sampler with an optimization budget of 50 trials.

Model deployment and results

Our model is now prepared and ready to be deployed to a platform of our choice. Potential deployment options would include building a web API around our model, deploying with a tool such as **PostgresML**, or using a cloud platform such as **AWS SageMaker**. These and other options are discussed in detail in the coming chapters.

We could also use the model as part of a data science report. See the previous section for details on writing a good report. Keep in mind the most important aspects of communicating data science results, as follows:

- Always report results in an unbiased and fair way
- Keep your audience in mind and focus on the report's details that provide them with the most value

Summary

This chapter presented two case studies on how to apply the data science process with LightGBM. The data science life cycle and the typical constituent steps were discussed in detail.

A case study involving wind turbine power generation was presented as an example of approaching a data problem while working through the life cycle. Feature engineering and how to handle outliers were discussed in detail. An example exploratory data analysis was performed with samples given for visualization. Model training and tuning were shown alongside a basic script for exporting and using the model as a program.

A second case study involving multi-class credit score classification was also presented. The data science process was again followed, with particular attention given to data cleaning and class imbalance problems in the dataset.

The next chapter discusses the AutoML framework FLAML and introduces the concept of machine learning pipelines.

References

[1]   N. V. Chawla, K. W. Bowyer, L. O. Hall, and W. P. Kegelmeyer, "SMOTE: Synthetic Minority Over-sampling Technique," *Journal of Artificial Intelligence Research*, vol. 16, p. 321–357, June 2002.

7

AutoML with LightGBM and FLAML

In the previous chapter, we discussed two case studies that showed end-to-end examples of how to approach data science problems. Of the steps involved in the typical data science life cycle, often, the most time-consuming tasks are preparing the data, finding the correct models, and tuning the models.

This chapter looks at the concept of automated machine learning. Automated machine learning systems seek to automate some or all parts of the machine learning life cycle. We will look at **FLAML**, a library that automates the process's model selection and tuning steps using efficient hyperparameter optimization algorithms.

Lastly, we will present a case study using FLAML and another open source tool called Featuretools. Practical usage of FLAML will be discussed and shown. We will also show FLAML's zero-shot AutoML functionality, which bypasses tuning altogether.

The main topics of this chapter are as follows:

- An introduction to automatic machine learning
- FLAML for AutoML
- Case study – using FLAML with LightGBM

Technical requirements

The chapter includes examples and code excerpts showcasing using FLAML with LightGBM for AutoML use cases. Complete examples and instructions for setting up a suitable environment for this chapter are available at https://github.com/PacktPublishing/Practical-Machine-Learning-with-LightGBM-and-Python/tree/main/chapter-7.

Automated machine learning

Automated machine learning (**AutoML**) is a burgeoning field that aims to automate complex aspects of ML workflows, allowing for more efficient and accessible deployment of ML models. The advent of AutoML reflects the increasing sophistication of artificial intelligence and ML technologies and their permeation into various industry and research sectors. It aims to alleviate some of the complex, time-consuming aspects of the data science process, allowing for broader usage and more accessible application of ML technologies.

For software engineers well versed in ML and data science processes, the increasing complexity of ML models and the expanding universe of algorithms can pose a significant challenge. Building a robust, high-performing model requires substantial expertise, time, and computational resources to select suitable algorithms, tune hyperparameters, and conduct in-depth comparisons. AutoML has emerged as a solution to these challenges, aiming to automate these complex, frequently labor-intensive tasks.

AutoML also serves to democratize the field of ML. By abstracting away some of the complexities of data engineering and model building and tuning, AutoML makes it possible for individuals and organizations with less experience in ML to leverage these powerful technologies. As a result, ML can be effective in a broader array of contexts, with more individuals and organizations capable of deploying ML solutions.

AutoML systems are available at various levels of complexity. Although all AutoML systems aim to simplify the ML workflow, most systems and tools only focus on parts of the workflow. Commonly, steps such as data preprocessing, feature engineering, model selection, and hyperparameter tuning are automated. Such automation saves time and can improve the robustness and performance of ML models by systematically exploring a more comprehensive array of options that may be overlooked or unexplored due to human biases or time constraints.

Automating feature engineering

As discussed in *Chapter 6, Solving Real-World Data Science Problems with LightGBM*, data cleaning and feature engineering are critical parts of the ML workflow. They involve dealing with unusable data, handling missing values, and creating meaningful features that can be fed into the model. Manual feature engineering can be particularly challenging and time-consuming. AutoML systems aim to handle these tasks effectively, enabling automated feature extraction and transformation, leading to more robust models.

Data cleaning automation is typically achieved by following specific well-known techniques for dealing with problems such as outliers and missing values. In previous chapters, we applied some of these techniques manually: outliers can be tested statistically and capped or truncated. Missing values are typically imputed using descriptive statistics such as the mean or the mode. AutoML systems either use heuristic algorithms and tests to select the best techniques to clean the data or take multiple approaches and tests that work best by training models against the data.

The methods for automating feature engineering are often similar: many possible transformations are applied to all existing features, and the usefulness of the generated features is tested after modeling. Examples of how transformations generate features can be found in the following case study.

Another method for automating feature engineering is extracting features using rules based on the data type of the features. For example, the day, week, month, and year could be extracted from a date field. Or the number of characters, lemmas, stems, or embeddings of word or sentence features could be calculated.

As you may notice, the application of feature engineering automation techniques relies on technical information about the features at hand, typically the data type, alongside correlation and relationships with other features. Importantly, there is no domain knowledge applied when creating new features. This highlights one of the shortcomings of AutoML: it cannot handle specific, domain-driven decisions that require human expertise. For example, consider a diabetes dataset with a feature for fasting blood sugar. A medical professional (domain expert) knows that an individual with a fasting blood sugar of 100 to 125 mg/dL is considered prediabetic, and any higher is considered diabetic. This continuous feature can be engineered to specific classes: normal, prediabetic, and diabetic, simplifying the data for modeling. A transformation like this is not possible to achieve with AutoML systems.

Automating model selection and tuning

Areas where AutoML is particularly useful are model selection and hyperparameter tuning. Given the plethora of algorithms available, choosing the best one for a particular dataset and problem can be daunting. AutoML systems use various techniques, including Bayesian optimization and meta-learning, to select the best model. They also automate the tuning of hyperparameters to maximize model performance.

AutoML systems can provide automated cross-validation, reducing the risk of overfitting and ensuring the model's generalizability to unseen data. Once the optimal model is selected and trained, many AutoML tools can also help with deployment, making the model available for inference on new data.

Beyond the initial model deployment, some AutoML solutions also provide value in ongoing model monitoring and maintenance. As real-world data evolves, models may suffer from drift, and their performance can degrade. AutoML can help monitor model performance and retrain the model as needed, ensuring that your ML system remains effective in the long run.

Risks of using AutoML systems

As mentioned previously, AutoML systems typically use no domain knowledge to aid in feature engineering, model selection, or other automation. Instead, a brute-force or scattershot approach of try and see is used.

The "black box" nature of some AutoML systems can also make it challenging to interpret decisions made by the system, making it less suitable for applications that require high levels of explainability.

Therefore, it's still essential to have a data scientist or domain expert in the loop, working alongside the AutoML system, to identify and act on opportunities where domain knowledge can lead to better models. However, AutoML systems sometimes hinder the data scientist instead of enabling them by creating one extra layer between the scientist and the data.

We've already seen one AutoML framework in action. Optuna, which we discussed in *Chapter 5, LightGBM Parameter Optimization with Optuna*, is an example of an AutoML framework focusing on hyperparameter tuning. In the next section, we discuss another AutoML framework: FLAML.

Introducing FLAML

FLAML (**Fast and Lightweight AutoML**) is a Python library developed by Microsoft Research [1]. It is designed to produce high-quality ML models with low computational cost automatically. The primary aim of FLAML is to minimize the resources required to tune hyperparameters and identify optimal ML models, making AutoML more accessible and cost-effective, particularly for users with budget constraints.

FLAML offers several key features that set it apart. One of these is its efficiency. It provides a fast and lightweight solution for ML tasks, minimizing the time and computational resources needed. It achieves this without compromising the quality of the models it produces. FLAML also emphasizes its versatility across various ML algorithms and various application domains.

The core of FLAML's efficiency lies in its novel, cost-effective search algorithms. These algorithms intelligently explore the hyperparameter space, initially focusing on "cheap" configurations. It gradually explores more "expensive" configurations as it gains more insights into the search space. This ensures a balanced exploration and exploitation, delivering optimized models within user-specified time and resource budgets.

FLAML also excels at the model selection process. It supports various ML algorithms, including XGBoost, LightGBM, CatBoost, RandomForest, and various linear models. The library can automatically choose the best algorithm for a given dataset and optimize its hyperparameters, providing users with an optimal model without extensive manual intervention.

FLAML provides a straightforward, intuitive API that integrates seamlessly with existing Python-based data science and ML workflows. Users specify the dataset, a time budget (in seconds), and the optimization task, and FLAML handles the rest. This user-friendliness and efficiency make it a practical choice for ML beginners and seasoned practitioners looking to expedite their workflows.

The novelty behind FLAML's efficiency comes from its **hyperparameter optimization** (**HPO**) algorithms. FLAML provides two HPO algorithms: **Cost Frugal Optimization** and **BlendSearch**.

Cost Frugal Optimization

Cost Frugal Optimization (**CFO**) is a local search method that leverages random direct search to explore the hyperparameter space [2]. The CFO algorithm starts with a low-cost hyperparameter configuration (for LightGBM, a low-cost configuration would, for instance, have few boosted trees). It takes randomized steps for a fixed number of iterations in the hyperparameter space toward higher cost parameter regions.

The CFO step size is adaptive, meaning the algorithm lowers the step size if there is no improvement for several iterations. Doing so means large step sizes aren't taken in unpromising directions with high cost.

CFO also utilizes random restarts. As a local search algorithm, CFO can get stuck in local optima. If no progress is made and the step size is already small, the algorithm restarts at a random point.

In summary, CFO quickly (with large step sizes) attempts to reach more promising regions in the search space, using as little of the optimization budget as possible (by starting in low-cost regions). CFO continues the search while the optimization budget allows, restarting in random areas if stagnation occurs. FLAML allows the user to set the optimization budget in seconds.

BlendSearch

FLAML provides an alternative to the CFO algorithm in BlendSearch. BlendSearch differs from CFO by running both a global and local search process using a multithreaded approach [3].

Similar to CFO, BlendSearch starts with a low-cost configuration and proceeds with a local search. However, unlike CFO, BlendSearch does not wait for the local search to stagnate before exploring new regions. Instead, a global search algorithm (such as Bayesian optimization) continually suggests new starting points. Starting points are filtered based on their distance to existing points and prioritized in terms of cost.

Each iteration of BlendSearch then chooses whether to continue a local search or start at a new global search point based on the performance in the previous iteration. Like CFO, configurations proposed by the global search method are validated for viability.

As BlendSearch uses global optimization, BlendSearch is less prone to getting stuck in local minima. BlendSearch is recommended over CFO if the hyperparameter search space is highly complex. It's often a good idea to try CFO first and only switch to BlendSearch if CFO is struggling.

FLAML limitations

Despite its advantages, FLAML also has its limitations. The library's automated processes may not consistently outperform manual tuning by experts, particularly for complex, domain-specific tasks. Also, as with other AutoML solutions, the interpretability of the produced models can be challenging, especially when dealing with models such as boosted trees or neural networks.

FLAML only performs the model selection and tuning part of the ML process. These are some of the most time-consuming parts of model development, but FLAML does not provide the functionality to perform feature engineering or data preparation.

The following section presents a case study of using FLAML with LightGBM, showcasing everyday use cases, different optimization algorithms, and FLAML's zero-shot AutoML.

Case study – using FLAML with LightGBM

We will use the Wind Turbine dataset from the previous chapter for the case study. The dataset is cleaned as before, imputing missing values and capping outliers to appropriate ranges. However, we take a different approach to feature engineering. To further explore AutoML, we use an open source framework called Featuretools.

Feature engineering

Featuretools (`https://featuretools.alteryx.com/en/stable/#`) is an open source framework for automated feature engineering. Specifically, Featuretools is well suited to transforming relational datasets and temporal data.

As discussed in the previous section, automated feature engineering tools typically use combinatorial transformations of features to generate new features for the dataset. Featuretools supports feature transformations through their **Deep Feature Synthesis** (**DFS**) process.

As an example, consider a dataset of online customer web sessions. Typical features that could be useful in such a dataset are the total sessions a customer visited the site for, or the month a customer signed up. Using Featuretools and DFS, this can be achieved using the following code (courtesy of `https://featuretools.alteryx.com/`):

```
feature_matrix, feature_defs = ft.dfs(
    entityset=es,
    target_dataframe_name="customers",
    agg_primitives=["count"],
    trans_primitives=["month"],
    max_depth=1,
)
feature_matrix
```

Two transformations are being applied here: a transformation for "`month`" and an aggregation for "`count`". With these transformations, the month would be automatically extracted from any dates present for a customer (such as the join date), and the count aggregations would be calculated for each customer (such as the number of sessions or transactions). Featuretools has a rich set of transformations and aggregations available. A complete list is available at `https://featuretools.alteryx.com/en/stable/api_reference.html`.

Let's see how we can use Featuretools to engineer the features for the Wind Turbine dataset.

Using Featuretools with the Wind Turbine dataset

We must perform two feature engineering tasks for our dataset: engineer features for the datetime field and encode categorical features. To get started, we create an `EntitySet` for our data:

```
es = ft.EntitySet(id="wind-turbine")
es = es.add_dataframe(
    dataframe_name="wind-turbine",
    dataframe=df,
    index="tracking_id"
)
```

`EntitySet` tells the Featuretools framework the entities and relationships we work with within the data. Customer is an example of an entity in the earlier example; for this case, it's Wind Turbines. We then pass the data frame and the column to be used as an index.

We then apply `dfs` and `encode_features` to engineer the features for our dataset:

```
feature_matrix, feature_defs = ft.dfs(
    entityset=es, target_dataframe_name="wind-turbine",
    trans_primitives=["day", "year", "month", "weekday"],
    max_depth=1)
feature_matrix_enc, features_enc = ft.encode_features(
    feature_matrix, feature_defs)
```

The preceding code extracts the day, year, month, and weekday for each of our wind turbine measurements. The feature encoding then automatically one-hot encodes the categorical features for our dataset, including the new datefields.

The following is an excerpt from the dataset column list showing some of the columns created by Featuretools:

```
...
'cloud_level = Low',
'cloud_level = Medium',
'cloud_level = Extremely Low',
'cloud_level is unknown',
'MONTH(datetime) = 1',
'MONTH(datetime) = 2',
...
'MONTH(datetime) = 8',
'MONTH(datetime) = 9',
'MONTH(datetime) = 11',
'MONTH(datetime) is unknown',
...
```

```
'YEAR(datetime) = 2019',
'YEAR(datetime) = 2018',
'YEAR(datetime) is unknown'
```

Note the one-hot encoding of categorical features: each value is now split into a separate column. This includes columns for unknown values (for example, YEAR(datetime) is unknown), which illustrates another way of dealing with missing values in categorical features. Instead of imputing a value by using something such as the mode, we have a column that signals to the model (true or false) that the value is missing.

The automated feature engineering has increased our column count from 22 columns to 66 columns. This illustrates another general caveat with automated feature engineering and AutoML: automation may lead to overcomplicated datasets. In *Chapter 6, Solving Real-World Data Science Problems with LightGBM*, we could encode features selectively based on our understanding of the learning algorithm. LightGBM can automatically handle categorical features; therefore, one-hot encoding is superfluous if LightGBM is the only learning algorithm used.

Additionally, the datefields could be handled numerically. By applying our knowledge of the problem and algorithm, we can reduce the dimensionality of the learning problem, thereby simplifying it. The ease of use of automated systems has to be balanced with the manual effort of expert feature engineering, which could save time later on.

The dataset is now ready for model development; we've completed the feature engineering for our dataset using only two lines of code.

FLAML AutoML

We will now look at model selection and tuning. We will use FLAML to compare five different models: LightGBM, RandomForest, XGBoost, ExtraTrees, and a limited-depth version of XGBoost. We would also like to find optimal parameters for the best model. This entire process is possible in two lines of code with FLAML:

```
automl = flaml.AutoML()
automl.fit(X, y, task="regression", time_budget=60)
```

The preceding code fits an optimal regression model within a time budget of 60 seconds. FLAML automatically uses a holdout set to calculate validation results and then proceeds with optimization, using CFO as the tuner by default.

The AutoML class provides "task-oriented AutoML." The user sets the learning task, and FLAML does the rest. Among others, the following tasks are supported: classification, regression, time-series forecasting and time-series classification, ranking, and NLP-related tasks such as summarization and word token classification.

The call to `fit` is customizable. For example, we could customize it as follows:

```
automl = flaml.AutoML()
custom_hp = {
    "learning_rate": {
        "domain": flaml.tune.loguniform(0.0001, 0.05)
    }
}
automl.fit(X, y, task="regression", time_budget=120,
           metric="mse",
           estimator_list=['lgbm', 'xgboost', 'rf'],
           custom_hp={
               "lgbm": custom_hp
           },
           hpo_method="bs")
```

Here, we customize the hyperparameter search space by explicitly declaring the learning rate as a log-scaled uniform variable within a range. Other options for setting the search space for parameters are uniform sampling, random integer sampling, and choice-based sampling for categorical parameters.

Furthermore, we set the estimator list to focus on only three modeling algorithms: LightGBM, Random Forest, and XGBoost. Lastly, we can customize the HPO algorithm, and here, we set it to BlendSearch, which uses the multithreaded optimization approach discussed earlier.

A complete list of customizations is available at `https://microsoft.github.io/FLAML/docs/reference/automl/automl/#automl-objects`.

Once `fit` has been called, we can use the AutoML-trained model as we would any other. FLAML provides a scikit-learn-style API for prediction and probability-based prediction (for classification problems).

The following code creates predictions from the given data and calculates metrics and feature importance:

```
y_pred = automl.predict(X)
print(f"r2: {1 - sklearn_metric_loss_score('r2',
    y_pred, y)}")
print(f"MSE: {sklearn_metric_loss_score('mse',
    y_pred, y)}")

r2: 0.9878605489721696
MSE: 0.08090827806554425
```

We can also get the best hyperparameter configuration for the winning model and for each of the models trialed by calling the following:

```
print(automl.best_config)
print(automl.best_config_per_estimator)
print(automl.time_to_find_best_model)
```

A final notable feature of FLAML is zero-shot AutoML, which bypasses the need for model tuning entirely.

Zero-shot AutoML

Zero-shot AutoML is a FLAML feature where hyperparameter optimization is not performed. Instead, suitable hyperparameter configurations are determined offline by analyzing the performance of an algorithm on a wide variety of datasets. The process can be described as follows:

1. Before building a model:

   - Train models on many datasets using AutoML
   - Store all datasets' hyperparameter configurations, evaluation results, and metadata as a zero-shot solution

2. When building a model for a new problem:

   - Use FLAML to analyze the new dataset against the zero-shot solution results and determine suitable hyperparameters
   - Train a model on the new dataset using the hyperparameters

The first step is performed only once for a given model type (such as LightGBM). Thereafter, a new model can be built for any new problem without tuning. The solution is "zero-shot" because suitable parameters are used on the first fit for a new dataset.

FLAML's zero-shot AutoML approach has many advantages:

- As mentioned, no tuning is involved, sparing much computational effort and time when solving a new problem
- Since no tuning is required, a validation dataset is not required either, and more of the data may be used for training
- Even less involvement is required by the user
- Often, no code changes are required, as we'll see next

Of course, creating the zero-shot solution for a model type is still arduous, requiring varied datasets and much computation to train many models. Fortunately, FLAML provides pretrained zero-shot solutions for many popular models, including LightGBM, XGBoost, and scikit-learn's random forests.

To use a zero-shot solution, replace the regular LightGBM import with the FLAML-wrapped version:

```
from flaml.default import LGBMRegressor

zs_model = LGBMRegressor()
zs_model.fit(X, y)
```

Calling `fit` analyzes the data in X, selects suitable parameters, and trains the model using those parameters. Training is performed only once, and no tuning is done.

This concludes our case study of FLAML. As we have seen, FLAML provides an intuitive API for sophisticated model selection and tuning functionality, which could spare much effort when working on an ML problem.

Summary

In summary, this chapter discussed AutoML systems and their uses. Typical approaches to automating feature engineering, model selection, and tuning were discussed. We also mentioned the risks and caveats associated with using these systems.

The chapter also introduced FLAML, a library for AutoML that provides tools for automating the model selection and tuning process. We also presented CFO and BlendSearch, two efficient hyperparameter optimization algorithms provided by FLAML.

The practicalities of applying FLAML were shown in the form of a case study. In addition to FLAML, we showcased an open source tool called Featuretools, which provides functionality to automate feature engineering. We showed how to develop optimized models in fixed-time budgets using FLAML. Finally, we provided examples of using FLAML's zero-shot AutoML functionality, which analyzes datasets against configurations for known problems to determine suitable hyperparameters, eliminating the need for model tuning.

The next chapter discusses building ML pipelines around LightGBM models, focusing on exporting, packaging, and deploying LightGBM models for production.

References

[1] C. Wang, Q. Wu, M. Weimer, and E. Zhu, "FLAML: A Fast and Lightweight AutoML Library," in MLSys, 2021.

[2] Q. Wu, C. Wang and S. Huang, Frugal Optimization for Cost-related Hyperparameters, 2020.

[3] C. Wang, Q. Wu, S. Huang, and A. Saied, "Economical Hyperparameter Optimization With Blended Search Strategy," in ICLR, 2021.

Part 3: Production-ready Machine Learning with LightGBM

In Part 3, we will delve into the practical applications of ML solutions in production environments. We will uncover the intricacies of machine learning pipelines, ensuring systematic data processing and model building for consistent results. MLOps, a confluence of DevOps and ML, takes center stage, highlighting the importance of deploying and maintaining robust ML systems in real-world scenarios. Through hands-on examples, we will explore the deployment of ML pipelines on platforms (like Google Cloud, Amazon SageMaker, and the innovative PostgresML) emphasizing the unique advantages each offers. Lastly, distributed computing and GPU-based training will be explored, showcasing methods to expedite training processes and manage larger datasets efficiently. This concluding part will emphasize the seamless integration of ML into practical, production-ready solutions, equipping readers with the knowledge to bring their models to life in dynamic environments.

This part will include the following chapters:

- *Chapter 8, Machine Learning Pipelines and MLOps with LightGBM*

- *Chapter 9, LightGBM MLOps with AWS SageMaker*

- *Chapter 10, LightGBM Models with PostgresML*

- *Chapter 11, Distributed and GPU-based Learning with LightGBM*

8

Machine Learning Pipelines and MLOps with LightGBM

This chapter shifts the focus from data science and modeling problems to building production services for our ML solutions. We introduce the concept of machine learning pipelines, a systematic approach to processing data, and building models that ensure consistency and correctness.

We also introduce the concept of MLOps, a practice that blends DevOps and ML and addresses the need to deploy and maintain production-capable ML systems.

The chapter includes an example of building an ML pipeline using scikit-learn, encapsulating data processing, model building, and tuning. We show how to wrap the pipeline in a web API, exposing a secure endpoint for prediction. Finally, we also look at the containerization of the system and deployment to Google Cloud.

The main topics of this chapter are as follows:

- Machine learning pipelines
- An overview of MLOps
- Deploying an ML pipeline for customer churn

Technical requirements

The chapter includes examples of creating scikit-learn pipelines, training LightGBM models, and building a FastAPI application. The requirements for setting up your environment can be found alongside the complete code examples at `https://github.com/PacktPublishing/Practical-Machine-Learning-with-LightGBM-and-Python/tree/main/chapter-8`.

Introducing machine learning pipelines

In *Chapter 6, Solving Real-World Data Science Problems with LightGBM*, we gave a detailed overview of the data science life cycle, which includes various steps to train an ML model. If we were to focus only on the steps required to train a model, given data that has already been collected, those would be as follows:

1. Data cleaning and preparation
2. Feature engineering
3. Model training and tuning
4. Model evaluation
5. Model deployment

In previous case studies, we applied these steps manually while working through a Jupyter notebook. However, what would happen if we shifted the context to a long-term ML project? If we had to repeat the process when new data becomes available, we'd have to follow the same procedure to build a model successfully.

Similarly, when we want to use the model to score new data, we must apply the steps correctly and with the correct parameters and configuration every time.

In a sense, these steps form a pipeline for data: data enters the pipeline, and a deployable model results from its completion.

Formally, an ML pipeline is a systematic and automated process that guides the workflow of an ML project. It involves several interconnected stages, encapsulating the steps listed previously.

An ML pipeline aims to ensure that these tasks are structured, reproducible, and efficient, making it easier to manage complex ML tasks. Pipelines are particularly beneficial when working with large datasets or when the steps to transform raw data into usable inputs for ML models are complex and must be repeated frequently, such as in a production environment.

There is some fluidity in the steps involved in a pipeline: steps may be added or removed depending on how the pipeline is utilized. Some pipelines include a data collection step, pulling data from various data sources or databases, and staging the data for ML modeling.

Many ML services and frameworks provide functionality and utilities to implement ML pipelines. Scikit-learn provides this functionality through its `Pipeline` class, which we will look at next.

Scikit-learn pipelines

Scikit-learn provides the `Pipeline` class as a tool to implement ML pipelines. The `Pipeline` class provides a unified interface to perform a sequence of data- and model-related tasks. Pipelines rely on scikit-learn's standard `fit` and `transform` interfaces to enable the chaining of operations. Each pipeline consists of any number of intermediate steps, which must be `transforms`. A transform must implement both `fit` and `transform`, and the `Pipeline` class each transform in turn, first passing the data to `fit` and then to `transform`. The final step, which usually entails fitting the model to the data, only needs to implement the `fit` method. The transformations are usually preprocessing steps that transform or augment the data.

The primary advantage of using scikit-learn pipelines is ensuring that the workflow is implemented clearly and in a reproducible manner. It helps avoid common mistakes, such as leaking statistics from the test data into the trained model during the preprocessing steps. By including the preprocessing steps within the pipeline, we ensure that the same steps are applied consistently during training and when the model is used to predict new data.

Furthermore, scikit-learn pipelines can be combined with tools for model selection and hyperparameter tuning, such as grid search and cross-validation. We can use grid search to automatically select the best parameters across the entire pipeline by defining a grid of parameters for the preprocessing steps and the final estimator. This can significantly simplify the code and reduce errors in a complex ML workflow. Tools such as FLAML also feature integration with scikit-learn pipelines.

For example, a simple pipeline can be created as follows:

```
from sklearn.pipeline import Pipeline
from sklearn.preprocessing import StandardScaler
from sklearn.linear_model import LinearRegression

pipeline = Pipeline(
    [
        ('scaler', StandardScaler()),
        ('linear', LinearRegression())
    ]
)
```

Here, the pipeline consists of two steps: a scaling step that standardizes the data and a final step that fits a linear regression model.

The power of scikit-learn's `Pipeline` is that it can, in turn, be used as we would any other estimator or model:

```
pipeline.fit(X_train, y_train)
pipeline.predict(X_train, y_train)
```

This provides us with a unified interface to all the steps encapsulated in the pipeline and makes reproducibility trivial. Furthermore, we can export the pipeline as we do for other scikit-learn models to enable deployment of the pipeline and all the steps it encapsulates:

```
import joblib
joblib.dump(pipeline, "linear_pipeline.pkl")
```

We will show more examples of using scikit-learn pipelines next.

Although we have spent much time addressing the concerns of working with data and building and tuning models, we haven't yet taken an in-depth look at what happens after a model is trained. It's here that the world of MLOps comes into play. The next section provides a detailed overview.

Understanding MLOps

Machine Learning Operations (**MLOps**) is a practice that blends the fields of ML and system operations. It is designed to standardize and streamline the life cycle of ML model development and deployment, thus increasing the efficiency and effectiveness of ML solutions within a business setting. In many ways, MLOps can be considered a response to the challenges associated with operationalizing ML, bringing DevOps principles into the ML world.

MLOps aims to bring together data scientists, who typically focus on model creation, experimentation, and evaluation, and operations professionals, who deal with deployment, monitoring, and maintenance. The goal is to facilitate better collaboration between these groups, leading to faster, more robust model deployment.

The importance of MLOps is underscored by the unique challenges presented by ML systems. Machine learning systems are more dynamic and less predictable than traditional software systems, leading to potential challenges in reliability and robustness, especially in a rapidly changing production environment.

A central goal of MLOps is to accelerate the ML life cycle, facilitating faster experimentation and deployment. This is achieved through the automation of ML pipelines. **Automation** can cover various stages, including data preprocessing, feature engineering, model training, model validation, and deployment. Another crucial aspect of MLOps is ensuring reproducibility. Given the dynamic nature of ML models, it can be challenging to replicate results exactly, especially when models are retrained with new data. MLOps emphasizes the importance of versioning code, data, and model configurations, which ensures that every experiment can be precisely reproduced, which is crucial for debugging and auditing.

Monitoring is also a vital part of MLOps. Once a model is deployed, *monitoring its performance and continuously validating its predictions is critical*. MLOps emphasizes the need for robust monitoring tools that can track model performance, input data quality, and other vital metrics. Anomalies in these metrics may indicate that a model needs to be retrained or debugged.

MLOps also encourages the use of robust testing practices for ML. ML testing includes traditional software testing practices, such as unit tests and integration tests, but also more ML-specific tests, such as validating the statistical properties of model predictions.

MLOps also focuses on managing and scaling ML deployments. In the real world, ML models may need to serve thousands or even millions of predictions per second. DevOps practices such as containerization and serverless computing platforms come into play here to facilitate deployment and scaling automation.

It's important to note how MLOps fits into the broader software ecosystem. Just like DevOps has bridged the gap between development and operations in software engineering, MLOps aims to do the same for ML. By promoting shared understanding and responsibilities, MLOps can lead to more successful ML projects.

MLOps is a rapidly evolving field becoming increasingly important as more businesses adopt ML. By applying principles from DevOps to the unique challenges of ML, MLOps provides a framework for managing the end-to-end ML life cycle, from initial experimentation to robust, scalable deployment. MLOps emphasizes standardization, automation, reproducibility, monitoring, testing, and collaboration to enable high-throughput ML systems.

We'll now look at a practical example of creating an ML pipeline using scikit-learn and deploying the pipeline behind a REST API.

Deploying an ML pipeline for customer churn

For our practical example, we'll use the telecommunication (**telco**) Customer Churn dataset we worked with in *Chapter 5, LightGBM Parameter Optimization with Optuna*. The dataset consists of descriptive information for each customer (such as gender, billing information, and charges) and whether the customer has left the telco provider (churn is *yes* or *no*). Our task is to build a classification model to predict churn.

Further, we'd like to deploy the model behind a REST API such that it can be integrated into a more extensive software system. The REST API should have an endpoint that makes predictions for data passed to the API.

We'll use **FastAPI**, a modern, high-performance Python web framework, to build our API. Finally, we'll deploy our model and API to Google Cloud Platform using Docker.

Building an ML pipeline using scikit-learn

We will start by building an ML pipeline using scikit-learn's `Pipeline` toolset. Our pipeline should encapsulate data cleaning and feature engineering steps, then build and tune an appropriate model.

We'll evaluate two algorithms for modeling: LightGBM and random forest, and as such, it's unnecessary to perform any scaling or normalization of the data. However, the dataset has a unique identifier for each customer, `customerID`, which we need to remove.

Further, the dataset consists of numerical and categorical features, and we must implement one-hot encoding for the categorical features.

Pipeline preprocessing steps

To perform these steps within a scikit-learn pipeline, we'll use `ColumnTransformer`. `ColumnTransformer` is a `Pipeline` transformer that operates only on a subset of the columns in the dataset. The transformer accepts a list of tuples in the form (name, transformer, columns). It applies the sub-transformers to the specified columns and concatenates the results such that all resultant features form part of the same result set.

For example, consider the following DataFrame and ColumnTransformer:

```
df = pd.DataFrame({
    "price": [29.99, 99.99, 19.99],
    "description": ["Luxury goods", "Outdoor goods",
        "Sports equipment"],
})
ct = ColumnTransformer(
    [("scaling", MinMaxScaler(), ["price"]),
     ("vectorize", TfidfVectorizer(), "description")])
transformed = ct.fit_transform(df)
```

Here, we have a DataFrame with two columns: price and description. A column transformer is created with two sub-transformers: a scaling transformer and a vectorizer. The scaling transformer applies min-max scaling only to the price column. The vectorizer applies TF-IDF vectorization only to the description column. When fit_transform is called, a *single* array is returned with a column for the scaled price and the columns representing the word vectors.

> **Note**
>
> TF-IDF, or **term frequency-inverse document frequency**, is just one way of extracting a feature from text. Analyzing and extracting features from text, and natural language processing in general, is a broad field within ML that we won't be delving into deeply here. You are encouraged to read further on the topic at https://scikit-learn.org/stable/modules/feature_extraction.html#text-feature-extraction.

We can set up our preprocessing for the Customer Churn dataset as a single ColumnTransformer. We first define the two individual transformers, id_transformer and encode_transformer, that apply to the ID columns and the categorical features:

```
id_transformer = (
    "customer_id",
    CustomerIdTransformer(id_columns),
    id_columns
)
encode_transformer = (
    "encoder",
    OneHotEncoder(sparse_output=False),
    categorical_features
)
```

And then combine the separate transformers into `ColumnTransformer`:

```
preprocessor = ColumnTransformer(
    transformers=[
        id_transformer,
        encode_transformer,
    ],
    remainder='passthrough'
)
```

`ColumnTransformer` is defined with the `remainder='passthrough'` parameter. The `remainder` parameter specifies what happens to the columns that `ColumnTransformer` does not transform. These columns are dropped by default, but we would like to pass them through, untouched, to include them in the dataset.

The encoding transformer creates and applies `OneHotEncoder` to the categorical features.

For illustrative purposes, we have created a custom transformer class to maintain the list of ID columns and drop them from the data during transformation.

The class is shown here:

```
class CustomerIdTransformer(BaseEstimator, TransformerMixin):
    def __init__(self, id_columns):
        self.id_columns = id_columns

    def fit(self, X, y=None):
        return self

    def transform(self, X, y=None):
        return X.drop(columns=self.id_columns, axis=1)
```

As we can see, the class extends `BaseEstimator` and `TranformerMixin` from the scikit-learn base classes and must implement `fit` and `transform`. Implementing these methods also makes it suitable as a transformer in a pipeline. Implementing `fit` is optional if required; in our case, nothing is done during `fit`. Our transformation step drops the relevant columns.

> **Note**
>
> It's important to encapsulate the functionality to drop irrelevant columns (in this case, the ID column) within the pipeline itself. When deploying the pipeline for production use, we expect these columns to be passed to the pipeline when making a prediction. Removing them as part of the pipeline simplifies our pipeline's usage for our model's consumers and reduces the chance of user mistakes.

This completes the transformations required for preprocessing, and we are ready to move on to the following steps: fitting and tuning the models.

Pipeline modeling steps

For the pipeline modeling part, we'll use FLAML. We'll also use the opportunity to show how parameters may be passed to steps within a pipeline. First, we define the settings for our AutoML model:

```python
automl_settings = {
    "time_budget": 120,
    "metric": "accuracy",
    "task": "classification",
    "estimator_list": ["lgbm", "rf"],
    "custom_hp": {
        "n_estimators": {
            "domain": flaml.tune.uniform(20, 500)
        }
    },
    "verbose": -1
}
```

The preceding code sets our time budget, optimization metric, and classification task for AutoML. We also limit the estimators to LightGBM and a random forest model. Finally, we customize the search space by specifying that n_estimators should be uniformly sampled between 20 and 500.

The pipeline requires the parameter for constituent steps to be prefixed with the step's name and a double underscore. We can set up a dictionary to pass these parameters to the AutoML class within our pipeline:

```python
pipeline_settings = {
    f"automl__{key}": value for key, value in
        automl_settings.items()
}
```

Here, automl is the name of the step in the pipeline. As such, for example, the parameters for time budget and metric are set as automl__time_budget: 120 and automl__metric: accuracy, respectively.

Finally, we can add FLAML's AutoML estimator:

```
automl = flaml.AutoML()
pipeline = Pipeline(
    steps=[("preprocessor", preprocessor),
           ("automl", automl)]
)
```

The final pipeline is shown in the following figure:

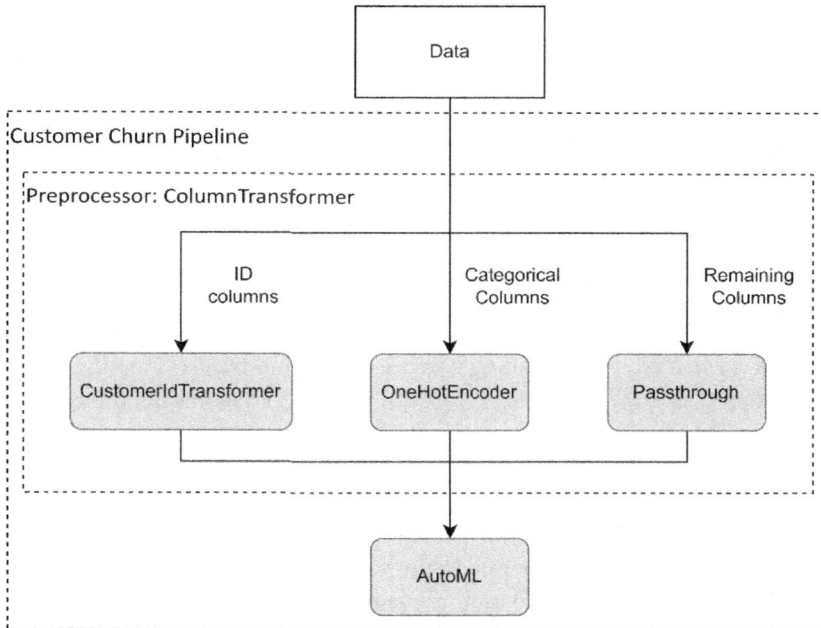

Figure 8.1 – Final ML pipeline for Customer Churn prediction

Figure 8.1 shows a *ColumnTransformer* that consists of two sub-transformers, feeding into the AutoML estimator.

Model training and validation

We are now ready to fit the pipeline to our data, passing the pipeline settings we set up earlier. Pipelines support the standard scikit-learn API so that we can call on the pipeline itself:

```
pipeline.fit(X, y, **pipeline_settings)
```

Running `fit` executes all the preprocessing steps and then passes the data for AutoML modeling and tuning. The single `Pipeline` object illustrates the power of an ML pipeline: the entire end-to-end process, including a trained and tuned model, is encapsulated and portable, and we can utilize the pipeline as we could a single model. For example, the following code performs F1 scoring for the training data:

```
print(f"F1: {f1_score(pipeline.predict(X), y,
    pos_label='Yes')}")
```

To export the pipeline, we joblib to serialize the model to a file:

```
joblib.dump(pipeline, "churn_pipeline.pkl")
```

Exporting the pipeline allows us to re-instantiate and use it within our production code. Next, we'll look at building an API for our model.

At this stage, our pipeline (which encapsulates preprocessing, training, optimization, and validation) is defined, and we are ready to deploy it to a system. We'll accomplish this by wrapping our model in an API with FastAPI.

Building an ML API using FastAPI

We will now look at building a REST API around our pipeline, enabling consumers of our pipeline to get predictions via web requests. Building a web API for a model also simplifies integration with other systems and services and is the standard method for integration in a microservices architecture.

To build the API, we use the Python library FastAPI.

FastAPI

FastAPI is a modern, high-performance web framework for building APIs with Python 3.6+. It was designed from the ground up to be easy to use and enable high-performance API development. The key features of FastAPI are its speed and ease of use, making it an excellent choice for developing robust, production-ready APIs. FastAPI widely adopts Python's type checking, which aids in catching errors early in the development process. It also uses these type hints to provide data validation, serialization, and documentation, reducing the boilerplate code developers need to write.

The performance of FastAPI is one of its defining features. It is on par with Node.js and significantly faster than traditional Python frameworks. This speed is achieved due to its use of Starlette for the web parts and Pydantic for the data parts, and its non-blocking nature makes it suitable for handling many concurrent requests.

FastAPI provides automatic interactive API documentation, a considerable advantage while developing complex APIs. Using FastAPI, developers gain access to automatically generated interactive API docs via Swagger UI. Swagger UI also provides functionality to interact with the REST resources without writing code or using external tooling. This feature makes FastAPI very developer-friendly and accelerates the development process.

FastAPI also supports industry-standard security protocols, such as OAuth2, and provides tooling to ease implementation. Much of FastAPI's tooling relies on its dependency injection system, allowing developers to manage dependencies and handle shared resources efficiently.

FastAPI is well suited to building web APIs and microservices for ML models due to its ease of use and high performance, allowing ML engineers to focus on the myriad of other concerns surrounding production ML deployments.

Building with FastAPI

To create a REST API with FastAPI, we can create a new Python script and instantiate the FastAPI instance. After the instance starts, we can load our model from the file:

```
app = FastAPI()
model = joblib.load("churn_pipeline.pkl")
```

Loading the model at the start of the application increases the startup time but ensures that the API is ready to serve requests when the application startup completes.

Next, we need to implement a REST endpoint to make predictions. Our endpoint accepts input data and returns the predictions as JSON. The input JSON is an array of JSON objects, as follows:

```
[
  {
    "customerID": "1580-BMCMR",
    ...
    "MonthlyCharges": 87.3,
    "TotalCharges": "1637.3"
  },
  {
    "customerID": "4304-XUMGI",
    ...
    "MonthlyCharges": 75.15,
    "TotalCharges": "3822.45"
  }
]
```

With FastAPI, we implement a REST endpoint by creating a function that takes the input data as parameters. FastAPI serializes the preceding JSON structure to a Python list of dictionaries. Therefore, our function signature is implemented as follows:

```
@app.post('/predict')
def predict_instances(
        instances: list[dict[str, str]]
):
```

We decorate the function using a FastAPI `post` decorator, specifying the endpoint path (`'/predict'`).

To make the actual predictions for the model, we convert the dictionaries to a DataFrame and perform the predictions:

```
instance_frame = pd.DataFrame(instances)
predictions = model.predict_proba(instance_frame)
```

We use `predict_proba` to get the probabilities for each class (Yes or No) since we want to send this additional information to the consumers of our API. Returning probabilities alongside predictions is a recommended practice, as this affords the API consumer more control over the use of the predictions. API consumers can decide what probability threshold is good enough for their application based on how the predictions are used.

To return the results as JSON, we construct a dictionary that FastAPI then serializes to JSON. We use NumPy's `argmax` to get the index of the highest probability to determine the predicted class and `amax` to get the highest probability itself:

```
results = {}
for i, row in enumerate(predictions):
    prediction = model.classes_[np.argmax(row)]
    probability = np.amax(row)
    results[i] = {"prediction": prediction,
        "probability": probability}

return results
```

The preceding code produces a `prediction` object for each data instance in the input list, using the position in the list as an index. When the endpoint is called, the following JSON is returned:

```
{
  "0": {
    "prediction": "Yes",
    "probability": 0.9758797243307111
  },
  "1": {
    "prediction": "No",
    "probability": 0.8896770039274629
  },
  "2": {
    "prediction": "No",
    "probability": 0.9149225087944103
  }
}
```

We have now built the core of the API endpoint. However, we must also pay attention to non-functional concerns such as security. Often, ML engineers neglect aspects such as security or performance and focus only on ML concerns. We mustn't make this mistake and must ensure we give these concerns the necessary attention.

Securing the API

To secure our endpoint, we'll make use of HTTP Basic authentication. We use a preset username and password, which we read from the environment. This allows us to securely pass these credentials to the application during deployment and avoids pitfalls such as hardcoding the credentials. Our endpoint also needs to be enhanced to accept credentials from the user. HTTP Basic authentication credentials are sent as an HTTP header.

We can implement this as follows. We first set up security for FastAPI and read the credentials from the environment:

```
security = HTTPBasic()
USER = bytes(os.getenv("CHURN_USER"), "utf-8")
PASSWORD = bytes(os.getenv("CHURN_PASSWORD"), "utf-8")
```

We then add the following to the endpoint function:

```
@app.post('/predict')
def predict_instances(
        credentials: Annotated[HTTPBasicCredentials,
            Depends(security)],
        instances: list[dict[str, str]]
):
    authenticate(credentials.username.encode("utf-8"),
        credentials.password.encode("utf-8"))
```

The authenticate function validates the received credentials against the API credentials we got from the environment. We can use Python's secrets library to do the validation:

```
def authenticate(username: bytes, password: bytes):
    valid_user = secrets.compare_digest(
        username, USER
    )
    valid_password = secrets.compare_digest(
        password, PASSWORD
    )
    if not (valid_user and valid_password):
        raise HTTPException(
            status_code=status.HTTP_401_UNAUTHORIZED,
            detail="Incorrect username or password",
```

```
        headers={"WWW-Authenticate": "Basic"},
    )
    return username
```

If the credentials are invalid, we throw an exception with HTTP status code 401, signaling that the consumer is not authorized.

Our API endpoint is now fully implemented, secured, and ready for deployment. To deploy our API, we'll containerize it using Docker.

Containerizing our API

We can build a Docker container for our API with the following Dockerfile:

```
FROM python:3.10-slim

RUN apt-get update && apt-get install -y --no-install-recommends apt-
utils
RUN apt-get -y install curl
RUN apt-get install libgomp1

WORKDIR /usr/src/app

COPY requirements.txt ./
RUN pip install --no-cache-dir -r requirements.txt
COPY . .

CMD [ "uvicorn", "telco_churn_api:app", "--host", "0.0.0.0", "--port",
"8080" ]
```

The Dockerfile is straightforward: we start with a base Python 3.10 image and install some OS dependencies that LightGBM needs (libgomp1). We then set up the FastAPI app: we copy the Python requirements file, install all of them, and then copy the necessary source files (using COPY . .).

Finally, we run a Uvicorn server, listening on all addresses on port 8080. Uvicorn is an ASGI web server implementation for Python that supports async I/O, significantly increasing the web server's throughput. We bind to port 8080, our deployment platform's default port.

We can build and run the Docker image using the following commands, passing the username and password environment variables:

```
docker build . -t churn_api:latest
docker run --rm -it -e CHURN_USER=***** -e CHURN_PASSWORD=**********
-p 8080:8080 churn_api:latest
```

The API should now be available on your localhost, on port 8080, secured behind the credentials you provide in the environment variables.

With our application containerized, we are ready to deploy our application to any platform that supports containers. For the churn application, we'll deploy it to Google Cloud Platform.

Deploying LightGBM to Google Cloud

We'll leverage the **Google Cloud Run** platform to deploy our application to Google Cloud Platform.

Google Cloud Run is a serverless platform that allows you to develop and run applications without worrying about infrastructure management. Cloud Run allows developers to run their applications in a secure, scalable, and zero-ops environment. Cloud Run is fully managed, meaning all infrastructure (such as servers and load balancers) is abstracted away, allowing users to focus on running their applications. Cloud Run also supports full autoscaling, and the number of running containers automatically increases to respond to increasing load. Cloud Run is also very cost-effective, as you are only charged when the container runs and serves requests.

To use Cloud Run, you need a Google Cloud account and need to create a Google Cloud project, enable billing, and set up and initialize the **Google Cloud CLI**. The following resources guide you through these steps:

- https://console.cloud.google.com/getting-started
- https://cloud.google.com/resource-manager/docs/creating-managing-projects
- https://cloud.google.com/sdk/docs/install
- https://cloud.google.com/sdk/docs/initializing

Once the Google Cloud setup is completed, we can deploy our API using the CLI. This can be accomplished using a single command:

```
gcloud run deploy --set-env-vars CHURN_USER=*****,CHURN_
PASSWORD=***********
```

Running the command prompts you for a service name and a region to deploy your service. We also set the environment variables needed for the security credentials. For deployment, Cloud Run creates Cloud Build for you, which automatically builds and stores the Docker container and then deploys it to Cloud Run.

Once the Cloud Run command completes, we have deployed a secure, scalable, RESTful web API serving our customer churn ML pipeline.

Summary

This chapter introduced ML pipelines, illustrating their advantages in enabling consistency, correctness, and portability when implementing ML solutions.

An overview was given on the nascent MLOps field, a practice combining DevOps and ML to realize tested, scalable, secure, and observable production ML systems.

Further, we discussed the scikit-learn `Pipeline` class, a toolset to implement ML pipelines using the familiar scikit-learn API.

A practical, end-to-end example of implementing an ML pipeline for customer churn was also given. We showed how to create a scikit-learn pipeline that performs preprocessing, modeling, and tuning and is exportable for a software system. We then built a secure RESTful web API using FastAPI that provides an endpoint for getting predictions from our customer churn pipeline. Finally, we deployed our API to Google Cloud Platform using the Cloud Run service.

Although our deployment is secure and fully scalable, with observability, metrics, and logs provided by Cloud Run, there are some ML-specific aspects our deployment does not address: model drift, model performance monitoring, and retraining.

In the next chapter, we look at a specialized ML cloud service with AWS SageMaker, which provides a platform-specific solution for building and hosting cloud-based ML pipelines.

LightGBM MLOps with AWS SageMaker

In *Chapter 8*, *Machine Learning Pipelines and MLOps with LightGBM*, we built an end-to-end ML pipeline using scikit-learn. We also looked at encapsulating the pipeline within a REST API and deployed our API to the cloud.

This chapter will look at developing and deploying a pipeline using **Amazon SageMaker**. SageMaker is a complete set of production services for developing, hosting, monitoring, and maintaining ML solutions provided by **Amazon Web Services (AWS)**.

We'll expand our capabilities with ML pipelines by looking at advanced topics such as detecting bias in a trained model and automating deployment to fully scalable, serverless web endpoints.

The following main topics will be covered in this chapter:

- An introduction to AWS and SageMaker
- Model explainability and bias
- Building an end-to-end pipeline with SageMaker

Technical requirements

This chapter dives deep into building ML models and pipelines using Amazon SageMaker. You need access to an Amazon account, and you must also configure a payment method. Note that running the example code for this chapter will incur costs on AWS. The complete notebooks and scripts for this chapter are available at https://github.com/PacktPublishing/Practical-Machine-Learning-with-LightGBM-and-Python/tree/main/chapter-9.

An introduction to AWS and SageMaker

This section provides a high-level overview of AWS and delves into SageMaker, AWS' ML offering.

AWS

AWS is one of the leading players in the global cloud computing marketplace. AWS offers many cloud-based products and services, including databases, **machine learning** (**ML**), analytics, networking, storage, developer tools, and enterprise applications. The idea behind AWS is to offer businesses an affordable and scalable solution to their computing needs, regardless of their size or industry.

A key advantage of AWS is elasticity, meaning servers and services can be stopped and started quickly and at will, scaling from zero machines to thousands. The elasticity of the services goes hand in hand with its primary pricing model of pay-as-you-go, meaning customers only pay for the services and resources they use without any upfront costs or long-term contracts. This elasticity and pricing allow businesses to scale computing needs as needed, on an ad hoc and granular level, and then only pay for what they use. This approach has transformed how businesses scale IT resources and applications, enabling them to react quickly to changing business needs without incurring the heavy costs traditionally associated with hardware and software procurement and maintenance.

Another advantage is the global reach of AWS. AWS services are available in many regions across the globe. Regions are geographically separated, and each region is further divided into availability zones. The region-zone setup allows users to create globally distributed and redundant infrastructure to maximize resilience and architect for disaster recovery. The regional data centers also allow users to create servers and services close to end users, minimizing latency.

Core services

The core AWS services provide computing, networking, and storage capability. AWS's compute services include **Amazon Elastic Compute Cloud** (**EC2**), which offers configurable virtual machines to customers, and **AWS Lambda**, a serverless compute platform that allows you to run code without the need to provision and manage servers. In ML, both EC2 instances and Lambda functions are often used to train and validate or serve models via API endpoints. The elastic nature of EC2 servers allows ML engineers to scale up training servers to many thousands, which can significantly speed up training or parameter-tuning tasks.

AWS's storage and database services, such as **Amazon Simple Storage Service** (**S3**) and **Amazon RDS** (**Relational Database Service**), offer reliable, scalable, and secure data storage solutions. These services manage storage infrastructure and offer high-level features such as backups, patch management, and vertical and horizontal scaling. S3 is a widely used service for data engineering and ML. S3 offers low-cost, highly redundant secure storage that scales beyond exabytes.

AWS also offers data warehousing solutions with **Amazon Redshift**. Large enterprises frequently use Redshift as a warehouse or the basis of a data lake, meaning it's often a data source for ML solutions.

AWS also offers networking services to help businesses meet complex networking and isolation needs. **AWS Direct Connect** allows customers to set up a dedicated network connection from a customer's site to the AWS cloud. Routing and name servers can be managed with Amazon Route 53, a flexible and scalable **Domain Name System** (**DNS**) service.

However, chief among the network services is **Amazon Virtual Private Cloud (VPC)**. VPCs offer customers the ability to configure completely isolated virtual networks. Customers can granularly configure subnetworks, routing tables, address ranges, gateways, and security groups. VPCs allow users to isolate their environment and cloud resources and control inbound and outbound traffic for increased security and privacy.

Security

A critical piece of any infrastructure equation is security. In terms of security, AWS provides a highly secure, scalable, and flexible cloud computing environment. AWS's security services, including **AWS Identity and Access Management (IAM)** and **Amazon Security Hub**, help customers protect their data and applications by implementing robust security measures.

AWS also complies with multiple international and industry-specific compliance standards, such as GDPR, HIPAA, and ISO 27001. Further, in terms of data governance, AWS makes it easy to comply with data residency and privacy requirements. Due to the regional structure of AWS, data can remain resident in specific countries, while engineers have access to the full suite of AWS services.

Machine learning

AWS also offers services focused on ML and **artificial intelligence (AI)**. Among these are many fully managed services for specific ML tasks. **AWS Comprehend** offers many **natural language processing (NLP)** services, such as document processing, named entity recognition, and sentiment analysis. **Amazon Lookout** is a service for anomaly detection in equipment, metrics, or images. Further, **Amazon Rekognition** offers services for machine vision use cases such as image classification and facial recognition.

Of particular interest to us is **Amazon SageMaker**, a complete ML platform that allows us to create, train, and deploy ML models in the Amazon cloud. The following section discusses SageMaker in detail.

SageMaker

Amazon SageMaker is an end-to-end ML platform that allows data scientists to work with data and develop, train, deploy, and monitor ML models. SageMaker is fully managed, so there is no need to provision or manage servers.

The primary appeal of Amazon SageMaker lies in its comprehensive nature as a platform. It encompasses all aspects of the ML process, including data labeling, model building, training, tuning, deployment, management, and monitoring. By taking care of these aspects, SageMaker allows developers and data scientists to focus on the core ML tasks instead of managing the infrastructure.

As we have discussed, the ML life cycle starts with data gathering, which often requires manual data labeling. For this, SageMaker provides a service called **SageMaker Ground Truth**. This service makes it easy to annotate ML datasets efficiently. It can significantly reduce the time and costs typically associated with data labeling by using automated labeling workflows, and it also offers a workforce for manual data labeling tasks. Further, SageMaker also provides the **Data Wrangler** service, which helps with data preparation and **exploratory data analysis (EDA)**. Data Wrangler provides functionality to query data from S3, Redshift, and other platforms and then cleanse, visualize, and understand the data from a single visual interface.

SageMaker provides a fully managed service for the model training phase that can handle large-scale, distributed model training via **Training Jobs**. The service is designed to be flexible and adaptable, allowing users to optimize their ML models as needed. Users only need to specify the location of their data, typically S3 and the ML algorithm, and SageMaker takes care of the rest of the training process. The model training service fully leverages the elastic nature of the underlying AWS infrastructure: many servers can be created quickly to perform training jobs and discarded after training is complete to save costs.

This paradigm also extends to hyperparameter tuning. To simplify hyperparameter optimization, SageMaker provides an automatic model-tuning feature. Many tuning algorithms are provided, such as Optuna or FLAML, and tuning can be run across multiple servers.

SageMaker also has support for a more fully AutoML experience via **SageMaker Autopilot**. Autopilot is a service that enables automatic model creation. A user only needs to provide the raw data and set the target; then, Autopilot automatically explores different solutions to find the best model. Autopilot provides complete visibility into the process so that data scientists can understand how the model is created and make any necessary adjustments.

Once a model has been trained and optimized, it must be deployed. SageMaker simplifies this process by providing a one-click deployment process. Users can quickly deploy their models to production with auto-scaling capabilities without worrying about the underlying infrastructure. This deployment autoscaling capability allows users to set metrics-based policies that increase or decrease backing servers. For instance, the deployment can be scaled up if the number of invocations within a period exceeds a specific threshold. SageMaker ensures the high availability of models and allows for A/B testing of models to compare different variants and decide on the best one. SageMaker also supports multi-model endpoints, allowing users to deploy multiple models on a single endpoint.

Amazon SageMaker also provides capabilities to monitor the model's performance and conduct analysis once deployed. **SageMaker Model Monitor** monitors the quality of deployed models continuously (for real-time endpoints) or in batches (for asynchronous jobs). Alerts can be defined to notify the user if metric thresholds are exceeded. Model Monitor can monitor data drift and model drift based on metrics such as accuracy.

Finally, SageMaker is both a platform within AWS and a software SDK. The SDK is available in both Python and R. The SageMaker SDK provides a range of built-in algorithms and frameworks, including support for the most popular algorithms in the ML community, such as XGBoost, TensorFlow, PyTorch, and MXNet. It also supports a marketplace where users can choose from a vast collection of algorithm and model packages shared by AWS and other SageMaker users.

A noteworthy part of SageMaker that simplifies one of the most important aspects of model development (bias and fairness) is **SageMaker Clarify**.

SageMaker Clarify

Amazon SageMaker Clarify is a tool that provides greater transparency into ML models. SageMaker Clarify aims to assist in understanding how ML models make predictions, thereby enabling model explainability and fairness.

One of the primary features of SageMaker Clarify is its capacity to provide model interpretability. It helps developers understand the relationships between the input data and the model's predictions. The service generates feature attributions that show how each feature in the dataset influences predictions, which can be critical in many domains, especially those where it's vital to understand the reasoning behind a model's prediction. In addition to providing insight into individual predictions, SageMaker Clarify offers global explanatory capabilities. It measures the importance of input features on a model's predictions in aggregate across the whole dataset. Feature impact analysis allows developers and data scientists to understand the overall behavior of a model, helping them interpret how different features drive model predictions on a global level.

Further, Clarify can help identify potential bias in trained models. The service includes pre-training and post-training bias metrics that help us understand if a model favors certain groups unfairly. It's best practice to check all new models for bias, but it is also imperative in regulated industries such as finance or healthcare, where biased predictions can have severe consequences.

Clarify provides model interpretability by using an advanced technique known as **SHapley Additive exPlanations** (**SHAP**).

SHAP

SHAP is a game theoretic approach to interpreting the output of any ML model [1]. SHAP aims to provide an understanding of the impact of individual features on a model's overall prediction.

Essentially, SHAP values assess the effect of a particular feature value by contrasting it with a baseline value for that feature, highlighting its contribution to the prediction. A SHAP value is a fair contribution allocation from each feature to the prediction for each instance. SHAP values are rooted in cooperative game theory, representing a solution to the following question:

"Given the difference a feature makes in predicting an outcome, what portion of that difference is attributable to each feature?"

These values are calculated using the concept of Shapley values from game theory. A Shapley value determines the significance of a feature by contrasting a model's predictions with the presence and absence of that feature. Yet, as the sequence in which a model encounters features can affect its prediction, Shapley values consider all possible orderings. Then, it assigns an importance value to a feature so that it equals the average marginal contribution of that feature across all possible coalitions.

There are several advantages to using SHAP for model interpretation. First, it offers consistency in interpretation. If the contribution of a feature changes, the attributed importance of that feature changes proportionally.

Secondly, SHAP guarantees local accuracy, which means the sum of the SHAP values for all features would equal the difference between the prediction and the average prediction for the dataset.

A great way to visualize SHAP values is by using SHAP summary plots. These plots provide a bird's-eye view of feature importance and what is driving it. They plot all the SHAP values for a feature on a graph for easy visualization. Each point on the graph represents a SHAP value for a feature and an instance. The position on the Y-axis is determined by the feature and on the X-axis by the SHAP value:

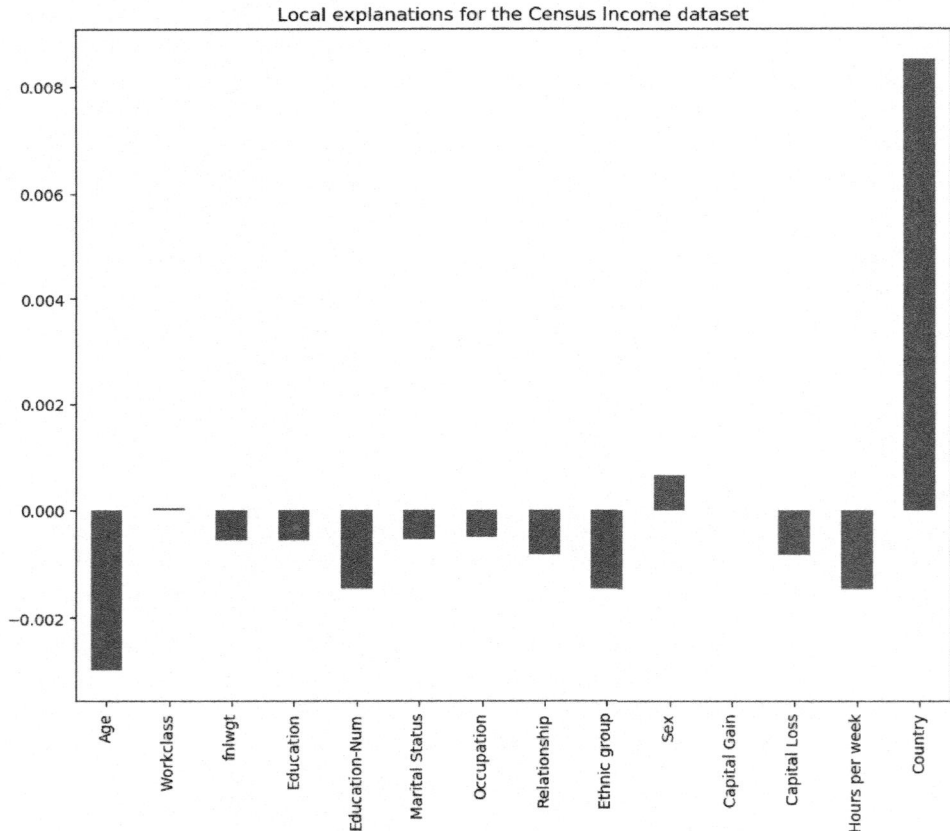

Figure 9.1 – Local explanation example for the Census Income dataset. Bars indicate SHAP values or the relative importance of each feature in predicting this specific instance

In the context of SageMaker Clarify, the service generates a set of SHAP values for each instance in your dataset when you run a clarification job. SageMaker Clarify can also provide global feature importance measures by aggregating SHAP values across the entire dataset.

SHAP values can help you understand complex model behavior, highlight potential issues, and improve your model over time. For example, by examining SHAP values, you might discover that a specific feature has a more significant effect on your model's predictions than expected, prompting you to explore why this might happen.

In this section, we looked at AWS and, more specifically, what the AWS ML family of services, SageMaker, offers. The functionality available in SageMaker, such as model explainability, bias detection, and monitoring, are components we have yet to implement in our ML pipelines. In the next section, we'll look at building a complete end-to-end LightGBM-based ML pipeline, including these crucial steps, using SageMaker.

Building a LightGBM ML pipeline with Amazon SageMaker

The dataset we'll use for our case study of building a SageMaker pipeline is the Census Income dataset from *Chapter 4, Comparing LightGBM, XGBoost, and Deep Learning*. This dataset is also available as a SageMaker sample dataset, so it's easy to work with on SageMaker if you are getting started.

The pipeline we'll build consists of the following steps:

1. Data preprocessing.
2. Model training and tuning.
3. Model evaluation.
4. Bias and explainability checks using Clarify.
5. Model registration within SageMaker.
6. Model deployment using an AWS Lambda.

Here's a graph showing the complete pipeline:

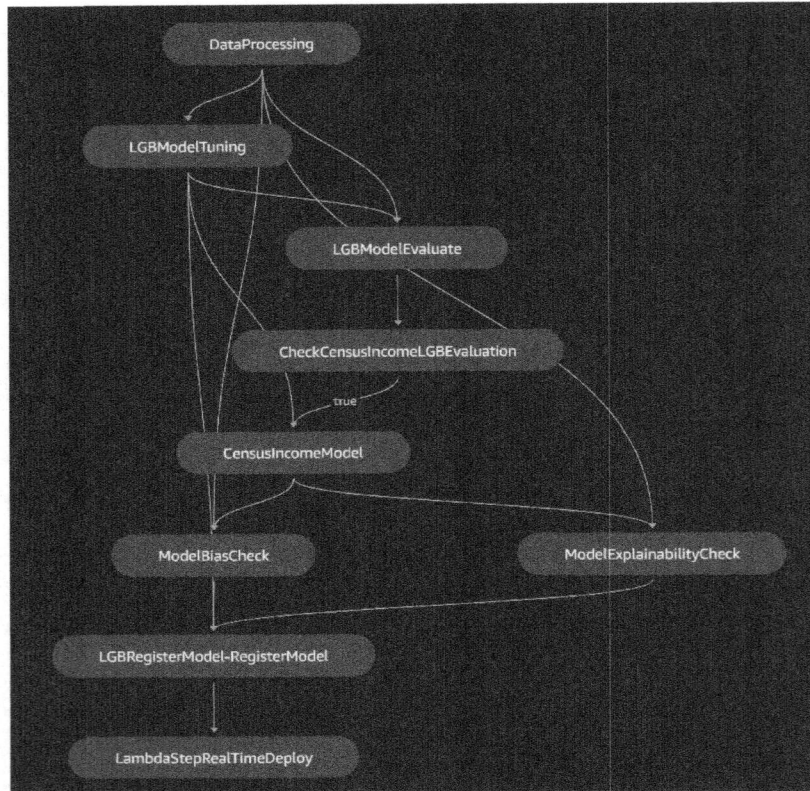

Figure 9.2 – SageMaker ML pipeline for Census Income classification

Our approach is to create the entire pipeline using a Jupyter Notebook running in SageMaker Studio. The sections that follow explain and go through the code for each pipeline step, starting with setting up the SageMaker session.

Setting up a SageMaker session

The following steps assume you have already created an AWS account and set up a SageMaker domain to get started. If not, the following documentation can be referenced to do so:

- Prerequisites: `https://docs.aws.amazon.com/sagemaker/latest/dg/gs-set-up.html`

- Onboarding to a SageMaker domain: `https://docs.aws.amazon.com/sagemaker/latest/dg/gs-studio-onboard.html`

We must initialize the SageMaker session and create S3, SageMaker, and SageMaker Runtime clients via `boto3` to get started:

```
sess = sagemaker.Session()
region = sess.boto_region_name
s3_client = boto3.client("s3", region_name=region)
sm_client = boto3.client("sagemaker", region_name=region)
sm_runtime_client = boto3.client("sagemaker-runtime")
```

We will use Amazon S3 to store our training data, source code, and all data and artifacts created by the pipeline, such as the serialized model. Our data and artifacts are split into a read bucket and a separate write bucket. This is a standard best practice as it separates the concerns for data storage.

SageMaker sessions have the concept of a default S3 bucket for the session. If no default bucket name is supplied, one is generated, and the bucket is created for you. Here, we're grabbing a reference to the bucket. This is our output or write bucket. The read bucket is a bucket we've created previously that stores our training data:

```
write_bucket = sess.default_bucket()
write_prefix = "census-income-pipeline"
read_bucket = "sagemaker-data"
read_prefix = "census-income"
```

The source code, configuration, and output of each of the steps in the pipeline are captured in folders within our S3 write bucket. It's useful to create variables for each S3 URI to avoid errors when repeatedly referring to data, like so:

```
input_data_key = f"s3://{read_bucket}/{read_prefix}"
census_income_data_uri = f"{input_data_key}/census-income.csv"
output_data_uri = f"s3://{write_bucket}/{write_prefix}/"
scripts_uri = f"s3://{write_bucket}/{write_prefix}/scripts"
```

SageMaker needs us to specify the compute instance types we want to use when running the jobs for training, processing, Clarify, and prediction. In our example, we're using m5.large instances. Most EC2 instance types can be used with SageMaker. However, a few special instance types that support GPUs and deep learning frameworks are also available:

```
train_model_id, train_model_version, train_scope = "lightgbm-
classification-model", "*", "training"
process_instance_type = "ml.m5.large"
train_instance_count = 1
train_instance_type = "ml.m5.large"
predictor_instance_count = 1
predictor_instance_type = "ml.m5.large"
clarify_instance_count = 1
clarify_instance_type = "ml.m5.large"
```

SageMaker uses standard EC2 instances for training but runs specific Docker images on the instances to provide ML functionality. Amazon SageMaker provides many prebuilt Docker images for various ML frameworks and stacks.

The SageMaker SDK also provides a function to search for images that are compatible with the instance type we need within the AWS region we are using. We can search for an image using `retrieve`:

```
train_image_uri = retrieve(
    region="us-east-1",
    framework=None,
    model_id=train_model_id,
    model_version=train_model_version,
    image_scope=train_scope,
    instance_type=train_instance_type
)
```

We specify None for the framework parameter as we manage the LightGBM installation ourselves.

To parameterize our pipeline, we must define SageMaker workflow parameters from the `sagemaker.workflow.parameters` package. Wrappers are available for various parameter types:

```
train_instance_type_param = ParameterString(
    name="TrainingInstanceType",
    default_value=train_instance_type)

train_instance_count_param = ParameterInteger(
    name="TrainingInstanceCount",
    default_value=train_instance_count)

deploy_instance_type_param = ParameterString(
    name="DeployInstanceType",
    default_value=predictor_instance_type)

deploy_instance_count_param = ParameterInteger(
    name="DeployInstanceCount",
    default_value=predictor_instance_count)
```

With our pipeline parameters, S3 data paths, and other configuration variables set, we can move on to creating our pipeline's preprocessing step.

Preprocessing step

Setting up our preprocessing step has two parts: creating a Python script that performs the preprocessing and creating a processor that is added to the pipeline.

The script we'll be using is a regular Python script with a main function. We'll use scikit-learn to do our preprocessing. The preprocessing script hasn't been entirely reproduced here but is available in our source code repository. Notably, when the pipeline executes the step, the data is retrieved from S3 and added to a local staging directory on the preprocessing instance. From here, we can read the data using standard pandas tooling:

```
local_dir = "/opt/ml/processing"
input_data_path = os.path.join("/opt/ml/processing/census-income",
"census-income.csv")

logger.info("Reading claims data from {}".format(input_data_path))
df = pd.read_csv(input_data_path)
```

Similarly, after processing is complete, we can write the results to a local directory, from which SageMaker retrieves it and uploads it to S3:

```
train_output_path = os.path.join(f"{local_dir}/train", "train.csv")
X_train.to_csv(train_output_path, index=False)
```

With a preprocessing script defined, we need to upload it to S3 for the pipeline to be able to use it:

```
s3_client.upload_file(
    Filename="src/preprocessing.py", Bucket=write_bucket,
Key=f"{write_prefix}/scripts/preprocessing.py"
)
```

We can define the preprocessing step as follows. First, we must create an SKLearnProcessor instance:

```
sklearn_processor = SKLearnProcessor(
    framework_version="0.23-1",
    role=sagemaker_role,
    instance_count=1,
    instance_type=process_instance_type,
    base_job_name=f"{base_job_name_prefix}-processing",
)
```

SKLearnProcessor handles the processing task for jobs that require scikit-learn. We specify the scikit-learn framework version and the instance type and count we defined earlier.

The processor is then added to ProcessingStep for use in the pipeline:

```
process_step = ProcessingStep(
    name="DataProcessing",
    processor=sklearn_processor,
    inputs=[...],
    outputs=[...],
```

```
    job_arguments=[
        "--train-ratio", "0.8",
        "--validation-ratio", "0.1",
        "--test-ratio", "0.1"
    ],
    code=f"s3://{write_bucket}/{write_prefix}/scripts/preprocessing.
py"
)
```

`inputs` and `outputs` are defined using the `ProcessingInput` and `ProcessingOutput` wrappers, as shown here:

```
inputs = [ ProcessingInput(source=bank_marketing_data_uri,
destination="/opt/ml/processing/bank-marketing") ]
outputs = [ ProcessingOutput(destination=f"{processing_output_uri}/
train_data", output_name="train_data",
                        source="/opt/ml/processing/train"), ... ]
```

`ProcessingStep` takes our scikit-learn processor and the inputs and outputs for the data. The `ProcessingInput` instances define the S3 source and local directory destination to facilitate copying the data (these are the same local directories our preprocessing script uses). Similarly, the `ProcessingOutput` instances take the local directory source and S3 destinations. We also set job arguments, which are passed to the preprocessing script as CLI arguments.

Having set up the preprocessing step, we can move on to training.

Model training and tuning

We define a training script in the same way as a preprocessing script: a Python script with a main function that uses our standard Python tools, such as scikit-learn, to train a LightGBM model. However, we also need to install the LightGBM library itself.

An alternative to installing the library is building it into a Docker image and using it as our training image in SageMaker. This is the canonical way of managing environments in SageMaker. However, it entails significant work and includes the long-term need to maintain the image over time. Alternatively, if we only need to install a handful of dependencies, we can do that directly from our training script, as shown here.

We must define a helper function to install packages and then use it to install LightGBM:

```
def install(package):
    subprocess.check_call([sys.executable, "-q", "-m", "pip",
"install", package])
install("lightgbm")
import lightgbm as lgb
```

This also has the advantage that we install the latest version (or a specific version) every time we run training.

With the package installed, the rest of the training script trains a standard LGBMClassifier on the data prepared by the preprocessing step. We can set up or train data and parameters from the arguments to the script:

```
train_df = pd.read_csv(f"{args.train_data_dir}/train.csv")
val_df = pd.read_csv(f"{args.validation_data_dir}/validation.csv")
params = {
    "n_estimators": args.n_estimators,
    "learning_rate": args.learning_rate,
    "num_leaves": args.num_leaves,
    "max_bin": args.max_bin,
}
```

Then, we must do standard scikit-learn cross-validation scoring, fit the model to the data, and output the training and validation scores:

```
X, y = prepare_data(train_df)
model = lgb.LGBMClassifier(**params)

scores = cross_val_score(model, X, y, scoring="f1_macro")
train_f1 = scores.mean()
model = model.fit(X, y)

X_test, y_test = prepare_data(val_df)
test_f1 = f1_score(y_test, model.predict(X_test))

print(f"[0]#011train-f1:{train_f1:.2f}")
print(f"[0]#011validation-f1:{test_f1:.2f}")
```

As shown here, the script accepts CLI arguments to set hyperparameters. This is used by the hyperparameter tuning step to set parameters during the optimization phase. We can use Python's ArgumentParser for this purpose:

```
parser = argparse.ArgumentParser()
parser.add_argument("--boosting_type", type=str, default="gbdt")
parser.add_argument("--objective", type=str, default="binary")
parser.add_argument("--n_estimators", type=int, default=200)
parser.add_argument("--learning_rate", type=float, default=0.001)
parser.add_argument("--num_leaves", type=int, default=30)
parser.add_argument("--max_bin", type=int, default=300)
```

We can also see that we log training and validation F1 scores, allowing SageMaker and CloudWatch to pull the data from logs for reporting and evaluation purposes.

Finally, we need to write out the results of the training in a JSON document. The results can then be used in subsequent pipeline processes and are shown as output from the job in the SageMaker interface. The JSON document is stored on disk, along with the serialized model file:

```
metrics_data = {"hyperparameters": params,
                "binary_classification_metrics":
{"validation:f1": {"value": test_f1},"train:f1": {"value":
train_f1}}
}
metrics_location = args.output_data_dir + "/metrics.json"
model_location = args.model_dir + "/lightgbm-model"
with open(metrics_location, "w") as f:
    json.dump(metrics_data, f)
with open(model_location, "wb") as f:
    joblib.dump(model, f)
```

As with the preprocessing step, the results are written to a local directory, where SageMaker picks them up and copies them to S3.

With the script defined, we can create the tuning step in the pipeline, which trains the model and tunes hyperparameters.

We must define a SageMaker Estimator that, similar to SKLearnProcessor, encapsulates the configuration for training, including a reference to the script (on S3):

```
static_hyperparams = {
    "boosting_type": "gbdt",
    "objective": "binary",
}
lgb_estimator = Estimator(
    source_dir="src",
    entry_point="lightgbm_train.py",
    output_path=estimator_output_uri,
    code_location=estimator_output_uri,
    hyperparameters=static_hyperparams,
    role=sagemaker_role,
    image_uri=train_image_uri,
    instance_count=train_instance_count,
    instance_type=train_instance_type,
    framework_version="1.3-1",
)
```

We can then define our SageMaker `HyperparameterTuner`, which performs the actual hyperparameter tuning. Similar to Optuna or FLAML, we must specify valid ranges for the hyperparameters using SageMaker wrappers:

```
hyperparameter_ranges = {
    "n_estimators": IntegerParameter(10, 400),
    "learning_rate": ContinuousParameter(0.0001, 0.5, scaling_
type="Logarithmic"),
    "num_leaves": IntegerParameter(2, 200),
    "max_bin": IntegerParameter(50, 500)
}
```

`HyperparameterTuner` can be set up as follows:

```
tuner_config_dict = {
    "estimator": lgb_estimator,
    "max_jobs": 20,
    "max_parallel_jobs": 2,
    "objective_metric_name": "validation-f1",
    "metric_definitions": [{"Name": "validation-f1", "Regex":
"validation-f1:([0-9\\.]+)"}],
    "hyperparameter_ranges": hyperparameter_ranges,
    "base_tuning_job_name": tuning_job_name_prefix,
    "strategy": "Random"
}
tuner = HyperparameterTuner(**tuner_config_dict)
```

SageMaker supports many strategies for hyperparameter tuning, including Hyperband tuning. More information can be found in the documentation for hyperparameter tuning: `https://docs.aws.amazon.com/sagemaker/latest/dg/automatic-model-tuning-how-it-works.html`. Here, we used random search, with a maximum job size of 20. It's here that AWS' elastic infrastructure can be used to significant benefit. If we increase the training instance count, SageMaker automatically distributes the training job across all machines. Provisioning additional machines has some overhead and increases cost, but it can also majorly reduce tuning time if we run thousands of trials.

The tuner's metric definitions define regular expressions that are used to pull the results metrics from the logs, as we showed in the training script earlier. The parameter optimization framework optimizes relative to the metrics defined here, minimizing or maximizing the metric.

With the hyperparameter tuner defined, we can create a `TuningStep` for inclusion into the pipeline:

```
tuning_step = TuningStep(
    name="LGBModelTuning",
    tuner=tuner,
    inputs={
```

```
        "train": TrainingInput(...),
        "validation": TrainingInput(...),
    }
)
```

The pipeline steps we've defined thus far prepare data and produce a trained model that's serialized to S3. The pipeline's next step is to create a SageMaker `Model` that wraps the model and is used for the evaluation, bias, and inference steps. This can be done as follows:

```
model = sagemaker.model.Model(
    image_uri=train_image_uri,
    model_data=tuning_step.get_top_model_s3_uri(
        top_k=0, s3_bucket=write_bucket, prefix=model_prefix
    ),
    sagemaker_session=sess,
    role=sagemaker_role
)
inputs = sagemaker.inputs.CreateModelInput(instance_type=deploy_
instance_type_param)
create_model_step = CreateModelStep(name="CensusIncomeModel",
model=model, inputs=inputs)
```

The `Model` instance encapsulates all the necessary configurations to deploy and run the model. We can see that `model_data` is taken from the top-performing model resulting from the tuning step.

The pipeline steps we've defined so far will produce processed data and train a tuned model. The layout for the processed data in S3 is shown in *Figure 9.3*:

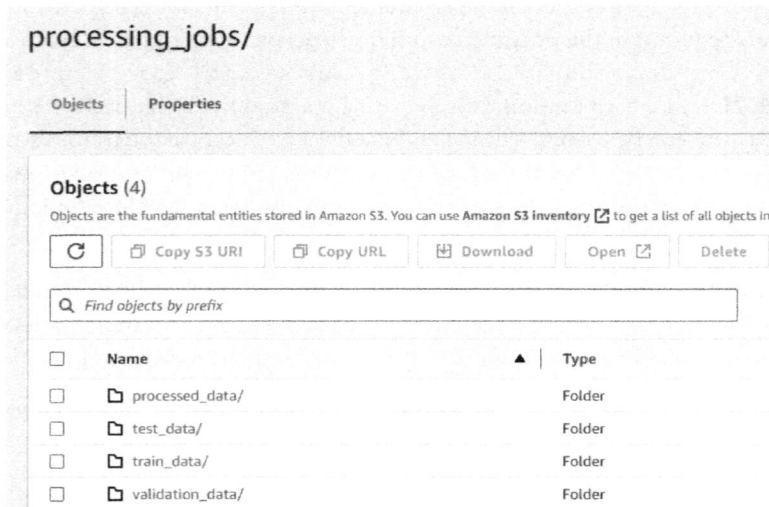

Figure 9.3 – S3 directory layout for the results of the processing jobs

We could proceed to the deployment step if we needed to. However, we will follow best practice and add quality gates to our pipeline that check the model's performance and bias and produce insights into its function.

Evaluation, bias, and explainability

So far, we've seen the general pattern of adding steps to a SageMaker pipeline: set up the configuration using SageMaker's configuration classes and then create the relevant pipeline step.

Bias configuration

To add bias checks to our pipeline, we must create the following configuration:

```
bias_config = clarify.BiasConfig(
    label_values_or_threshold=[1], facet_name="Sex", facet_values_or_
threshold=[0], group_name="Age"
)
model_predictions_config = sagemaker.clarify.
ModelPredictedLabelConfig(probability_threshold=0.5)
model_bias_check_config = ModelBiasCheckConfig(
    data_config=model_bias_data_config,
    data_bias_config=bias_config,
    model_config=model_config,
    model_predicted_label_config=model_predictions_config,
    methods=["DPPL"]
)
```

BiasConfig describes which facets (features) we want to check for bias. We've selected Sex and Age, which are always essential facets to check when working with demographic data.

ModeLBiasCheckConfig wraps the data configuration, model configuration, and bias confirmation for the bias check step. It also sets the method to use for the bias check. Here, we use the **difference in positive proportions in predicted labels (DPPL)**.

The DPPL is a metric that's used to gauge if a model predicts outcomes differently for varying facets of data. The DPPL is calculated as the difference between the proportion of positive predictions for facet "a" and facet "d." It helps assess whether there's bias in the model predictions after training by comparing them with the initial bias present in the dataset. For instance, if a model predicting eligibility for a home loan predicts positive outcomes for 70% of male applicants (facet "a") and 60% for female applicants (facet "d"), the 10% difference could indicate bias against facet "d."

The DPPL formula is represented as follows:

$$DPPL = q'_a - q'_d$$

Here, q'_a is the predicted proportion of facet "a" receiving a positive outcome, and q'_d is the analogous proportion for facet "d." For binary and multicategory facet labels, normalized DPPL values fall between [-1, 1], while continuous labels vary over the interval (-∞, +∞). A positive DPPL value suggests a higher proportion of positive predictions for facet "a" versus "d," indicating a positive bias. Conversely, a negative DPPL indicates a higher proportion of positive predictions for facet "d," signifying a negative bias. A DPPL near zero points to a relatively equal proportion of positive predictions for both facets, with a value of zero implying perfect demographic parity.

You can add the bias check to the pipeline using `ClarifyCheckStep`:

```
model_bias_check_step = ClarifyCheckStep(
    name="ModelBiasCheck",
    clarify_check_config=model_bias_check_config,
    check_job_config=check_job_config,
    skip_check=skip_check_model_bias_param,
    register_new_baseline=register_new_baseline_model_bias_param,
    supplied_baseline_constraints=supplied_baseline_constraints_model_
bias_param
)
```

Explainability configuration

The configuration for explainability is very similar. Instead of creating `BiasConfig`, we must create `SHAPConfig`:

```
shap_config = sagemaker.clarify.SHAPConfig(
    seed=829,
    num_samples=100,
    agg_method="mean_abs",
    save_local_shap_values=True
)
```

Alongside `SHAPConfig`, we must create `ModelExplainabilityCheckConfig` to calculate the SHAP values and create an explainability report:

```
model_explainability_config = ModelExplainabilityCheckConfig(
    data_config=model_explainability_data_config,
    model_config=model_config,
    explainability_config=shap_config
)
```

Everything is then combined using `ClarifyCheckStep`:

```
model_explainability_step = ClarifyCheckStep(
    name="ModelExplainabilityCheck",
    clarify_check_config=model_explainability_config,
```

```
    check_job_config=check_job_config,
    skip_check=skip_check_model_explainability_param,
    register_new_baseline=register_new_baseline_model_explainability_
param,
    supplied_baseline_constraints=supplied_baseline_constraints_model_
explainability_param
)
```

Evaluation

Finally, we also need to evaluate our model against test data. The evaluation script is very similar to the training script, except it pulls the tuned model from S3 for scoring. The script consists of a main function with two steps. First, we must bootstrap the trained model and perform the scoring (in our case, calculating the F1 score):

```
...
    test_f1 = f1_score(y_test, model.predict(X_test))

    # Calculate model evaluation score
    logger.debug("Calculating F1 score.")
    metric_dict = {
        "classification_metrics": {"f1": {"value": test_f1}}
    }
```

Then, we must output the results to a JSON file:

```
# Save model evaluation metrics
output_dir = "/opt/ml/processing/evaluation"
pathlib.Path(output_dir).mkdir(parents=True, exist_ok=True)

logger.info("Writing evaluation report with F1: %f", test_f1)
evaluation_path = f"{output_dir}/evaluation.json"
with open(evaluation_path, "w") as f:
    f.write(json.dumps(metric_dict))
```

The evaluation JSON is used for reporting and subsequent steps that rely on the evaluation metrics.

Deploying and monitoring the LightGBM model

We are now ready to add our pipeline's final steps for supporting deployment. The deployment part of the pipeline consists of three steps:

1. Registering the model in SageMaker.

2. A conditional check to validate that the model evaluation surpasses a minimum threshold.

3. Deploying a model endpoint using an AWS Lambda function.

Model registration

To deploy our model, we first need to register our model in SageMaker's **Model Registry**.

SageMaker's Model Registry is a central repository where you can manage and deploy your models.

The Model Registry provides the following core functionality:

- **Model versioning**: Every time a model is trained and registered, it's assigned a version in the Model Registry. This helps you keep track of different iterations of your models, which is useful when you need to compare model performance, roll back to previous versions, or maintain reproducibility in your ML projects.

- **Approval workflow**: The Model Registry supports an approval workflow, where models can be marked as "Pending Manual Approval," "Approved," or "Rejected." This allows teams to effectively manage the life cycle of their models and ensure that only approved models are deployed.

- **Model catalog**: The Model Registry acts as a catalog where all your models are centrally stored and accessible. Each model in the registry has metadata associated with it, such as the training data used, hyperparameters, and performance metrics.

While registering our model, we attach the metrics that were calculated from our evaluation step. These metrics are also used for model drift detection.

Two types of drift are possible: **data drift** and **model drift**.

Data drift refers to a change in the statistical distribution of the incoming data compared to our model's training data. For example, if the training data had a male/female split of 60% to 40%, but the data used for prediction is skewed to 80% male and 20% female, it's possible that drift occurred.

Model drift is a phenomenon where the statistical properties of the target variable, which the model tries to predict, change over time in unforeseen ways, causing model performance to degrade.

Both data and model drift can occur due to environmental changes, societal behaviors, product usage, or other factors not accounted for during model training.

SageMaker supports continuous monitoring of drift. SageMaker calculates the statistical distribution of both incoming data and the predictions we are making. Both are compared against the distributions present in the training data. Should drift be detected, SageMaker can produce alerts to AWS CloudWatch.

We can configure our metrics as follows:

```
model_metrics = ModelMetrics(
    bias_post_training=MetricsSource(
        s3_uri=model_bias_check_step.properties.
CalculatedBaselineConstraints,
        content_type="application/json"
    ),
```

```
    explainability=MetricsSource(
        s3_uri=model_explainability_step.properties.
CalculatedBaselineConstraints,
        content_type="application/json"
    ),
)
```

Then, for the drift metrics, we must set up `DriftCheckBaselines`:

```
drift_check_baselines = DriftCheckBaselines(
    bias_post_training_constraints=MetricsSource(    s3_uri=model_bias_
check_step.properties.BaselineUsedForDriftCheckConstraints, content_
type="application/json",
    ),
    explainability_constraints=MetricsSource(        s3_uri=model_
explainability_step.properties.BaselineUsedForDriftCheckConstraints,
content_type="application/json",
    ),
    explainability_config_file=FileSource(        s3_uri=model_
explainability_config.monitoring_analysis_config_uri, content_
type="application/json",
    ))
```

Then, we must create a model registration step with the following code:

```
register_step = RegisterModel(
    name="LGBRegisterModel",
    estimator=lgb_estimator,
    model_data=tuning_step.get_top_model_s3_uri(
        top_k=0, s3_bucket=write_bucket, prefix=model_prefix
    ),
    content_types=["text/csv"],
    response_types=["text/csv"],
    inference_instances=[predictor_instance_type],
    transform_instances=[predictor_instance_type],
    model_package_group_name=model_package_group_name,
    approval_status=model_approval_status_param,
    model_metrics=model_metrics,
    drift_check_baselines=drift_check_baselines
)
```

Model validation

The conditional check uses the evaluation data from the evaluation step to determine whether the model is suitable for deployment:

```
cond_gte = ConditionGreaterThanOrEqualTo(
    left=JsonGet(
        step_name=evaluation_step.name,
        property_file=evaluation_report,
        json_path="classification_metrics.f1.value",
    ),
    right=0.9,
)
condition_step = ConditionStep(
    name="CheckCensusIncomeLGBEvaluation",
    conditions=[cond_gte],
    if_steps=[create_model_step, register_step, lambda_deploy_step],
    else_steps=[]
)
```

Here, we created ConditionStep and compared the F1 score against a threshold of 0.9. Deployment can proceed if the model has an F1 score higher than the threshold.

Deployment with AWS Lambda

The deployment script is a standard AWS Lambda script in Python that defines a lambda_handler function that obtains a client connection to SageMaker and proceeds to create the model endpoint:

```
def lambda_handler(event, context):
    sm_client = boto3.client("sagemaker")
...
    create_endpoint_config_response = sm_client.create_endpoint_
config(
        EndpointConfigName=endpoint_config_name,
        ProductionVariants=[{
            "VariantName": "Alltraffic",
            "ModelName": model_name,
            "InitialInstanceCount": instance_count,
            "InstanceType": instance_type,
            "InitialVariantWeight": 1}])
    create_endpoint_response = sm_client.create_endpoint(
        EndpointName=endpoint_name,
        EndpointConfigName=endpoint_config_name)
```

Notably, the Lambda function does not serve requests for the model. It only creates the model endpoint within SageMaker.

In SageMaker, an **endpoint** is a web service to get predictions from your models. Once a model is trained and the training job is complete, you need to deploy the model to make real-time or batch predictions. Deployment in SageMaker parlance means setting up an endpoint – a hosted, production-ready model.

An endpoint in SageMaker is a scalable and secure RESTful API that you can use to send real-time inference requests to your models. Your applications can access an endpoint to make predictions directly via the REST API or AWS SDKs. It can scale instances up and down as needed, providing flexibility and cost-effectiveness.

SageMaker also supports multi-model endpoints, which can deploy multiple models on a single endpoint. This feature can significantly save on costs if many models are used infrequently or are not resource-intensive.

With the Lambda script defined, it can be incorporated into the pipeline using LambdaStep:

```
lambda_deploy_step = LambdaStep(
    name="LambdaStepRealTimeDeploy",
    lambda_func=func,
    inputs={
        "model_name": pipeline_model_name,
        "endpoint_config_name": endpoint_config_name,
        "endpoint_name": endpoint_name,
        "model_package_arn": register_step.steps[0].properties.
ModelPackageArn,
        "role": sagemaker_role,
        "instance_type": deploy_instance_type_param,
        "instance_count": deploy_instance_count_param
    }
)
```

> **Note**
>
> A model endpoint incurs cost as soon as it's deployed for the duration of its deployment. Once you run your pipeline, an endpoint is created as a result. If you are only experimenting with or testing your pipeline, you should delete the endpoint once you're done.

Creating and running the pipeline

All of our pipeline steps are now in place, which means we can create the pipeline itself. The Pipeline construct takes the name and parameters we've already defined:

```
pipeline = Pipeline(
    name=pipeline_name,
    parameters=[process_instance_type_param,
                train_instance_type_param,
                train_instance_count_param,
                deploy_instance_type_param,
                deploy_instance_count_param,
                clarify_instance_type_param,
```

```
                    skip_check_model_bias_param,
                    register_new_baseline_model_bias_
    param,              supplied_baseline_constraints_model_bias_param,
                    skip_check_model_explainability_
    param,              register_new_baseline_model_explainability_
    param,              supplied_baseline_constraints_model_
    explainability_param,
                    model_approval_status_param],
```

We must also pass all the steps we've defined as a list parameter and finally upsert the pipeline:

```
    steps=[
        process_step,
        train_step,
        evaluation_step,
        condition_step
    ],
    sagemaker_session=sess)
pipeline.upsert(role_arn=sagemaker_role)
```

Executing the pipeline is done by calling the start method:

```
start_response = pipeline.start(parameters=dict(
        SkipModelBiasCheck=True,
        RegisterNewModelBiasBaseline=True,
        SkipModelExplainabilityCheck=True,
        RegisterNewModelExplainabilityBaseline=True))
```

Note the conditions we defined here. When running the pipeline for the first time, we must skip the model bias and explainability checks while registering new bias and explainability baselines.

Both checks require an existing baseline to run (otherwise, there is no data to check against). Once baselines have been established, we can disable skipping the checks in subsequent runs.

More information on the model life cycle and creating baselines can be found at https://docs. aws.amazon.com/sagemaker/latest/dg/pipelines-quality-clarify-baseline-lifecycle.html.

Results

When the pipeline is executed, you can view the execution graph to see the status of each step:

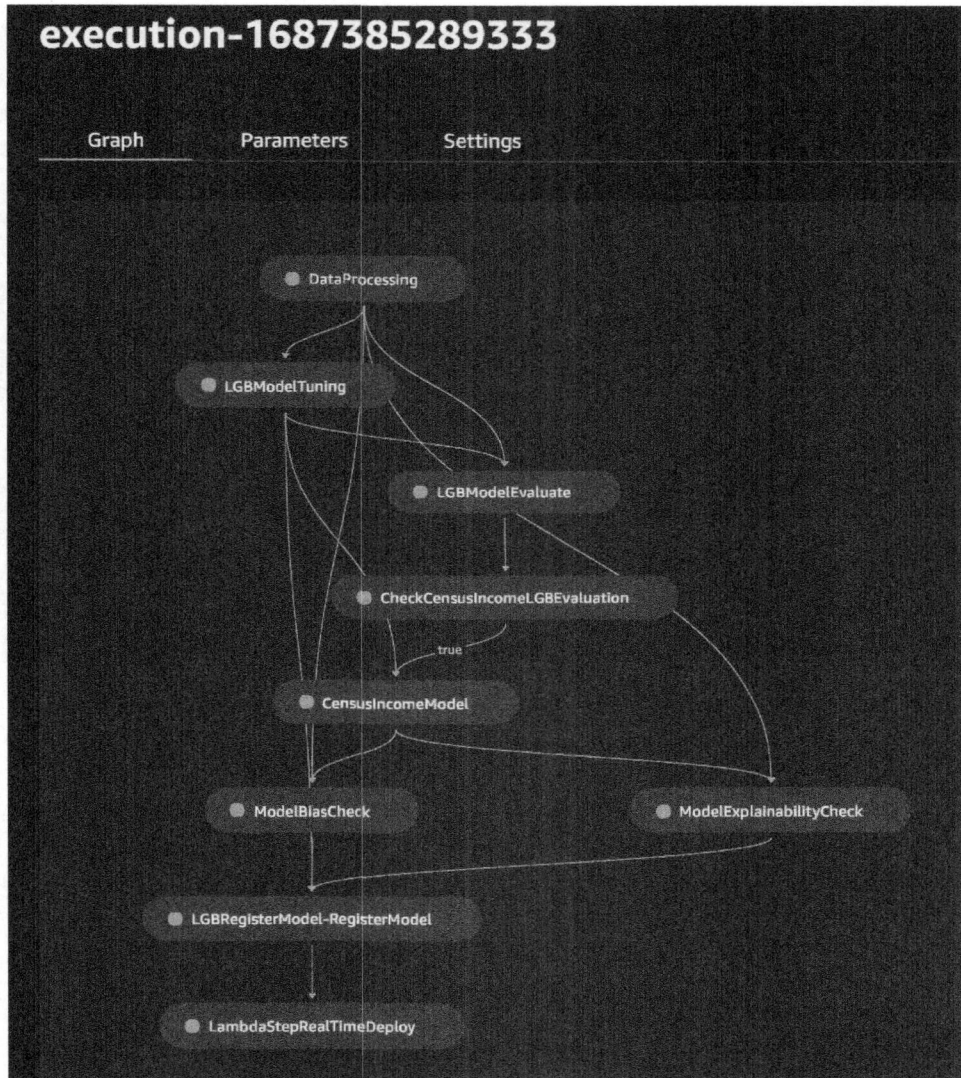

Figure 9.4 – Successful execution of the LightGBM Census Income pipeline

We can also see the model itself registered in the Model Registry once the pipeline completes:

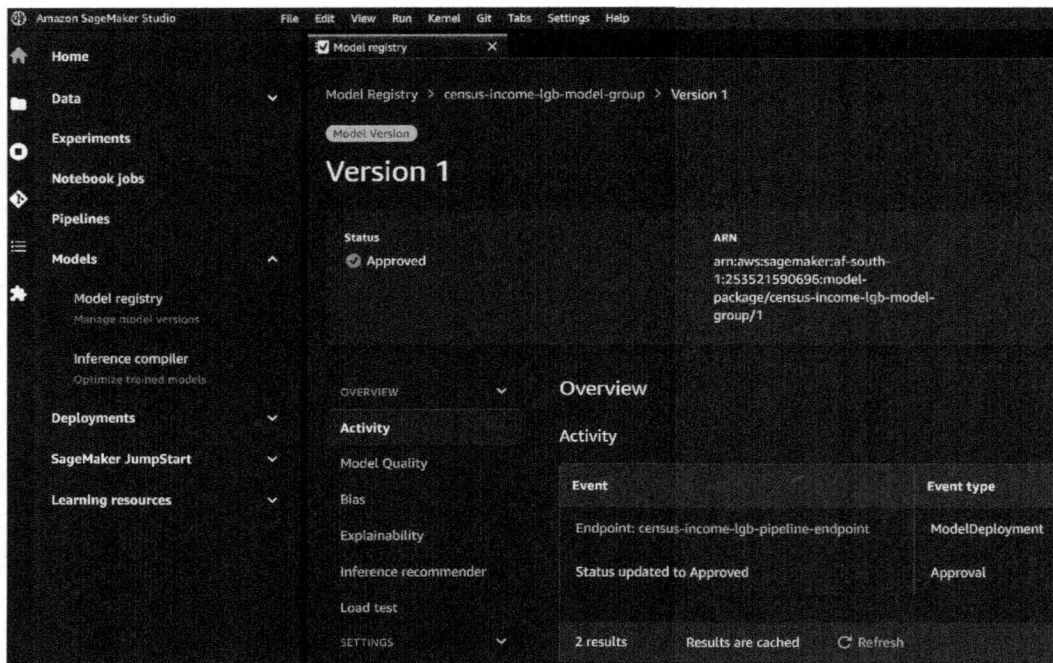

Figure 9.5 – SageMaker Model Registry showing the approved
Census Income model and the related endpoint

The bias and explainability reports can be viewed when a model is selected. *Figure 9.6* shows the bias report for the model that was created by the pipeline. We can see a slight imbalance in the DPPL for sex, but less than the class imbalance in the training data. The report indicates there isn't strong evidence for bias:

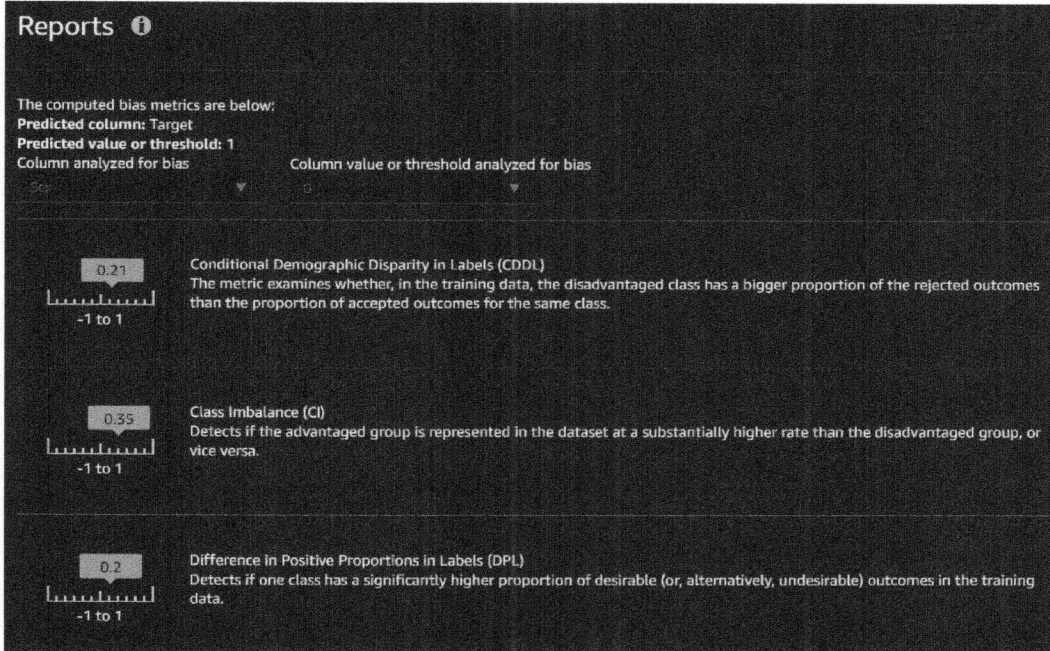

Figure 9.6 – Bias report for the Census Income model. We can see a slight imbalance
in the DPPL but less than the class imbalance in the training data

The explainability report, as shown in *Figure 9.7*, shows the importance of each feature in terms of SHAP values. Here, we can see that the **Capital Gain** and **Country** features are dominant regarding importance to predictions:

Explainability ⓘ

FEATURE IMPORTANCE

Explaining your model's predictions
Amazon SageMaker Studio helps you understand your machine learning model by portraying the imp

Predicted column: label0

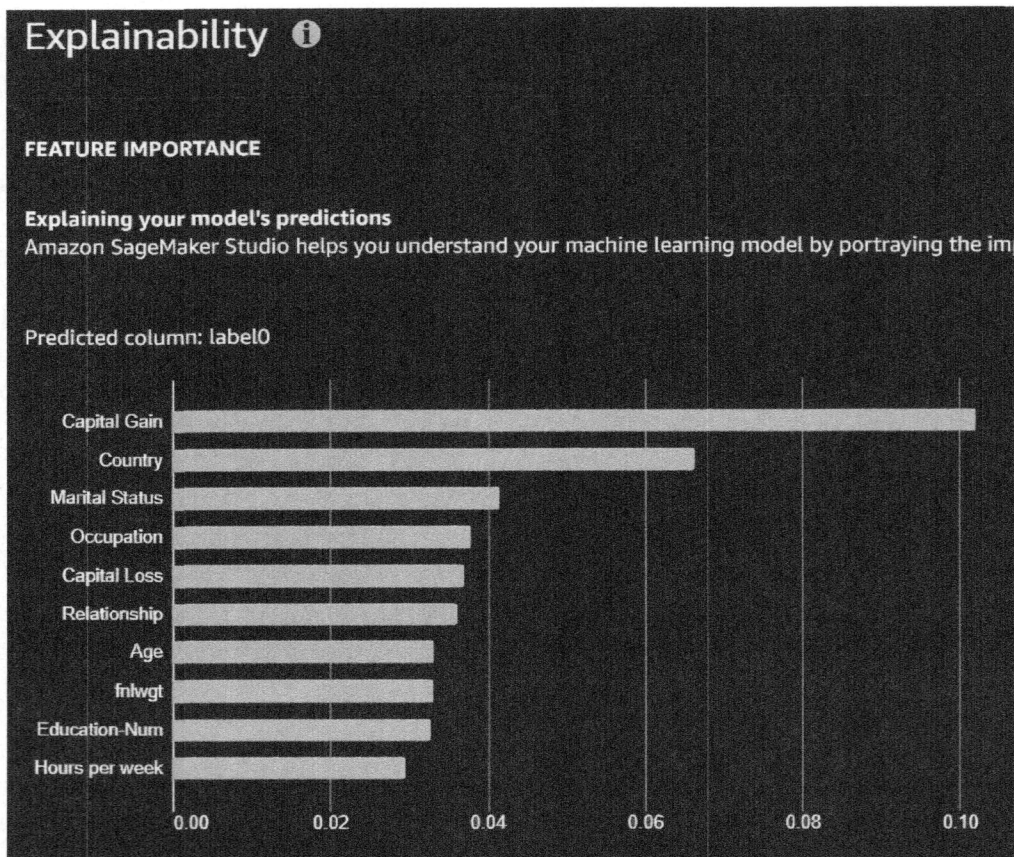

Figure 9.7 – Explainability report for the Census Income model showing the
dominant importance of the Capital Gain and Country features

The bias and explainability reports can also be downloaded in PDF format, which can easily be shared with business or non-technical stakeholders.

Making predictions using the endpoint

Of course, our deployed model is not very useful if we can't make any predictions using it. We can make predictions with the deployed model via REST calls or the Python SDK. Here is an example of using the Python SDK:

```
predictor = sagemaker.predictor.Predictor(endpoint_
name,                                                sagemaker_
session=sess, serializer=CSVSerializer(),
                deserializer=CSVDeserializer())
```

```
payload = test_df.drop(["Target"], axis=1).iloc[:5]
result = predictor.predict(payload.values)
```

We obtain a SageMaker `Predictor` using the endpoint name and the session. Then, we can call `predict`, passing a NumPy array (obtained from a test DataFrame in this case).

With that, we have created a complete, end-to-end, production-ready pipeline using SageMaker. Our pipeline includes data preprocessing, automatic model tuning, bias validation, drift detection, and a fully scalable deployment.

Summary

This chapter introduced AWS and Amazon SageMaker as a platform for building and deploying ML solutions. An overview of the SageMaker service was given, including the Clarify service, which provides advanced features such as model bias checks and explainability.

We then proceeded to build a complete ML pipeline with the SageMaker service. The pipeline includes all steps of the ML life cycle, including data preparation, model training, tuning, model evaluation, bias checks, explainability reports, validation against test data, and deployment to cloud-native, scalable infrastructure.

Specific examples were given to build each step within the pipeline, emphasizing full automation, looking to enable straightforward retraining and constant monitoring of data and model processes.

The next chapter looks at another MLOps platform called **PostgresML**. PostgresML offers ML capabilities on top of a staple of the server landscape: the Postgres database.

References

[1]   S. M. Lundberg and S.-I. Lee, A Unified Approach to Interpreting Model Predictions, in Advances in Neural Information Processing Systems 30, I. Guyon, U. V. Luxburg, S. Bengio, H. Wallach, R. Fergus, S. Vishwanathan and R. Garnett, Eds., Curran Associates, Inc., 2017, p. 4765–4774.

[2]   R. P. Moro and P. Cortez, Bank Marketing, 2012.

10
LightGBM Models with PostgresML

In this chapter, we'll look at a unique MLOps platform called **PostgresML**. PostgresML is a Postgres database extension that allows you to train and deploy ML models using SQL.

PostgresML and SQL are a significant departure from the scikit-learn style of programming we've used throughout this book. However, as we'll see in this chapter, performing ML model development and deployment at the database level has significant advantages regarding data movement requirements and inferencing latency.

The main topics in this chapter are as follows:

- An overview of PostgresML
- Getting started with PostgresML
- A customer churn case study with PostgresML and LightGBM

Technical requirements

This chapter includes practical examples of working with PostgresML. Docker will be used to set up a PostgresML environment and is recommended to run the examples. The code for this chapter is available at `https://github.com/PacktPublishing/Practical-Machine-Learning-with-LightGBM-and-Python/tree/main/chapter-10`.

Introducing PostgresML

PostgresML (`https://postgresml.org/`) is an extension for Postgres that allows practitioners to implement the entire ML life cycle on top of a Postgres database for text and tabular data.

PostgresML utilizes SQL as the interface to train models, create deployments, and make predictions. The use of SQL means model and data operations can be combined seamlessly and fit naturally into Postgres DB data engineering environments.

There are many advantages to having a shared data and ML platform. As we saw in the previous chapter, with SageMaker, significant effort is spent on moving data around. This is a common problem in ML environments where data, especially transactional data, lives in production databases, and complex data engineering workflows need to be created to extract data from production sources, transform the data for ML use, and load the data into a store that's accessible to the ML platform (such as S3 for SageMaker).

By combining the data store with the ML platform, PostgresML does away with moving data from one platform to another, saving significant time, effort, storage, and potentially egress costs.

Further, modeling from live transactional data means that training data is always up to date (read directly from the system of record) instead of gated behind a refresh. This eliminates errors that stem from working with outdated data or data being transformed or loaded incorrectly by ETL jobs.

Latency and round trips

A typical pattern for model deployment, which we've illustrated in earlier chapters, is deploying models behind a web API. In microservice terms, the model deployment is just another service that can be composed of other services to realize the overall system goal.

Deployment as a web service has several advantages. First, interoperability with other systems is straightforward via network calls when using web standards such as REST. Second, it allows you to independently deploy the model code, isolated from the rest of the system, affording resilience and independent scaling.

However, deploying models as separate services also has a significant downside: latency and network round trips.

Let's consider an e-commerce example. A common ML problem in e-commerce settings is fraud detection. Here is a system architecture diagram of a simple e-commerce system:

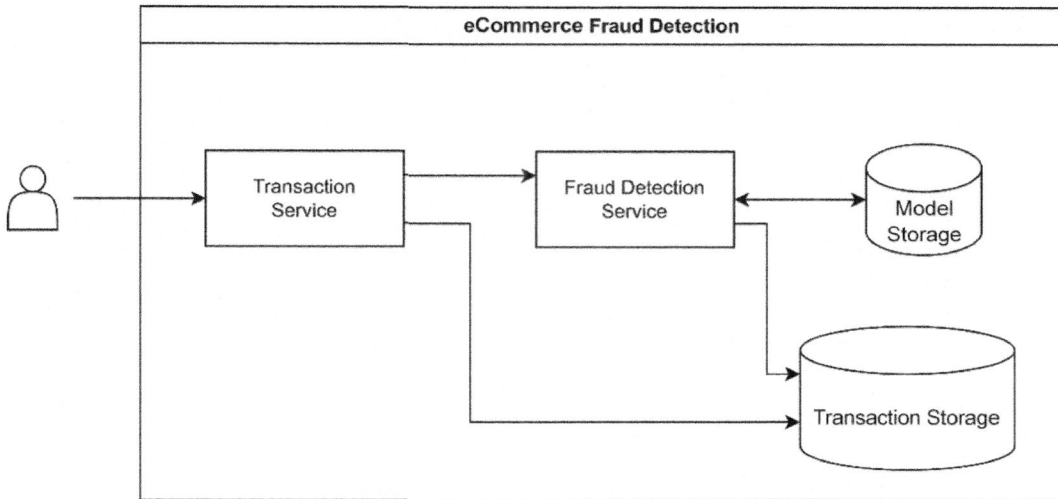

Figure 10.1 – Simplified e-commerce system architecture illustrating the interaction between functional services (transaction) and an ML-driven service (fraud detection)

Considering the architecture in *Figure 10.1*, the flow for a new transaction proceeds as follows:

1. The transaction is sent to the transaction service.
2. The transaction service calls the fraud detection service with the details of the new transaction.
3. The fraud detection service receives the new transaction, loads the relevant model from model storage (if needed), loads historical data from the transaction storage, and responds to the transaction service with the prediction.
4. The transaction service receives the fraud prediction and stores the transaction with the relevant classification.

A few variations on this workflow might exist. However, due to the separation of the transaction and fraud detection services, many network round trips have to be made to process a new transaction. Making the fraud prediction also requires fetching historical data from the transaction storage to feed to the model.

The networking call latency and round trips add significant overhead to the transaction. If the goal is to achieve a low-latency or real-time system, significantly more complex architectural components are required – for example, caching for the model and transactional data and higher throughput web services.

With PostgresML, the architecture may be simplified as follows:

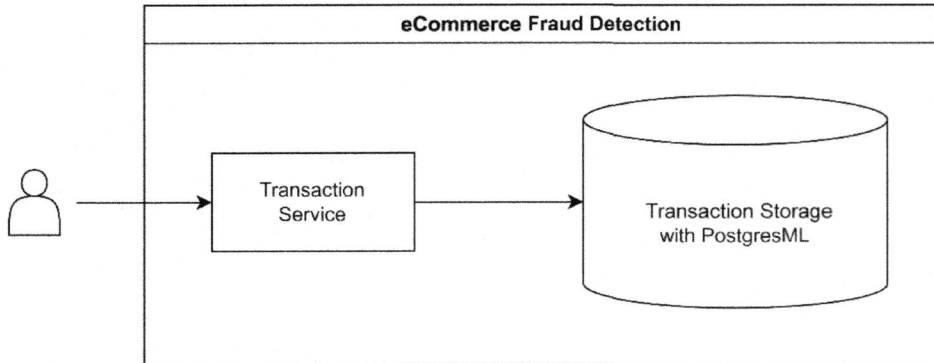

Figure 10.2 – Combining the ML services with data storage using
PostgresML allows for a more straightforward system design

Although this example is an oversimplification, the point is that significant overhead is added to the overall process of leveraging ML models in a service-oriented architecture with separate model services.

Through PostgresML, we can eliminate the need for separate model storage and overheads of loading models and, importantly, combine data storage calls and predictions into a single call on the data storage layer with no network overhead in between. PostgresML's benchmarks found that the simplified architecture improved performance by a factor of 40 within a cloud environment [1].

However, there are also downsides to this architecture. First, the database is now a single point of failure. If the database is unavailable, all models and predictive capabilities are also unavailable. Second, the architecture mixes the concerns of data storage and ML modeling and inference. Depending on the use case, training and deploying ML models has different server infrastructure needs compared to serving SQL queries and storing data. The mixture of concerns might force you to compromise on one or the other responsibilities or significantly increase database infrastructure costs to support all use cases.

In this section, we introduced PostgresML and explained, at a conceptual level, the advantages of combining our data store and ML service. Now, we'll look at practically setting up and getting started with PostgresML, alongside some basic functionality.

Getting started with PostgresML

PostgresML, of course, relies on PostgreSQL being installed. PostgresML requires PostgreSQL 11, with newer versions also supported. PostgresML also requires Python 3.7+ to be installed on your system. Both ARM and Intel/AMD architectures are supported.

> **Note**
>
> This section provides an overview of the steps and dependencies required to start working with PostgresML and the features at the time of writing. For up-to-date information, check out the official website: `https://postgresml.org/`. The simplest way to run PostgresML is to use Docker. For more information, check out the *Quick Start with Docker* documentation: `https://postgresml.org/docs/guides/setup/quick_start_with_docker`.

The extension can be installed with official package tools (such as APT) or compiled from sources. Once all the dependencies and the extension have been installed, `postgresql.conf` must be updated to load the PostgresML library, and the database server must be restarted:

```
shared_preload_libraries = 'pgml,pg_stat_statements'
sudo service postgresql restart
```

With PostgresML installed, the extension must be created within the database you plan to use. This can be done in the regular PostgreSQL way from a SQL console:

```
CREATE EXTENSION pgml;
```

Verify the installation, like so:

```
SELECT pgml.version();
```

Training models

Now, let's look at the features provided by PostgresML. As stated in the introduction, PostgresML has a SQL API. The following code examples should be run in a SQL console.

The extension function for training a model is as follows:

```
pgml.train(
    project_name TEXT,
    task TEXT DEFAULT NULL,
    relation_name TEXT DEFAULT NULL,
    y_column_name TEXT DEFAULT NULL,
    algorithm TEXT DEFAULT 'linear',
    hyperparams JSONB DEFAULT '{}'::JSONB,
    search TEXT DEFAULT NULL,
    search_params JSONB DEFAULT '{}'::JSONB,
    search_args JSONB DEFAULT '{}'::JSONB,
    preprocess JSONB DEFAULT '{}'::JSONB,
    test_size REAL DEFAULT 0.25,
    test_sampling TEXT DEFAULT 'random'
)
```

We need to supply `project_name` as the first parameter. PostgresML organizes models and deployments into projects, and projects are uniquely identified by their names.

Next, we specify the model's `task`: either classification or regression. `relation_name` and `y_column_name` set up the data for the training run. The relation is the table or view where the data is defined, and the Y column's name specifies the target column within the relation.

These are the only required parameters for training. Training a linear model (the default) can be done as follows:

```
SELECT * FROM pgml.train(
    project_name => 'Regression Project',
    task => 'regression',
    relation_name => pgml.diabetes',
    y_column_name => 'target'
);
```

When `pgml.train` is called, PostgresML copies the data into the `pgml` schema: this ensures all training runs are reproducible and enables training to be rerun using different algorithms or parameters but the same data. `relation_name` and `task` are also only required the very first time training is done for a project. To train a second model for a project, we can simplify the training call like so:

```
SELECT * FROM pgml.train(
    'Regression Project ',
    algorithm => 'lightgbm'
);
```

When calling this code, a LightGBM regression model is trained on the same data.

The algorithm parameter sets the learning algorithm to use. PostgresML supports various algorithms, including LightGBM, XGBoost, scikit-learn's random forests and extra trees, **support vector machines (SVMs)**, linear models, and unsupervised algorithms such as K-means clustering.

By default, 25% of the data is used as a test set, and the test data is selected at random. This can be controlled with the `test_size` and `test_sampling` parameters. Alternative test sampling methods select data from the first or last rows.

Hyperparameter optimization

PostgresML supports performing **hyperparameter optimization (HPO)** during the training run. The search parameters control the HPO process. Two search strategies are supported via `search`: grid search and random search. To set the hyperparameter ranges for the HPO, a JSON object is used with the `search_params` parameter. HPO parameters are specified using `search_args`. Here's an example:

```
SELECT * FROM pgml.train('Regression Project',
```

```
            algorithm => 'lightgbm',
            search => 'random',
            search_args => '{"n_iter": 100 }',
            search_params => '{
                    "learning_rate": [0.001, 0.1, 0.5],
                    "n_estimators": [20, 100, 200]
            }'
);
```

Preprocessing

PostgresML also supports performing certain types of preprocessing when training a model. As with the training data and configuration, the preprocessing is also stored with the project, so the same preprocessing can be applied when using a model for predictions.

Regarding pre-processing, PostgresML supports encoding categorical variables, imputing missing values, and scaling numerical values. Preprocessing rules are set using a JSON object via the `preprocess` parameter, as follows:

```
SELECT pgml.train(
...
preprocess => '{
        "model": {"encode": {"ordinal": ["Ford", "Kia",
            "Volkswagen"]}}
        "price": {"impute": "mean", scale: "standard"}
        "fuel_economy": {"scale": "standard"}
    }'
);
```

Here, we applied ordinal encoding for the model feature. Alternatively, PostgresML also supports one-hot encoding and target encoding. We also imported missing values (as indicated by NULL in the column) using the mean of the price and applied standard (normal) scaling to the price and the fuel economy features.

Deploying and prediction

PostgresML automatically calculates appropriate metrics on the test set after training, including R^2, the F1 score, precision, recall, ROC_AUC, accuracy and log loss. PostgresML will then automatically deploy the model after training if the key metric for the model (R^2 for regression and F1 for classification) improves over the currently deployed model.

However, deployments can also be managed manually for a project with the pgml.deploy function:

```
pgml.deploy(
    project_name TEXT,
```

```
    strategy TEXT DEFAULT 'best_score',
    algorithm TEXT DEFAULT NULL
)
```

The deployment strategies supported by PostgresML are `best_score`, which immediately deploys the model with the best key metrics; `most_recent`, which deploys the most recently trained model; and `rollback`, which rolls back the current deployment to the previously deployed model.

With a model deployed, predictions can be made with the `pgml.predict` function:

```
pgml.predict (
    project_name TEXT,
    features REAL[]
)
```

The `pgml.predict` function accepts the project name and the features for prediction. Features may be either arrays or composite types.

PostgresML dashboard

PostgresML provides a web-based dashboard for a more accessible interface to PostgresML features. The dashboard is deployed separately from PostgreSQL and is not required for administration or fully utilizing PostgresML features as all functionality is also accessible via SQL queries.

The dashboard provides access to a list of projects, models, deployments, and data snapshots. More details can also be found on trained models via the dashboard, including hyperparameter settings and training metrics:

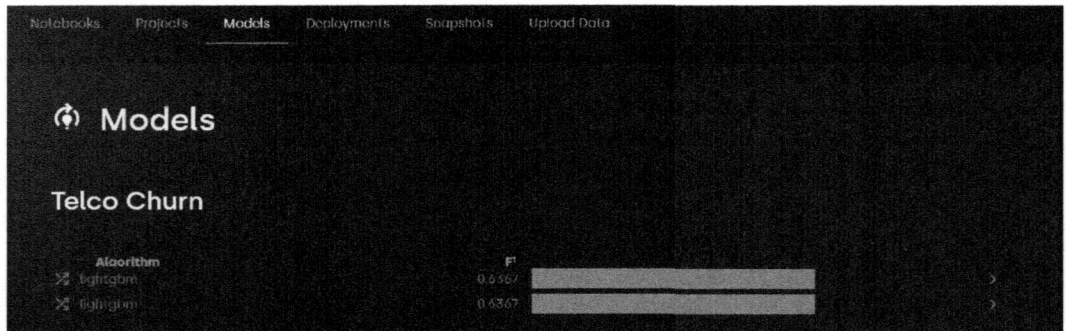

Figure 10.3 – PostgresML dashboard showing a list of trained models

Besides offering a view of projects, models, and deployments, the dashboard also allows the creation of SQL notebooks, similar to Jupyter Notebooks. These SQL notebooks provide a simple interface to interact with PostgresML if another SQL console is not readily available.

This concludes our section on getting started with PostgresML. Next, we'll look at an end-to-end case study of training and deploying a PostgresML model.

Case study – customer churn with PostgresML

Let's revisit the customer churn problem for a telecommunications provider. As a reminder, the dataset consists of customers and their account and cost information associated with the telecommunication provider.

Data loading and preprocessing

Our data will typically already be available within the PostgreSQL database in a real-world setting. However, for our example, we will start by loading the data. First, we must create the table the data is loaded into:

```
CREATE TABLE pgml.telco_churn
(
    customerid       VARCHAR(100),
    gender           VARCHAR(100),
    seniorcitizen    BOOLEAN,
    partner          VARCHAR(10),
    dependents       VARCHAR(10),
    tenure           REAL,
...
    monthlycharges   VARCHAR(50),
    totalcharges     VARCHAR(50),
    churn            VARCHAR(10)
);
```

Note that in our table structure, for a few of our columns, the types do not match what we may expect: for example, monthly and total charges should be real values. We'll address this during our preprocessing.

Next, we can load our CSV data into the table. PostgreSQL provides a COPY statement for this purpose:

```
COPY pgml.telco_churn (customerid,
                       gender,
                       seniorcitizen,
                       partner,
...
                       streamingtv,
                       streamingmovies,
                       contract,
                       paperlessbilling,
                       paymentmethod,
```

```
                        monthlycharges,
                        totalcharges,
                        churn
) FROM '/tmp/telco-churn.csv'
DELIMITER ','
CSV HEADER;
```

Running this statement reads the CSV file and adds the data to our table.

> **Note**
>
> If you run PostgresML in a Docker container (which is recommended to get started), the CSV file must first be copied to the container runtime. This can be done with the following command (substituting your own container name):
>
> ```
> docker cp telco/telco-churn.csv postgresml-postgres-1:/tmp/
> telco-churn.csv.
> ```

With the data loaded, we can perform our preprocessing. We perform this in three steps: cleaning data directly in the table, creating a table view that coerces the data to appropriate types, and using PostgresML's preprocessing functionality:

```
UPDATE pgml.telco_churn
SET totalcharges = NULL
WHERE totalcharges = ' ';
```

We must replace the empty text values in total charges with NULL, allowing PostgresML to impute the values later:

```
CREATE VIEW pgml.telco_churn_data AS
SELECT gender,
       seniorcitizen,
       CAST(CASE partner
               WHEN 'Yes' THEN true
               WHEN 'No' THEN false
           END AS BOOLEAN) AS partner,
...
       CAST(monthlycharges AS REAL),
       CAST(totalcharges AS REAL),
       CAST(CASE churn
               WHEN 'Yes' THEN true
               WHEN 'No' THEN false
           END AS BOOLEAN) AS churn
FROM pgml.telco_churn;
```

We then create a view to prepare the data for training. Notably, two type transformations are performed: features with `Yes/No` values are mapped to booleans, and we cast our monthly and total charges to `REAL` values (after mapping the text values to `NULL`). We also exclude `CustomerId` from the view as this can't be used for training.

Training and hyperparameter optimization

We can train our LightGBM model as follows:

```
SELECT *
FROM pgml.train('Telco Churn',
                task => 'classification',
                relation_name => 'pgml.telco_churn_data',
                y_column_name => 'churn',
                algorithm => 'lightgbm',
                preprocess => '{"totalcharges": {"impute": "mean"} }',
                search => 'random',
                search_args => '{"n_iter": 500 }',
                search_params => '{
                        "num_leaves": [2, 4, 8, 16, 32, 64]
                }'
    );
```

We set the view as our relation, with the churn column being our target feature. For preprocessing, we use the mean to ask PostgresML to impute missing values for the `totalcharges` feature.

We also set up hyperparameter optimization using 500 iterations of a random search with the specified search parameter ranges.

After completing training, we will be able to see our trained and deployed model in the dashboard:

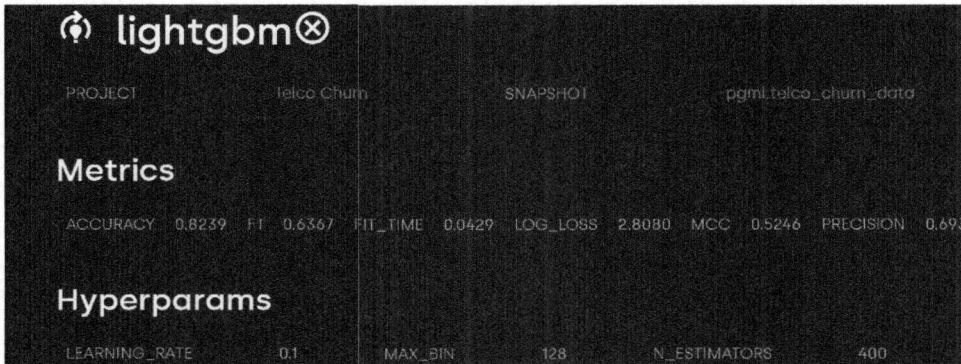

Figure 10.4 – Trained LightGBM model, as seen in the PostgresML dashboard

The dashboard shows the metrics for our model and the best-performing hyperparameters. Our model achieved an F1 score of 0.6367 and an accuracy of 0.8239.

The same information can also be retrieved with the following SQL query should the dashboard be unavailable:

```
SELECT metrics, hyperparams
FROM pgml.models m
LEFT OUTER JOIN pgml.projects p on p.id = m.project_id
WHERE p.name = 'Telco Churn';
```

Our model is automatically deployed when trained and is ready to make predictions.

Predictions

We can make predictions manually using a composite type as the feature data. This can be done as follows:

```
SELECT pgml.predict(
            'Telco Churn',
            ROW (
                CAST('Male' AS VARCHAR(30)),
                1,
...
                CAST('Electronic check' AS VARCHAR(30)),
                CAST(20.25 AS REAL),
                CAST(4107.25 AS REAL)
                )
        ) AS prediction;
```

We use the PostgreSQL ROW expression to set up the data, casting literals to the correct types for our model.

However, the more common way to leverage a PostgresML model is to incorporate predictions into regular business queries. For example, here, we've selected all the data from the original customer data table and added the prediction for each row using the pgml.predict function:

```
SELECT *,
       pgml.predict(
            'Telco Churn',
            ROW (
                gender,
                seniorcitizen,
...
                paymentmethod,
```

```
                    CAST(monthlycharges AS REAL),
                    CAST(totalcharges AS REAL)
                    )
            ) AS prediction
 FROM pgml.telco_churn;
```

Similar to calling the predict function manually, we use the ROW expression to pass data to the pgml.predict function but select the data from the table.

This also clearly illustrates the advantage of using PostgresML: a consumer of the ML model could query new customer data alongside the predictions with minimal overhead and in the same business transaction with a single network call.

Summary

This chapter provided an overview of PostgresML, a unique MLOps platform that allows training and calling models from SQL queries on top of an existing PostgreSQL database.

We discussed the platform's advantages in simplifying an ML-enabled landscape and reducing overhead and network latency in a service-oriented architecture. An overview of the core features and the API was provided.

This chapter concluded with a practical example of leveraging PostgresML for a classification problem, illustrating how to train a LightGBM model, perform hyperparameter optimization, deploy it, and leverage it for predictions in a handful of SQL queries.

In the next chapter, we will look at distributed and GPU-based learning with LightGBM.

References

[1]   *PostgresML is 8-40x faster than Python HTTP microservices, [Online]. Available at https://postgresml.org/blog/postgresml-is-8x-faster-than-python-http-microservices.*

11

Distributed and GPU-Based Learning with LightGBM

This chapter looks at training LightGBM models on distributed computing clusters and GPUs. Distributed computing can significantly speed up training workloads and enable the training of much larger datasets than the memory available on a single machine. We'll look at leveraging Dask for distributed computing and LightGBM's support for GPU-based training.

The topics covered in the chapter are as follows:

- Distributed learning with LightGBM and Dask
- GPU training for LightGBM

Technical requirements

The chapter includes examples of training and running LightGBM models on distributed computing clusters and GPUs. A Dask environment and GPUs are required to run the examples. Complete code examples are available at https://github.com/PacktPublishing/Practical-Machine-Learning-with-LightGBM-and-Python/tree/main/chapter-11.

Distributed learning with LightGBM and Dask

Dask is an open-source Python library for distributed computing. It's designed to integrate seamlessly with existing Python libraries and tools, including scikit-learn and LightGBM. This section looks at running distributed training workloads for LightGBM using Dask.

Dask (https://www.dask.org/) allows you to set up clusters on both a single machine and across many machines. Running Dask on a single machine is the default and requires no setup. However, workloads that run on a single-machine cluster (or scheduler) can readily be run with a distributed scheduler.

Dask offers many ways to run a distributed cluster, including integrating Kubernetes, MPI, or automatic provisioning into a hyperscalar such as AWS or Google Cloud Platform.

When running on a single machine, Dask still distributes the workload across multiple threads, which can significantly speed up workloads.

Dask provides cluster management utility classes to set up a cluster easily. A local cluster can be run as follows:

```
cluster = LocalCluster(n_workers=4, threads_per_worker=2)
client = Client(cluster)
```

The preceding code creates a local cluster with four workers, configuring each worker to run two threads. The cluster runs on localhost, with the scheduler running on port 8786 by default. The host IP and port can be configured using parameters. In addition to running the scheduler, Dask also starts a diagnostic dashboard that's implemented using Bokeh (https://docs.bokeh.org/en/latest/). By default, the dashboard runs on port 8787. We can check the **Workers** page to see the status of our running cluster, as shown in *Figure 11.1*.

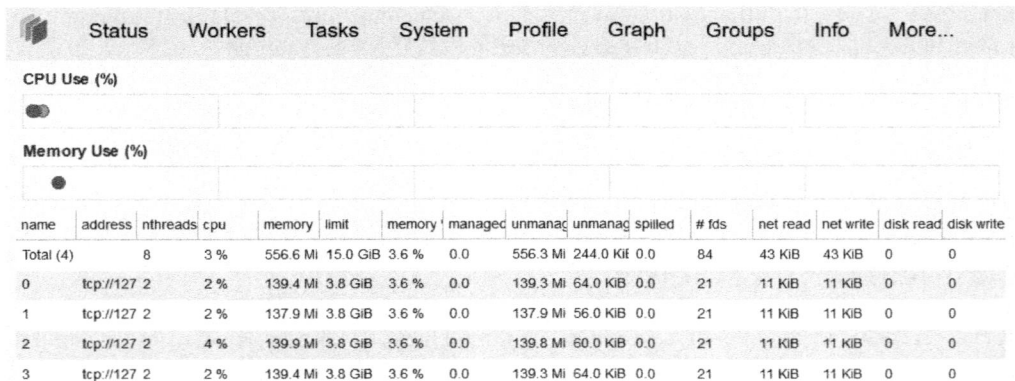

	Status	Workers	Tasks	System	Profile	Graph	Groups	Info	More...

CPU Use (%)

Memory Use (%)

name	address	nthreads	cpu	memory	limit	memory	managed	unmanag	unmanag	spilled	# fds	net read	net write	disk read	disk write
Total (4)		8	3 %	556.6 Mi	15.0 GiB	3.6 %	0.0	556.3 Mi	244.0 KiF	0.0	84	43 KiB	43 KiB	0	0
0	tcp://127	2	2 %	139.4 Mi	3.8 GiB	3.6 %	0.0	139.3 Mi	64.0 KiB	0.0	21	11 KiB	11 KiB	0	0
1	tcp://127	2	2 %	137.9 Mi	3.8 GiB	3.6 %	0.0	137.9 Mi	56.0 KiB	0.0	21	11 KiB	11 KiB	0	0
2	tcp://127	2	4 %	139.9 Mi	3.8 GiB	3.6 %	0.0	139.8 Mi	60.0 KiB	0.0	21	11 KiB	11 KiB	0	0
3	tcp://127	2	2 %	139.4 Mi	3.8 GiB	3.6 %	0.0	139.3 Mi	64.0 KiB	0.0	21	11 KiB	11 KiB	0	0

Figure 11.1 – Dask diagnostics dashboard showing four running
workers with some technical statistics for each

With a cluster up and running, we can prepare our data for use on the distributed cluster.

Dask offers its own implementation of a data frame called the Dask DataFrame. A Dask DataFrame comprises many smaller pandas DataFrames, which are split based on the index. Each part can be stored on disk or distributed across a network, which allows working with much larger datasets than can fit into a single machine's memory. Operations performed on the Dask DataFrame are automatically distributed to the pandas DataFrames.

> **Note**
>
> When your dataset fits into RAM, using standard pandas DataFrames instead of a Dask DataFrame is recommended.

We can create a Dask DataFrame by loading a CSV file. Note that the CSV file may be located on S3 or HDFS and can be very large. The following code creates a Dask DataFrame from a CSV file:

```
import dask.dataframe as dd
df = dd.read_csv("covtype/covtype.csv", blocksize="64MB")
```

Here, we also specify the block size for loading the CSV file. The block size sets the chunks the dataset is divided into and gives us granular control over the memory of individual DataFrame parts. When calling df.shape, we get an interesting result:

```
df.shape
# (Delayed('int-a0031d1f-945d-42b4-af29-ea5e40148f3f'), 55)
```

The number of columns is returned as a number. However, looking at the number of rows, we got a wrapper class called Delayed. This illustrates that even though we've created the DataFrame, the data is not loaded into memory. Instead, Dask loads the data as needed on the workers that use the data. We can force Dask to compute the row count as follows:

```
df.shape[0].compute()
# 581012
```

With the data available in a DataFrame, we can prepare it for training. We split our data into a training and test set using the train_test_split function from dask_ml:

```
X = df.iloc[:, :-1]
y = df.iloc[:, -1]
X_train, X_test, y_train, y_test = dask_ml.model_selection.train_test_
split(X, y)
```

Although the function from dask_ml mirrors the functionality of scikit-learn's train_test_split, the Dask version maintains the distributed nature of the underlying Dask DataFrame.

Our cluster is now set up, and the data is prepared for training. We can now look toward training our LightGBM model.

The LightGBM library team offers and maintains Dask versions of each available learning algorithm: DaskLGBMRegressor, DaskLGBMClassifier, and DaskLGBMRanker. These are wrappers around the standard LightGBM scikit-learn interface with additional functionality to specify the Dask cluster client to use.

When LightGBM runs on a Dask cluster, training occurs with one LightGBM worker per Dask worker. LightGBM concatenates all data partitions on a single worker into a single dataset, and each LightGBM worker uses the local dataset independently.

Each LightGBM worker then works in concert to train a single LightGBM model, using the Dask cluster to communicate. When data parallel training is performed (as is the case with Dask), LightGBM uses a **Reduce-Scatter** strategy:

1. During the histogram-building phase, each worker builds histograms for different non-overlapping features. Then, a **Reduce-Scatter** operation is performed: each worker shares a part of its histogram with each other worker.

2. After the **Reduce-Scatter**, each worker has a complete histogram for a subset of features and then finds the best split for these features.

3. Finally, a gathering operation is performed: each worker shares its best split with all other workers, so all workers have all the best splits.

The best feature split is chosen, and the data is partitioned accordingly.

Fortunately, the complexity of the distributed algorithm is hidden from us, and the training code is identical to the scikit-learn training code we're used to:

```
dask_model = lgb.DaskLGBMClassifier(n_estimators=200, client=client)
dask_model.fit(X_train, y_train)
```

Running the preceding code trains the LightGBM model, and we can see the progress by checking the **Status** page of the Dask dashboard, as shown in *Figure 11.2*.

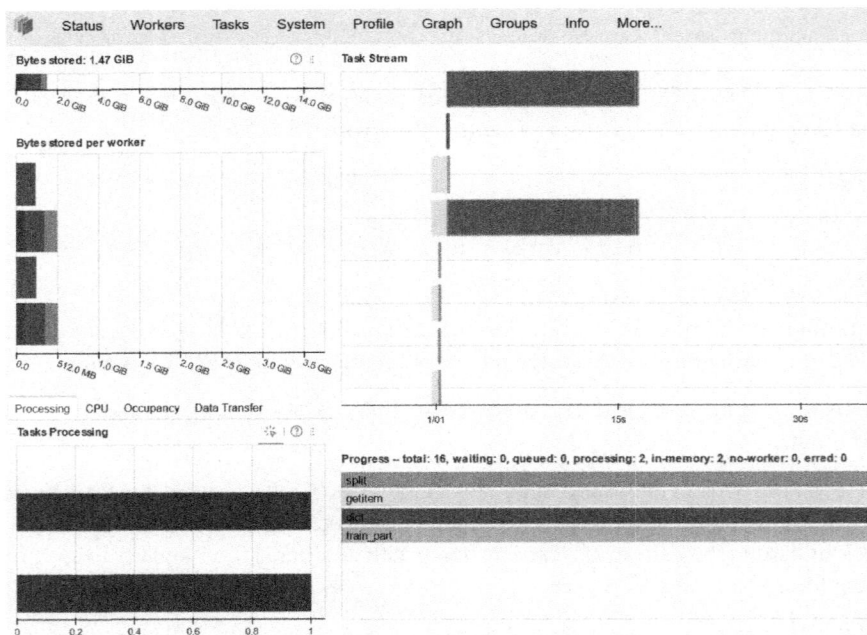

Figure 11.2 – Status page of the Dask dashboard showing the task stream while a LightGBM model is training

Dask LightGBM models can be fully serialized using **Pickle** or **joblib**, and we can save the model to disk as follows:

```
with open("dask-model.pkl", "wb") as f:
        pickle.dump(dask_model, f)
```

Predictions can be made by calling the `predict` method of the model. Note that the Dask model expects a Dask DataFrame or array:

```
predictions = dask_model.predict(X_test)
```

Similar to getting the shape of a Dask DataFrame, the prediction operation is also delayed and only calculated when needed. We can use `compute` to get the prediction values:

```
predictions.compute()
```

This concludes our look at leveraging Dask for distributed training with LightGBM. With Dask, LightGBM can train models on massive datasets well beyond the computing power of a single server. Dask scales alongside your needs, so you can start with your local laptop and move to a high-performance computing environment or cloud infrastructure as your data grows. Further, as shown previously, Dask is designed to work harmoniously with established Python libraries such as pandas, NumPy, and scikit-learn, providing a familiar environment for data scientists while extending the capabilities of these tools.

Next, we'll look at speeding up LightGBM training when large models need to be trained using the GPU.

GPU training for LightGBM

The LightGBM library has native support for training the model on a GPU [1]. Two GPU platforms are supported: GPU via OpenCL and CUDA. Leveraging the GPU via OpenCL offers support for the broadest range of GPUs (including AMD GPUs) and is significantly faster than running the model on a CPU. However, the CUDA platform offers the fastest runtime if you have an NVIDIA GPU available.

Setting up LightGBM for the GPU

Setting up your environment to use the GPU can be a bit tricky, but we'll review the core steps here.

> **Note**
>
> The GPU setup steps discussed here are offered as a guide and overview of the process of setting up your environment. The exact version number of libraries and drivers listed here may be outdated, and it's recommended that you review the official documentation for up-to-date versions: `https://lightgbm.readthedocs.io/en/latest/GPU-Tutorial.html`.

In order to use the GPU, we have to *compile and build the LightGBM library from the source code*. The following instructions assume an Ubuntu Linux build environment; steps for other platforms are similar. Before we can build the library, we must install a few dependencies.

Importantly, first, install the GPU drivers for your environment. If you have an NVIDIA GPU, also install CUDA. Instructions for doing so are available from the respective vendor sites:

- `https://docs.nvidia.com/cuda/`

- `https://www.amd.com/en/support`

Next, we need to install the OpenCL headers:

```
sudo apt install --no-install-recommends
sudo apt install --no-install-recommends nvidia-opencl-dev opencl-
headers
```

Finally, install the library build dependencies:

```
sudo apt install --no-install-recommends git cmake build-essential
libboost-dev libboost-system-dev libboost-filesystem-dev
```

We are now ready to compile the LightGBM library with GPU support. Clone the repository and build the library, setting the USE_GPU flag:

```
git clone --recursive https://github.com/microsoft/LightGBM
cd LightGBM
mkdir build
cd build
cmake -DUSE_GPU=1 ..
make -j$(nproc)
cd ..
```

As mentioned in *Chapter 2, Ensemble Learning – Bagging and Boosting*, LightGBM is a C++ library with a Python interface. With the preceding instructions, we have built the library with GPU support, but we must build and install the Python package to use the library from Python (including the scikit-learn API):

```
cd python-package/
python setup.py install --user --precompile
```

Running LightGBM on the GPU

Running training code on the GPU is straightforward. We set the device parameter to either gpu or cuda:

```
model = lgb.LGBMClassifier(
        n_estimators=150,
        device="cuda",
        is_enable_sparse=False
)
model = model.fit(X_train, y_train)
```

As shown in the preceding code, we turn off LightGBM's sparse matrix optimization by setting `is_enable_sparse` to `False`. LightGBM's sparse features are not supported on GPU devices. Further, depending on your dataset, you might get the following warning stating that `multi_logloss` is not implemented:

```
Metric multi_logloss is not implemented in cuda version. Fall back to
evaluation on CPU.
```

Notably, the fallback performed is only for evaluation and not training; training is still performed on the GPU. We can validate that the GPU is used by checking `nvidia-smi` (for NVIDIA GPUs):

```
+-----------------------------------------------------------------------------+
| NVIDIA-SMI 525.116.04   Driver Version: 525.116.04   CUDA Version: 12.0     |
|-------------------------------+----------------------+----------------------+
| GPU  Name        Persistence-M| Bus-Id        Disp.A | Volatile Uncorr. ECC |
| Fan  Temp  Perf  Pwr:Usage/Cap|         Memory-Usage | GPU-Util  Compute M. |
|                               |                      |               MIG M. |
|===============================+======================+======================|
|   0  Quadro P5000        Off  | 00000000:00:05.0 Off |                  Off  |
| 26%   40C    P0    56W / 180W |   4674MiB / 16384MiB |     40%      Default  |
|                               |                      |                  N/A  |
+-------------------------------+----------------------+----------------------+
```

Figure 11.3 – nvidia-smi output while LightGBM training is running
(as we can see, the GPU utilization is at 40%)

The speed-up achieved depends on your GPU. The training time was reduced from 171 s to 11 s (a 15-times speed-up) for 150 iterations on the Forest Cover dataset.

The immense performance gain stemming from using a GPU is especially useful when performing parameter tuning. We can use GPU-based training with, for instance, Optuna to significantly accelerate the search for optimal parameters. All that's needed is to move the model training in the `objective` function to the GPU device. When defining the objective function, we specify our Optuna parameter ranges as per usual:

```
def objective(trial):
        lambda_l1 = trial.suggest_float(
                'lambda_l1', 1e-8, 10.0, log=True),
```

```
        lambda_l2 = trial.suggest_float(
            'lambda_l2', 1e-8, 10.0, log=True),
...
```

We then create the model with the Optuna parameters and make sure to specify the device as cuda (or gpu):

```
model = lgb.LGBMClassifier(
    force_row_wise=True,
    boosting_type=boosting_type,
    n_estimators=n_estimators,
    lambda_l1=lambda_l1,
    lambda_l2=lambda_l2,
...

    learning_rate=learning_rate,
    max_bin=max_bin,
    device="cuda")
```

The last part of the objective function is to return the cross-validated scores:

```
scores = cross_val_score(model, X_train, y_train, scoring="f1_macro")
return scores.mean()
```

We can then run a parameter study as we would normally:

```
sampler = optuna.samplers.TPESampler()
pruner = optuna.pruners.HyperbandPruner(
        min_resource=10, max_resource=400, reduction_factor=3)

study = optuna.create_study(
        direction='maximize', sampler=sampler,
        pruner=pruner
)
study.optimize(objective(), n_trials=10, gc_after_trial=True, n_
jobs=1)
```

Importantly, we also set the n_jobs parameter to 1 here, as running parallel jobs leveraging the GPU could cause unnecessary contention and overhead.

There are a few noteworthy best practices for getting the best performance when training on a GPU:

- Always verify that the GPU is being used. LightGBM returns to CPU training if the GPU is unavailable despite setting device=gpu. A good way of checking is with a tool such as nvidia-smi, as shown previously, or comparing training times to reference benchmarks.

- Use a much smaller `max_bin` size. Large datasets reduce the impact of a smaller `max_bin` size, and the smaller number of bins benefits training on the GPU. Similarly, use single-precision floats for increased performance if your GPU supports it.

- GPU training works best for large, dense datasets. Data needs to be moved to the GPU's VRAM for training, and if the dataset is too small, the overhead involved with moving the data is too significant.

- Avoid one-hot encoding of feature columns, as this leads to sparse feature matrices, which do not work well on the GPU.

This concludes our section on how to use the GPU with LightGBM. Although the setup might be more complex, GPUs offer a significant boost in training speed due to their ability to handle thousands of threads simultaneously, allowing for efficient parallel processing, especially with large datasets. The massive parallelism of GPUs is particularly beneficial for histogram-based algorithms in LightGBM, making operations such as building histograms more efficient and effective.

Summary

In this chapter, we discussed two ways of accelerating computing with LightGBM. The first is large-scale distributed training across many machines using the Python library Dask. We showed how to set up a Dask cluster, how data can be distributed to the cluster using the Dask DataFrame, and how to run LightGBM on the cluster.

Second, we also looked at how to leverage the GPU with LightGBM. Notably, the GPU setup is complex, but significant speed-up can be achieved when it's available. We also discussed some best practices for training LightGBM models on the GPU.

References

[1]   H. Zhang, S. Si, and C.-J. Hsieh, *GPU-acceleration for Large-scale Tree Boosting, 2017.*

Index

‹packt›

Other Books You May Enjoy

If you enjoyed this book, you may be interested in these other books by Packt:

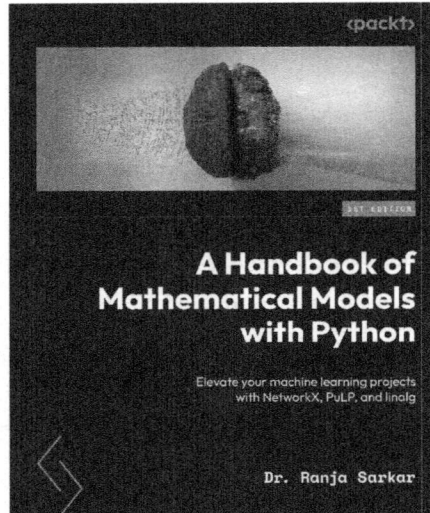

A Handbook of Mathematical Models with Python

Dr. Ranja Sarkar

ISBN: 9781804616703

- Understand core concepts of mathematical models and their relevance in solving problems
- Explore various approaches to modeling and learning using Python
- Work with tested mathematical tools to gather meaningful insights
- Blend mathematical modeling with machine learning to find optimal solutions to business problems
- Optimize ML models built with business data, apply them to understand their impact on the business, and address critical questions
- Apply mathematical optimization for data-scarce problems where the objective and constraints are known

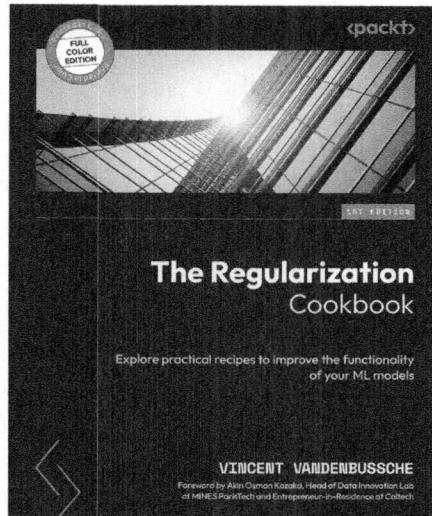

The Regularization Cookbook

Vincent Vandenbussche

ISBN: 9781837634088

- Diagnose overfitting and the need for regularization
- Regularize common linear models such as logistic regression
- Understand regularizing tree-based models such as XGBoost
- Uncover the secrets of structured data to regularize ML models
- Explore general techniques to regularize deep learning models
- Discover specific regularization techniques for NLP problems using transformers
- Understand the regularization in computer vision models and CNN architectures
- Apply cutting-edge computer vision regularization with generative models

Packt is searching for authors like you

If you're interested in becoming an author for Packt, please visit authors.packtpub.com and apply today. We have worked with thousands of developers and tech professionals, just like you, to help them share their insight with the global tech community. You can make a general application, apply for a specific hot topic that we are recruiting an author for, or submit your own idea.

Share Your Thoughts

Now you've finished *Machine Learning with LightGBM and Python*, we'd love to hear your thoughts! Scan the QR code below to go straight to the Amazon review page for this book and share your feedback or leave a review on the site that you purchased it from.

https://packt.link/r/1-800-56474-0

Your review is important to us and the tech community and will help us make sure we're delivering excellent quality content.

Download a free PDF copy of this book

Thanks for purchasing this book!

Do you like to read on the go but are unable to carry your print books everywhere? Is your eBook purchase not compatible with the device of your choice?

Don't worry, now with every Packt book you get a DRM-free PDF version of that book at no cost.

Read anywhere, any place, on any device. Search, copy, and paste code from your favorite technical books directly into your application.

The perks don't stop there, you can get exclusive access to discounts, newsletters, and great free content in your inbox daily

Follow these simple steps to get the benefits:

1. Scan the QR code or visit the link below

https://packt.link/free-ebook/9781800564749

1. Submit your proof of purchase
2. That's it! We'll send your free PDF and other benefits to your email directly

Printed in Great Britain
by Amazon